Alexander Balloch Grosart, George Herbert

The Complete Works in Verse and Prose of George Herbert

In three Volumes. Vol. II

Alexander Balloch Grosart, George Herbert

The Complete Works in Verse and Prose of George Herbert
In three Volumes. Vol. II

ISBN/EAN: 9783744727310

Printed in Europe, USA, Canada, Australia, Japan

Cover: Foto ©ninafisch / pixelio.de

More available books at **www.hansebooks.com**

THE

COMPLETE WORKS OF GEORGE HERBERT.

VOL. II. VERSE.

ESSAY ON THE LIFE AND WRITINGS.
THE CHURCH MILITANT.
LILIES OF THE TEMPLE. PSALMS.
SECULAR POEMS: WITH ADDITIONS FROM MSS. PARENTALIA.
ANTI-TAMI-CAMI-CATEGORIA AND EPIGRAMMATA APOLOGETICA.
ALIA POEMATA LATINA. PASSIO DISCERPTA. LUCUS.
WITH TRANSLATIONS OF THE WHOLE.
GLOSSARIAL INDEX.

Richard and Lady Magdalene Herbert.

Father and Mother of George Herbert.

From the Monument in Montgomery Church.

The Fuller Worthies' Library.

THE COMPLETE WORKS

IN VERSE AND PROSE

OF

GEORGE HERBERT.

FOR THE FIRST TIME FULLY COLLECTED AND COLLATED WITH
THE ORIGINAL AND EARLY EDITIONS AND MSS.
AND MUCH ENLARGED WITH

I. HITHERTO UNPRINTED AND INEDITED POEMS AND PROSE FROM
THE WILLIAMS MSS. ETC.
II. TRANSLATION OF THE WHOLE OF THE LATIN AND GREEK VERSE
AND LATIN PROSE.
III. MEMORIAL-INTRODUCTION, ESSAY ON LIFE AND WRITINGS, AND
NOTES AND ILLUSTRATIONS.
IV. IN QUARTO, PORTRAITS ON STEEL, AND OTHER SPECIALLY-
PREPARED ILLUSTRATIONS AND FACSIMILES.

Edited by the

REV. ALEXANDER B. GROSART,
ST. GEORGE'S, BLACKBURN, LANCASHIRE.

IN THREE VOLUMES.

VOL. II. VERSE.

PRINTED FOR PRIVATE CIRCULATION.
1874.
100 *copies only.*

CONTENTS.

Richard Herbert and Lady Magdalene his Wife.

Montgomery Church.

ESSAY ON THE LIFE AND WRITINGS OF
GEORGE HERBERT.

In our Memorial-Introduction (Vol. I.) and in the anno-
tated Life by Izaak Walton (Vol. III.), the outward
Facts of the Biography of GEORGE HERBERT are given,
it will perhaps be admitted, with more fulness and accu-
racy of detail than hitherto. I propose now to offer the
Reader a Study of the Life in relation to the Writings,
and of the Writings in relation to the Life, in order to
arrive at a deeper knowledge and a more adequate esti-
mate of both. Thus far, narrative and criticism alike have
been to a large extent traditional and repeatative. It is
surely about time that such a Life and such Writings
were submitted to a searching and deliberate examination,
that we may understand the secret of the still unspent
and unique POWER of these lowly and unpretentious Writ-
ings—after well nigh two and a half centuries—and the
abiding and ever-growing wealth of affectionate reverence
cherished toward the Man so long subsequent to the in-
evitable passing-away of the 'glamour' of personal me-
mories—as of Barnabas Oley and Izaak Walton ; e.g. in
the United States of America, in Canada and Nova Sco-
tia, in Australia and New Zealand, in India and through-

out the English-speaking colonies, the lovers of HERBERT are as numerous and as ardent as in the mother-country.[1] None the less is this desirable, in that it affords opportunity of bringing together many scattered remarks of eminent Admirers, contemporary and recent.

These FIVE things seem to invite thought and critical examination :

I. THE ORIGINAL AND EARLY EDITIONS AND MSS. OF THE WRITINGS AND OUR TEXT.

II. THE STORY OF THE LIFE, AS REVEALING HIS ORIGINAL AND ULTIMATE CHARACTER, PUBLIC AND PRIVATE.

III. THE ANTI-TAMI-CAMI-CATEGORIA CONTROVERSY, AND ITS SIGNIFICANCES AND BEARINGS.

IV. THE CHARACTERISTICS OF HERBERT'S WRITINGS, VERSE AND PROSE.

V. EARLY AND LATER ESTIMATES.

1. *The original and early editions and* MSS. *of the Writings and our text.*

Like Sir Philip Sidney's, nearly the whole of GEORGE HERBERT's Writings were published posthumously, although, with such loving Editors and guardians as Nicholas Ferrar and Barnabas Oley, it were almost a wrong to follow T. P., on publishing the ΑΠΟΣΠΑΣΜΑΤΙΑ SACRA of Bishop Andrewes (1657, folio), in calling them 'posthumous and *orphan*.'[2]   The University Collections, as of the

---

[1] To the praise of G. W. Childs, Esq., of Philadelphia, U.S.A., be it recorded that on learning the wish of the Dean of Westminster and others to place a memorial-window in our great Abbey, in honour of GEORGE HERBERT and WILLIAM COWPER, as Westminster-School boys, he spontaneously and large-heartedly expressed his readiness to furnish such a window at his own cost.   The generous offer was cordially accepted.

[2] Even so (presumably) well-informed a writer as the author of the Paper on HERBERT in the Retrospective Review (vol. iii. pp. 215-222) has fallen into the error of saying, 'His poems were

Lamentations for Prince Henry (1612), and on the death
of Queen Anne (1619), and the like, contained the well-
known but not at all remarkable Latin Verse, given in
their places; and as an appendix to Dean Donne's Funeral
Sermon for Lady Danvers, the 'Parentalia' were added
(1627). Probably others were less or more circulated in
manuscript, as was the *mode* even onward: the Melville
Epigrams must have been thus circulated (as will appear
hereafter). But substantially the Writings of GEORGE
HERBERT were given to the world not by their Author, but
by Friends. At a time when the Press travailled with the
superabundance of books, this initial fact in the biblio-
graphy of these Writings is noticeable, perhaps praise-
worthy. Nevertheless, there can be no doubt that the
posthumousness of HERBERT'S books placed them under
inevitable disadvantages as compared with, *e.g.* Robert
Herrick's 'Hesperides,' or Henry Vaughan's 'Silex Scinti-
lans' or 'Olar Iscanus.' As every one knows who has had
to do with the Press, what is written is one thing, and what
is printed quite another; that the latter gives a different
look and character to the whole, so much so that faults pre-
viously overlooked come out startlingly and accusingly in
the proof-sheets. There are things in 'The Temple' that one
feels persuaded would have been cleared of their obscurity;
while other things must have been felt to be incongruous,
not to speak of occasional instances of mean symbolisms in

---

published during his lifetime' (p. 217). In the Christian Remem-
brancer for July 1862 (vol. xliv. p. 105), the writer of a thought-
ful paper on GEORGE HERBERT and his Times remarks of this: 'It is
characteristic of his modesty, or, more strictly speaking, of the vic-
tory which he won over his naturally eager and ambitious tempera-
ment, that they were [nearly] all posthumous in publication.'
Again: 'The too frequent recurrence of anti-climax, and even down-
right bathos, at the end of many [?] of the poems, indicates that
they were never properly revised by the "last hand" of the author
(p. 129).

even the finest poems—reminding of a lark that has just
been soaring and singing, singing and soaring, all a-thrill
with the ecstasy of its divinely-given music, dropping down
not into the yellowing corn or daisied grass, but right on
the bare-trodden highway : and so too with false rhymes,
and at least one missing line (in 107. The Size, l. 40). The
Writings of HERBERT claim indulgence, therefore, as not
having passed in their printed form beneath his own eyes.
Very touching is Izaak Walton's narrative of the death-
bed delivery of the 'little book,' which was to be after-
wards known as 'The Temple.' Visited by a 'Mr. Dun-
con'—of whom it is pity we know so very little—he sent
a pathetic message to his 'brother Ferrar,' soliciting a
continuance of his 'daily prayers' for him, and telling him
all was 'well' and in 'peace.' 'Having said this,' we read,
'he did, with so sweet a humility as seemed to exalt him,
bow down to Mr. Duncon, and, with a thoughtful and con-
tented look, say to him, "Sir, I pray deliver this little book
to my dear brother Ferrar, and tell him he shall find in it
a picture of the many spiritual conflicts that have passed
betwixt God and my soul, before I could subject mine to
the will of Jesus my Master, in Whose service I have now
found perfect freedom. Desire him to read it : and then,
if he can think it may turn to the advantage of any de-
jected poor soul, let it be made public ; if not, let him
burn it ; for I and it are less than the least of God's mer-
cies."' Thus meanly did this humble man think of this
excellent book, which now bears the name of 'The Tem-
plo, or Sacred Poems and Private Ejaculations ;' of which
Mr. Ferrar would say, 'There was in it the picture of a
divine soul in every page, and that the whole book was
such a harmony of holy passions as would enrich the world
with pleasure and piety.' Good Nicholas Ferrar has fur-
ther given his estimate of the 'little book' thus confided to
him, in the golden Epistle as from 'The Printers to the
Reader' (Vol. I pp. 3-5). It would appear that he lost no

time after the burial of HERBERT (3d March 1632)[1] in
preparing it for the Press ; for immediately the Manuscript,
as written out for Ferrar, was submitted by him for 'Li-
cense'—now deposited in the Bodleian.[2] There was a little
difficulty, and consequent brief delay, in obtaining the
necessary authority, as thus told by Walton, in its state-
ment, removal, and result : ' This ought to be noted, that
when Mr. Ferrar sent this book to Cambridge to be licensed
for the press, the Vice-Chancellor would by no means allow
the two so much noted verses (in the ' Church Militant,'
ll. 239, 240),

> " Religion stands a-tiptoe in our land,
>   Ready to pass to the American strand,"

to be printed, and Mr. Ferrar would by no means allow
the book to be printed and want them ; but after some
time, and some arguments for and against their being
made public, the Vice-Chancellor said : " I knew Mr. HER-
BERT well, and know that he was a divine poet ; but I hope
the world will not take him to be an inspired prophet, and
therefore I license the whole book." So that it came to
be printed without the diminution or addition of a syllable
since it was delivered into the hands of Mr. Duncon, save
only that Mr. Ferrar hath added the excellent preface that
is printed before it.' The ' after some time' must have
been very inconsiderable, seeing that, almost certainly,
' The Temple' was in print and (at least) privately circu-
lated in 1632. At BRAND's Sale there was a copy with a
second title-page, which is described as having 1632 printed
on it (Lowndes, s. n.) ; and I have myself seen two copies

---

[1] In our Memorial-Introduction (Vol. I.) we accept the date of
the burial, 3d March 1632, usually given ; but see our Note in the
annotated Life of Walton in Vol. III. for further details and queries.

[2] See its title-page, &c. in Vol. I. p. 233 ; where are also a few
Various Readings.

contemporaneously marked 1632 on the undated title-page.[1] That title-page was *literatim* as follows :

THE

T E M P L E.

SACRED POEMS

AND

PRIVATE EJA-

CULATIONS.

By Mr. George Herbert
Late Oratour of the Universitie.

Psal. 29.
*In his Temple doth every
man speak of his honour.*

Cambridge :
Printed by *Thomas Buck*
and *Roger Daniel :*
¶ And are to be sold by *Francis
Green*, stationer in
Cambridge.

In Vol. I. pp. 1, 2 will be found similarly the title-pages of the first dated edition and of the second, both belonging

[1] Hence I have, in Notes and Illustrations, designated the undated edition of 'The Temple' as of 1632.

to 1633. There are minute typographical differences in
the three title-pages ; but collation shows that the undated
copies of 1632 and the first dated edition of 1633 corre-
spond, and are indeed the same book throughout. The
conclusion accordingly is, that the types were kept stand-
ing for the first dated edition.[1] But the second edition of
1633 (so named), though answering page to page and line
to line, is a distinct impression, *i.e.* was not the same set-
ting up. In all likelihood the undated copies consisted
of a very few issued as gifts for intimate friends. Then
came early in 1633 the first edition proper, and then in
the same year the second (as above) : the third followed in
1634 ; fourth in 1635; fifth in 1638; sixth in 1641 ; seventh
in 1656 ; eighth in 1660 ; ninth in 1667 ; tenth in 1674 ;
eleventh in 1679 ; twelfth in 1703 ; thirteenth in 1709.
The first to the sixth edition's text remained the same :
from 1640, 'The Synagogue' of Christopher Harvey ac-
companied 'The Temple ;' from 1656 onward, there were
orthographical alterations ; in 1660 was ' an Alphabeticall
Table for ready finding out chief places ;' in 1674 (see our
Preface) the priceless gift of R. White's portrait of HER-
BERT first appeared ; and also two (sorry) illustrations to
the Church Threshold and The Altar: in 1679 began such
corruptions of the text as ' gore' for 'doore' in The Thanks-
giving (l. 6), and ' My' for ' Thy' (l. 29), and so increasingly ;

[1] A Writer of a Paper on GEORGE HERBERT and his Times, in
the Christian Remembrancer for July 1862 (vol. xliv. pp. 133-137),
states: ' "The Temple" was first given to the world in 1633, by
Nicholas Ferrar, HERBERT's literary executor; under his editorship it
was printed by his daughters and other members of his household,
or " Protestant Nunnery," as it has been called, at Little Gidden, in
Northamptonshire, and then published at Cambridge, after being, of
course, formally licensed by the Vice-Chancellor's "imprimatur" '
(pp. 106-7). There is no authority whatever for this alleged printing
privately at Little Gidding. The undated copies are expressly stated
to be ' Printed by Thomas Buck' (as *supra*). Curiously enough there
is no ' imprimatur' in any of the editions of ' The Temple.'

the loss being that Pickering (1835, 1838, &c.) reprinted
the vitiated text; and even Dr. George Macdonald (in
'Antiphon') did not detect the blunders.[1] It adds to the
significance of these multiplied editions, that earlier the
troubles of Charles I. in Scotland, deepening into the cla-
mour and confusions of the Civil War—shadows of which
darkened portentously over the closing weeks of HER-
BERT'S life—and later the profligacy and sensualism of The
Restoration and the reign of Charles II., seemed to render
it improbable that a fit audience should be found, how-
ever 'few,' for, in relation to the Commonwealth, so churchly,
and, in relation to the Restoration, so pure and true a book.
I like to accept the Fact, as declarative of 'hidden ones'
who still clave to the Lord, after the type of the olden
revelation to Elijah of the ' seven thousand,' when he in
his anguish and loneliness imagined there was not another
besides himself who believed in the One living and True
God. When Walton first wrote the Life (or about forty
years after HERBERT'S death), 'more than twenty thousand
of them' had been ' sold since the first impression.' Well-
thumbed and worn are the few copies of these earlier edi-
tions that have come down to us. Lowly hands handled,
lowly hearts received the devout teaching; and I do not
doubt ' The Temple' helped many and many a pilgrim
Zionward to 'sing' when perchance only sobs and groans
had fallen. I do not know that it is needful to record the
numerous editions, complete and incomplete, from 1709
to 1873. They have nothing special about them : only be
it ever remembered that to William Pickering belongs the
praise of having been the first to aim at a complete col-
lection of the Writings of GEORGE HERBERT.

    Returning now upon the MS. of ' The Temple' as
' licensed,' the printed text of 1632-3 corresponds with it
pretty closely, departures being mainly orthographical.
The Manuscript cannot, however, have been the ' printer's

____

[1] ' Antiphon,' pp. 190-1.

copy,' for it is stainless and uncrushed, as well as occasion-
ally differing in its readings. Being a folio, too, it cannot
have been the 'little book' placed in Mr. Duncon's hands
by the dying Poet. That, it is to be feared, has irrecover-
ably gone, with many other of the Little Gidding trea-
sures of the Ferrars. But of scarcely less interest is a
MS. now in the Williams Library, London, whence it
has been our privilege to draw so much hitherto unknown
unprinted Poetry, English and Latin. I must here describe
the 'little volume' (12mo). It records on the front fly-leaf
that it was presented by Dr. Mapletoft to a Rev. John
Jones (of Sheephall, Herts), who was donor of very many
MSS. and books to the same Library. Mr. Jones has pre-
fixed this note (in pencil): 'This book came originally
from the family of Little Gidding, and was probably
bound there. Q. whether this be not the manuscript copy
that was sent by Mr. Herbert a little before his death to
Mr. Nic. Ferrar. See Mr. Herbert's Life.'[1] Again, on
verso of p. 101 is the following note: 'The following sup-
posed to be Mr. Herbert's own writing. See the records
in the custody of yᵉ University Orator at Cambridge.'
With reference to the former note, we can testify that the
binding (plain brown calf, with a single line of gold round
the borders and a double line of tooling) is self-evidently
amateur, and corresponds otherwise with other Little Gid-
ding books that I possess and have seen. But as this
volume does not contain one half of the Poems as published
in 'The Temple,' Mr. Jones's query must be answered in

---

[1] So in the Third Report of the Royal Commission on Historical
Manuscripts, 1872, p. 368. The inscription is as follows: 'Don.
Jni Jones, Cler. & Museo V. Cl. D. H. M. Venantodûn. qui ob.
1730.' That is, 'A gift to John Jones, Clerk, from the study
(Library) of Dr. H. Mapletoft, Huntingdon, who died 1730.' For
notices of the Ferrars, mainly from Professor Mayor's 'Nicholas
Ferrar' (1855), see our annotated 'Life of Herbert,' by Walton (in
Vol. III.); also of the Mapletofts.

the negative. It seems to have been an earlier form of
the Manuscript. With reference to the latter note, the
suggested comparison with the Orator's Books at Cam-
bridge and my familiarity with HERBERT'S handwriting,
enable me to attest that the whole of the latter portion
is in his own autograph ; while the earlier portion has a
number of characteristic corrections of the amanuensis'
MS. Our Facsimile (in the quarto) is true in its reproduc-
tion of two pages of the holograph MS.; and it will be ob-
served that the appended signature (from another MS.)
gives the somewhat curious form of 'ε' (*e*)—a form never
wanting in any of the MSS. of HERBERT that have been
examined by me, albeit his autograph proper varies more
than almost any that I have met with.[1]

Our 'Various Readings' from the Williams MS. (before
Notes and Illustrations, in Vol. I.), and the Six never-
before-printed English sacred poems, with another version
of ' The Song' for Easter, and the 'Passio Discerpta,'—
which may be interpreted as meaning the Passion or Re-
deeming Love of the Lord Jesus, taken to pieces as one
might a passion-flower, petal by petal ; or, more freely,
that the Poet celebrates certain leading incidents in the
great and awful story ; and ' Lucus,'—which may intend a
Sacred Grove, with perhaps a sub-reference to the trans-
figuring light of the Divine presence there, and so reminds
of Phineas Fletcher's ' Sylva Poetica,' and Milton's later—
will certify of our rare good fortune in the discovery or
recovery of this ' little book.' It must often and often
have been handled by visitors of the Williams Library,

---

[1] In the Memorial-Introduction (Vol. I. p. xliv.) it is seen that
HERBERT signed 'Harbert,' and that his name was so written con-
temporaneously : in other University MSS. he signs 'Herberte' and
' Herbert:' in others (certainly his) the character of the writing dif-
fers considerably from these and from the Williams MS. See onward
about a copy of King James's Works, alleged to have belonged to
our successive HERBERTS.

but no one seems to have really read it until the present Editor did so. If William Pickering was in ecstasies over his small 'find' from Dr. Bliss, of 'The Paradox' from a Rawlinson MS., what would not his enthusiasm have been over this treasure-trove! Except the further details of the contents of the MS. below, more need not be repeated here, inasmuch as the WHOLE are given in this volume in their places, and in the first volume.[1]

[1] See Vol. I. pp. 219-231. These further little particulars may be recorded here. There comes first the fly-leaf, with the inscription in note on p. xix. ; a second leaf, with Mr. Jones's pencil-note, as before ; next the Dedication (six lines) ; The Church-Porch, folios 1-13 ; blank page 14, and on verso four lines headed 'Perirranterium;' folio 15, four lines headed 'Superliminare,' and on verso The Altar ; then successively The Sacrifice, folios 16-22 ; on verso The Thanksgiving to folio 23 ; The Second Thanksgiving [or The Reprisall], folio 24 ; on verso The Passion (two) to folio 25 ; on verso Good-Friday ; The Sinner, folio 26 ; on verso Easter (two) to folio 27 ; on verso and folio 28, Easter Wings ; on verso Holy Baptisme (two) to folio 29 ; on verso Love 1 and 2, to folio 30 ; The Holy Communion, verso to folio 31 (No. I. of the new Pieces) ; Church Musick, folio 32 ; verso The Christian Temper (two) to folio 33 ; Prayer (three) to folio 35 ; Imploiment verso to folio 36 ; verso Whitsunday to folio 37 ; verso and to folio 38 The Holy Scriptures, 1 and 2 ; verso Love, to folio 39 (No. II. of the new Poems); folio 39 to 40, Sinne ; verso Trinity Sunday (two, latter No. III. of the new Pieces) to folio 40 ; verso Repentance, to folio 41 ; verso Praise ; folio 42, Nature ; verso Grace, to folio 43 ; folio 43, Mattens ; Even-song, folio 44 (No. IV. of the new Poems) ; Christmas-day, folio 45 ; verso Church Monuments, to folio 46 ; Frailty, folio 46 ; folio 47, Content, to folio 48 ; Poetry, folio 48 ; verso Affliction, to folio 50 ; verso Humility, to folio 51 ; verso Sunday, to folio 52 ; Jordan, folio 53 ; verso Deniall, to folio 54 ; verso Ungratefulnes, to folio 55 ; verso Imploiment, to folio 56 ; A Wreath, folio 56 ; verso To all Angels and Saints, to folio 57 ; verso The Pearle, to folio 58 ; verso Tentation, to folio 59 ; verso The World, to folio 60 ; folio 60, Coloss. iii. 3 ; verso Faith, to folio 61 ; Lent, folio 62 to 63 ; verso Man, to folio 64 ; Ode, folio 65 ; verso Affliction, to folio 66 ; Sinne, folio 66 ; verso Charmes and Knots, to folio 67 ; verso Unkindnes, to folio 68 ; verso Mortification, to folio 69 ; verso The

Other two MSS. fall next to be described ; neither, it is believed, hitherto known. The first is a translation into Latin of The Church Militant ; the other a later adaptation of nearly the entire Poems of The Temple for singing and praise. Of these successively.

(*a*) Latin translation of The Church Militant. This is deposited in the Library of Durham Cathedral. The title-page runs :

D. G. HERBERTI

HAUD PRIDEM ORATORIS

ACADEMIAE CANTABRIGIENSIS

CARMINIS

QUOD INSCRIBITUR

ECCLESIA MILITARIS

VERSIO LATINA.

HOR. IN EPIST.

Indignor quicquam reprehendi, non quia crasse,
Compositum illepidere putetur; sed quia nuper
At veniam quo laude peto: laudatus abunde
Non fastiditus si tibi, Lector, ero.

OVID: *in Trist.*

1634.

An Epistle-dedicatory (in Latin) is dated ' Ex Collegio D. Petri Cantabrigiae Calend. Jan. MDCXXXIIII°.' It is ad-

---

Publican, to folio 71 ; verso Prayer, to folio 72 ; verso Obedience, to folio 73 ; Invention, folio 74 ; verso Perfection, The Elixir, to folio 75 ; verso The Knell (No. V. of the new English Pieces) ; Perseverance, folio 76 (No. VI. of the new English Poems) ; verso Death, to folio 77 ; verso Doomsday, to folio 78 ; verso Judgment ; folio 79, Heaven ; verso Love ; folio 80 to 82 (1st page) blank ; then The Church Militant, verso to folio 89, including L'Envoy (N.B. ll. 239-40), are emphatically dot-marked with a heavy pencil) ; folios 100-101 blank ; on verso Mr. Jones's pencil-note ; Passio Discerpta, folios 102-107 ; verso to 119, Lucus ; verso and folios 120-129 blank.

dressed, 'Amplissimo viro et Augustissimo Regi Carolo a Secretiaribus Consiliis Heroi Pendentissimo D. Johanni Cooke, honoratissimo suo Maecenati εὐδαιμονεῖν.' The translator is 'Jacobus Leeke.' This Sir John Cooke was probably of the family of Highnam, to the Sir Robert Cooke of which, HERBERT'S widow was married. It is to be regretted that the Epistle tells more of him than of HERBERT; yet this much may be recalled here, that this Sir John Cooke was Secretary of State to Charles I. from 1625 to 1632; that he was son of Richard Cooke of Trusley, co. Derby, and a brother of George Cooke, successively Bishop of Bristol and Hereford; and that his sister Dorothy was wife of Valentine Carey, Bishop of Exeter. Notwithstanding Leeke's superlatives, there was really nothing notable about him. Leaving it to the curious in such things to consult the original Latin, the Epistle follows in English, seeing it is a noteworthy memorial of our Worthy thus early :

'To that most noble man and to that most wise hero, Sir John Cooke (of his most august Majesty King Charles's Privy Council)—his own most honoured Mæcenas, all happiness! There are not wanting people nowadays, most noble Sir, who, when they feel themselves bound by a kindness, take upon them that they have made an abundant return of thanks so long as they boast that, with their interminable praises and mighty flourish of words, they exalt from earth, and place amid the inhabitants of heaven, even while he is yet living, their Mæcenas, illustrious in himself, and needing no testimonial from petty ability which creeps along the ground :—people, however, who perceive not meanwhile, much less consider sufficiently (mere beggars of the purchasable smoke of kindness), that they have not so much painted in fair colours one who deserves the utmost from them, as told a story in an exaggerated manner, and incurred the shameful suspicion of flattery. As to you, most honoured Sir, thy wisdom affects not those who love to " protest too much," much less endures those troublesome trumpeters of thy virtues. You are such an one as all who know you know that you were not born to catch at empty breaths (of praise), much less that you are at all influenced by a flattering tickling of the ears, except to hatred and loathing. You would rather have the council of your wisdom, dignity, goodness, in fine, of all the virtues which adorn a man, (seated) in your conscience, than (dwelling) on the lips of a crier; in your own individual mind you would rather have a noble testimony to shine forth than in another man's printed page. Since then this way does not lie open to me (without some risk of forfeiting your feeling and regard towards me) for proving my gratitude for the remarkable favour (which is never likely to escape from my mind) with which your kindness not long ago treated me ; nay, since whatever my poor ability may have suggested to my stammering inexperience is beneath your merits and unhoped-for frankness towards me, this only remains to me to prove my real regard and the expression of everlasting duty,—to dedicate to your Highness these recent attempts of my idle Muse.

It is a familiar anecdote of Alexander the Great that he did not reject poor Milo's drop of water offered even in the palms of his hands, but valued it amongst the greatest gifts of the richest men. You in like manner, most noble Sir, if you will not disdain to take in good part this drop sought from the streams of the Muses, have made me happy to the point of envy : and if, with such a favouring gale of your most pleasant and kindly countenance as you have hitherto enriched my mind withal, you should not hesitate to rise and breathe upon this Translation of the illustrious Herbertian Muse, you will make me hope at length to present, not as now, one little drop from the streams of the Muses with a poor and unskilful hand, but hereafter to draw whole vessels full from the very fountains, to offer for your acceptance. May God, All-good, Almighty, keep you in safety as long as possible—a glorious example of true godliness and an eminent ornament of the state. So never will cease to pray your Highness's most devoted   JAMES LEEKE.'

Sooth to say, the translation of ' The Church Militant' is in no way memorable. This slight specimen must suffice :

> 'Sentitur Pietatis apex: alata supremo
> Ungue premit nostram hanc tellurem, ad America vergens
> Littora; quum Baccho, Veneri, Geniisque, litatur
> Omnimodis, odia in furcas rumpentia, et effrons
> Peccatum, lamiae, Circeaque murmura, dirae
> Perfidiae (horroris certissima signa futuri)
> Nostra perimplerint ad apertas pocula fibras :

Sequana quando rapax saturabit Tibridis unda
Iugluviem, Thamisisque procis utrisque receptis
Intactas putido vitiabit flumine Nymphas:
Quando nova hanc quatiet male-suada tyrannide gente
Ausonia, et veteres repetito crimine fastus
Farserit, ut liceat venturo [dicier] anno,   [dici ex]
Quod Gallis scelus et fractis dominabitur Anglis :
Tunc, tunc occiduos exul properabit ad Indos
Relligio: subeunt horum faelicia nostris
Tempora temporibus : Deus alme, his providus omnem
Dempsisti remoram, laceratae hinc fulva parentis
Viscera mittendo, dirae irritamina culpae.
Nam male conveniunt, nec in una sede morantur
Auri sacra fames, et Gratia, sacra salutis' &c.[1]

What of further translation Leeke designed was done in
more scholarly fashion in Dr. Dillingham's now somewhat
rare book, viz. Poemata Varii Argumenti, &c. 1678.

(b) *A* MS. *adaptation of most of ' The Temple' for
singing and praise.* This ' translation,' as the writer calls
it, was written, as shown by the several dates given in it,
in the years 1681-2. The ' Church Porch' ended, he says,
' scripsi partim domi partim apud Hasleborow diebus . . .
et Feb. 12, 1680-1 ;' and after ' The Sacrifice,' ' scripsi
Feb. 7, et nunc ult° ejusd. 1680-1 summi Honoris ergo
Beatissimo Jesu hic pono.' Another of the larger pieces,
' Providence,' is dated March 3, 1680-1. Thereafter there
appears to have been a cessation, and a steady resumption
of the task in 1682. ' Humilitie,' p. 82, is dated Mar. 28,
1682 ; ' Constancy,' p. 86, Mar. 30, 1682 ; ' Lent,' p. 108,
May 30, 1682 ; ' An Offering,' p. 180, Oct. 17, 1682 ; ' Love,'
p. 222, Dec. 12, 1682. ' The Church Militant' is dated
Dec. 14, 1682 ; this, like ' The Sacrifice,' having been in
part translated contemporaneously with portions of ' The
Temple.'

[1] There is also a translation by Leeke in the same MS. entitled
' Ejusdem D. G. Herberti Poematis cui titulum inscripsit Parasche-
ven ηsταφρασιs'—poor.

Before the date at p. 86 is ' ita I. B.,' and this, and that he sometimes went to Haselbrough, and that he was a Puritan, and probably a Nonconformist, is all we learn of the ' Translator.' His Puritanism (at least) is quaintly shown on several occasions. In the margin of ' Lent,' and opposite ll. 34-41, our text (vol. i. p. 98), he writes : ' In my poor judg^t the Poetry is better than the Reason : therefore, though I translate it as piously intended, yet I cannot say y^t I am like minded wth ye worthy Author : May 30, 1682.' In ' The British Church' (ibid. p. 124), ll. 9-12 are added to as in the third line following :

> ' Outlandish looks may not compare,
>   For all they either painted are,
>   As Popish ones : or though more blest,
>   To me appears as under-drest :'

and not content with this, a mark at ' under-drest' gives in the margin ' non ita mihi vero.' Afterwards we have :

> ' She in the valley is so shy
>   Of dressing, that her hair doth ly
>   About her ears (her modesty
>   Doth, in my thoughts, appear thereby) ;'

where the (. . . .) is an interpolation, and ' my' is noted as ' the translator, who in this is not like-minded wth the Rever^d Author.' And again we have :

> ' But, dearest mother, w^t those misse
>   The mean thy praise and glory is,
>   And long may be. I wish no worse,
>   Yet think it rather breaths a curse :'

and opposite the last line is this :—' not the author, but ut s[upra]. Lastly, in ' Aaron' (ibid. p. 200), l. 10 is thus written :

> ' Poore Priest, *this is my case*, for] *thus am I drest*.'

The commendable fidelity with which I. B. endeavours to follow his author, and which results as above in a mingling of incompatibles when he differs in opinion, is shown throughout. In the versification he alters as little as his intent will permit, sometimes varying only a line in four or five. In the ' Foil' he writes :

> ' Yet how we toil,
>   As if grief foul
>   Were not to the soul
>   Nor virtue oyl:'

and, apparently on account of the change in the last line, gives in the margin HERBERT'S words, ' Yet in [. . . .] nor virtue winning.' So in ' Affliction' (ibid. p. 82), words struck out for metre's sake are placed in the margin, and occasionally such are made to serve as an explanatory gloss, as in Ephes. iv. 30 (p. 164) :

> ' Marbles can weep; and surely strings
>   Have more bowels than such hard things:'

' bowels' in margin. Such carefulness, however, occurs mainly in the latter half of the volume. To the question, Why all this trouble to alter and care to preserve? The answer appears to be, To change HERBERT'S Poems into a Hymnal in metres adapted to the usual psalm tunes. This is shown, first, by the notings, more frequent in the early part, such as The Church Porch: ' sing it as the cxiii. Psalm ;' Church Lock and Key, ' as cxlviii. ;' the Church Floore, ' comon Tune ;' The Windows, ' as Pas. [*sic*] xxv.;' and so on, for in all about fourteen instances. But it is still more shown, second, by this, that there is no ' transation' of those in metres requiring no alteration, but only a reference, such as at p. 213; The Rose, p. 172 ; Discipline, p. 173 ; The Invitation, p. 174, where the pagination agrees with 1633 edition of The Temple and onward. For this cause about twenty-two pieces are omitted, besides those next to be noticed. Thirdly, we have still better evidence in such as these: The Quiddity [not translated], p. 61, ' is to the 100 Ps.,' Submission ; ' Note this is already in the ordinary Psalm-tune ;' Time [not translated], ' This, wth some little care, may be sung as the 100

Psalm, vide p. 115 [of printed book].' Two or three others have similar notes; and as HERBERT'S 'Easter' is in two metres, and the latter one a psalm metre, the translator alters the first to accord with the second, and then says, 'cætera vide to the same tune already, pag. 33 [of printed book];' and the same is done with the other double piece, 'Good-Friday,' with this note: 'The other 3 [verses] are to the same tune in print already, vid. p. 31.' These and the frequent references in the altered poems to the page of the printed book also show that the latter was intended to be consulted as the complement of the MS. One entry distinctly shows this: 'Whitsunda [*sic*] p. 51:

> "Listen, sweet dove, unto my song," &c.

Vid. cætera in libro—onely take out the words thus enclosed [ⵔ].' On examination, these words are found to be the fifth foot in each fourth line of HERBERT.

I note all these things, not because of the intrinsic value of the 'translation,' but because, like Leeke's translation of The Church Militant into Latin, they add to the proofs of the esteem in which we know HERBERT'S poems were held. Of the 'translation' itself not much can be said in its praise. As already stated, where it can be done, lines are kept intact; elsewhere a too-short line is eked out by added syllables, as in 'Sunday,' or as in 'Whitsunday,' a too-long line is shortened. 'Frailty' and 'The Starre' are also good examples of both processes. But even in such cases we find strange and even laughable devices, as in 'Mary Magdalen' and 'Affliction.' In two or three instances we find, too, words like 'jus—t' thus written to rhyme with 'us.' But it is when he has to recast the whole metre that the 'Translator' is fully shown, as in 'Constancy.' In such cases we must reverse his own note, and say, 'in our poor judgment HERBERT'S Reason is better than the translator's Poetry.' Philologically it may be noted, *en passant*, that *Fall* is glossed in the margin *Autumn*, thus showing that the present 'Americanism' was then dropping out of use in England (1682). The following specimens will illustrate I. B.'s mode of working and his own powers, viz. a stanza from several, showing examples from slight alteration to extreme change :

1. Mary Magdalen.

She being stain'd herself so vild,
    Why did she strive to make Him clean?
Who surely could not be defil'd :
    Why kept she not her tears (I mean)?   (st. 4.)

2. Sunday.

O day most calm, most sweet, most bright,
    The fruit of this, the next world's bud;
Th' endorsement of supreme delight,
    Writ by a friend, and wth His blood:
The couch of Time, Care's balm and bay;
    The week were dark but for thy light;
Thy torch alone [doth] show the way
    Thitherward where there is no night.   (st. 1.)

3. Affliction.

My heart did heave, and presently
    these words came forth, 'O God!'
By which I knew assuredly
    that Thou wast wth the rod,
And in the grief wch it produc't,
    to guide and govern it ;
And well did'st know how Thou couldst use 't
    to my relief (as fit).   (st. 1.)

4. Frailty. Com. tune.

Lord, in my silence how do I
    despise what upon trust
Is stil'd honour, riches, or
    fair eyes, but is fair dust!
I do surname them gilded clay,
    dear earth, fine hay or grasse ;
In all I think my foot doth tread
    upon their very head.   (st. 1.)

5. Constancy.

Who is the honest man ?
    he that doth constantly
And strongly also can
    pursue what's good ; I, I,
    That is most true
        to God Most High
        his neighbour nigh,
himself (in view).   (st. 1.)

6. The Star.

Bright spark shot from a brighter place,
Where beams surround my Saviour's face,
Canst thou be any other where
So well bestow'd as thou art there?   (st. 1.)

The MS. is very neatly and carefully written. The handwriting is not the same throughout, and there is just a possibility that parts of the ' translation' are by different hands ; but, taking all into consideration, it is more probable that the translator was one, but the scribes more than one. The present owner of the MS. has given it a dainty morocco skin, and I wish to acknowledge my sense of obligation to him (F. W. Cosens, Esq., London) for the use of this literary curiosity.

Of the Prose of Herbert in the original and early editions account is given in the several places. They are all now of considerable rarity.

Our Text of Verse and Prose is a careful reproduction of the original editions, with the results of collation of after-editions and MSS. in our Notes and Illustrations. The original and early editions of both Verse and Prose, but especially the Verse, deserve commendation for their accuracy. When we print for the first time, our anxious aim has been to be true to the MSS. In wording and orthography throughout, our Text is faithful to both. Two slight departures ought perhaps to be named, viz. from the profuse italics and capitals, which belong to the printers, not to HERBERT (as proved by his MSS.); and that where the ' ed' might be misread, we have elided, as ' perplex'd,' not ' perplexed.' The punctuation has been reduced from chaos to some order, it is hoped. Repeatedly, over-punctuation destroys sense and sound in the printed texts. I pass next to

II. *The story of the Life, as revealing his original and ultimate character, public and private.*

In delivering the ' little book,' to wit a MS. of ' The Temple,' it will be remembered the dying HERBERT used these remarkable words to his visitor, Mr. Duncon : ' Sir, I pray deliver this little book to my dear Brother Farrer [Ferrar], and tell him he shall find in it a picture of the many spiritual conflicts that have passed between God and my soul, before I could subject mine to the will of Jesus, my Master : in Whose service I have now found perfect freedom.' There was beautiful humility in this, but, like all genuine humility, it rested on the deepest truth and reality of personal experience. GEORGE HERBERT was perhaps at that moment, and from his induction to Bemerton, one of the holiest men in Christendom and the most John-like spirit in the Church of England, or in any Church. Nevertheless, it is to miss the teaching of his Life as well as the innermost meanings of his Writings, to forget ' the many spiritual conflicts' commemorated in his Poems, and the emphasis of the ' *now*' in his grateful as adoring profession, ' in Whose service I have *now* found perfect freedom.' That is to say, if, as I think, all must recognise in GEORGE HERBERT one whom we inevitably think of as a St. John in his ultimate tenderness and lovingness, equally must it be recalled that as, until the grace and masterdom of The Master transformed and transfigured him, St. John was originally bold, proud, fierce, self-conscious, so it was out of intense, prolonged, backsliding-marked conflict our Worthy became what he

did become, unworldly, humble, meek, gentle, tender, holy:
' my fierce youth' is his own confession (136. The Answer).
Izaak Walton did not know the subject of his ' Life' so
well as he himself did, or he never should have spoken of
him as at Westminster ' natively' good and gentle.   I can
accept nearly all his golden-mouthed Biographer's praise
of him even thus early, when he tells us that at School
' the beauties of his pretty behaviour and wit shin'd and
became so eminent and lovely in this his innocent age,
that he seem'd to be mark'd out for piety, and to have the
care of heaven and of a particular angel to guard and guide
him.' The power of his Mother's example and instruction
repressed that inborn haughtiness and lofty self-estimate
which flashed out very soon ; but the motherly power *was*
needed, there were haughtiness and pride to be repressed.
For if we take note of young Master Edward's presump-
tion in holding a 'dispute' in Logic at the University almost
immediately on his entrance there (twelfth or fourteenth
year), there was still more presumption in Master GEORGE
while at Westminster School answering and ' reproving'
Andrew Melville for daring to condemn the ultra-
Ritualism of King James in his Royal Chapel.   As will
appear, the renowned Divine and Scholar was thus ' re-
proved' by GEORGE HERBERT in his eleventh or twelfth
year. Effrontery or impudence is the only word for the
like of that ; and it is to be recalled, as symptomatic of
the native character—a character that showed itself simi-
larly and even more egregiously later.   When in his six-
teenth year, a Letter and double-Sonnet are extremely
noteworthy and suggéstive.   It seems clear that he was a
versifier from a very early date, probably as early as
Abraham Cowley or Pope were : and here is his verdict
to his Mother on the poetry that was then being pub-
lished : 'I fear the heat of my late Ague hath dryed up
those springs by which scholars say the Muses use to take
up their habitations. However, I need not their help to

reprove the vanity of those many love-poems that are
daily writ and consecrated to Venus ; nor to bewail that so
few are writ that look towards God and Heaven. For my
own part, my meaning, deer mother, is, in these sonnets,
to declare my resolution to be, That my poor abilities in
Poetry shall be all and ever consecrated to God's glory.'
This Letter (of which Walton gives only these sentences)
was written ' in the first year of his going to Cambridge,'
and the accompanying Sonnets ' for a New Year's gift.'
The ' first year' was 1608, or say his sixteenth year ; and
if the phrase ' poore abilities in poetry' is a foil to the for-
wardness and frowardness of his eleventh or twelfth year,
one has an inevitable suspicion that it was only a phrase,
and that Master George regarded his Sonnets as well
worthy of being sent as a New Year's gift.   There cer-
tainly is thought in them and his abidingly-characteristic
quaintness of wording, while the sentiment is admirable.
This double-Sonnet is such a land-mark in his life as to
demand a place here, that it may be studied :

'My God, where is that ancient heat towards Thee
    Wherewith whole shoals of martyrs once did burn,
Besides their other flames ?   Doth poetrie
    Wear Venus' liverie, onely serve her turn ?
    Why are not sonnets made of Thee, and layes
    Upon Thine altar burnt?   Cannot Thy love
Heighten a spirit to sound out Thy praise
    As well as any she ? Cannot Thy Dove
Outstrip their Cupid easilie in flight ?
    Or, since Thy wayes are deep, and still the same,
    Will not a verse runne smooth that bears Thy Name ?
Why doth that fire, which by Thy power and might
    Each breast does feel, no braver fuel choose
    Then that which one day worms may chance refuse ?

Sure, Lord, there is enough in Thee to drie
    Oceans of ink ; for, as the Deluge did
Cover the earth, so doth Thy Majestic.
    Each cloud distills Thy praise, and doth forbid

Poets to turn it to another use;
  Roses and lilies speak Thee, and to make
A pair of cheeks of them is Thy abuse.
  Why should I women's eyes for crystal take?
Such poor invention burns in their low minde,
  Whose fire is wild, and doth not upward go
  To praise, and on Thee, Lord, some ink bestow.
Open the bones, and you shall nothing finde
  In the best face but filth; when, Lord, in Thee
  The beauty lies in the discoverie.'

With reference to the sweeping condemnation of the 'Love-Poems' of the period, all familiar with them must agree that the youthful Censor was not without warrant; yet must it be kept in mind that Edmund Spenser's 'Twelve Books' of 'The Faerie Queene,' with, for the first time, 'Two Cantoes of Mutabilitie,' were at the very time in the press of 'H. L. for Matthew Lownes,' while Michael Drayton's pure Poems, 'newly corrected by the author,' bear the same date; and so with some of the supremest of the productions of Shakespeare and Jonson and the Elizabethan Worthies; while the alleged Love-songs 'daily writ and consecrated to Venus' are unknown or slight in proportion. Then, in respect of the 'Resolution,' when we come to examine into its carrying out, there is disappointment. Years follow years, and while he found time to go on with his 'Epigrams-Apologetical' in answer to Anti-Tami-Cami-Categoria, one is struck with the all but utter absence of Christian thinking as of Christian feeling therein. He is quick, keen, sarcastic, effective in unyielding defence of Ceremonial and Rite and Dignity; but there is scarcely a thrill of emotion, scarcely a recognition of the real end for which a Church exists. So, too, with his 'Epicidivm' celebration of Prince Henry. With such a nation-stirring death for text, what a great poem-sermon he might have preached! It is as pagan as if it had been written by Virgil or Horace, and more sycophantic than ever were they to a Cæsar. Even as far on as 1627, when

the 'Parentalia' appeared, there is wealth of filial venera-
tion and filial sorrow over his illustrious lady-mother ; but
there are the merest scintillations of Christian faith and
hope : precious scintillations, yet only aggravating the gene-
ral lack. The artist excels the poet, and the poet hides the
Christian. I cannot marvel that of the 'Parentalia,' as of
the 'Epigrams-Apologetical,' even so revering a friend as
Archdeacon Barnabas Oley felt constrained to pronounce
this judgment : 'those many Latin and Greek verses, the
obsequious [=funereal] Parentalia he made and printed in
her memory : which, though they be good, very good, yet
(to speak freely even of this man I so much honour) they
be dull or dead in comparison of his Temple Poems. And
no marvel. To write those, he made his ink with water of
Helicon ; but these inspirations prophetical were distilled
from above. In those, are weak motions of Nature ; in
these, raptures of grace ; in those he writ [of] flesh and
blood—a frail earthly woman, though a mother ; but in
these he praised his heavenly Father, the God of men and
angels, and the Lord Jesus Christ his Master.' Strongly
put, certainly, is this ; yet there is extremely notable and
extremely sad truth in it. Nor does it vindicate HERBERT to
allege that the *mode* of the day was to imitate the classic
writers, and so to speak of God as Jove, and more than
that, to make Christians talk like heathens ; for the *grava-
men* of our charge as the sting of our regret, not to say
wonder, is, that GEORGE HERBERT should not have risen
above such mere classicality, especially in the celebration
of his own lady-mother. I am compelled to look beneath
the logical inconsistency of all this with a really Christian
or Christ-tending life, to a still over-mastering earthliness,
even on the borders of *the* change of changes. We may
be very sure that if his Christianhood had been all in all
to him, he would have contrived to make it give cha-
racter to his (then) writings, as Shakespeare has it of
Antony :

> ' His delights
> Were dolphin-like ; *they show'd his back above*
> The element they liv'd in.'   (Antony and Cleopatra, v. 2.)

We are thus brought back to our starting-point, viz. that of GEORGE HERBERT, however true of his ultimate character, it was untrue what Walton says : ' In this morning of that short day of his life, he seem'd to be mark'd out for vertue and to become the care of heaven ; for God still kept his soul in so holy a frame, that he may and ought to be a pattern of vertue to all Posterity.' This is linked on to the Letter and double-Sonnet ; but the 'holy frame' came very much later ; the 'pattern' was not for Posterity until after ' *many spiritual conflicts.*' The ' Resolution' of his sixteenth year was self-evidently overborne by circumstances ; and when circumstances overbear a man he proves himself to be weak, and not free of blame.   In accord with this is the double set of Facts, which must be weighed by all who would understand the problem of this so unique Life and co-equally unique Writings : (*a*) The recurring declaration of his intention to give himself to the service of the Church ; (*b*) The contemporaneous paying court to the Court, and shouldering it with rivals to win political place.

(*a*) *The recurring declaration of his intention to give himself to the service of the Church.* His ' Letters' (in Vol. III.), as annotated, bring this out strikingly. Thus, in one of probably many to his stepfather (Sir John Danvers), he tells, with fine simpleness, of his book-hunger ; and one responds to it sympathetically as these words are read and re-read : ' I protest and vow I even study thrift, and yet I am scarce able, with much ado, to make one half year's allowance shake hands with the other ; and yet if a book of four or five shillings come in my way I buy it, though I fast for it ; yea, sometimes of ten shillings ; but, alas, sir, what is that to those infinite volumes of Divinity, which yet every day grow and swell bigger?' The closing allusion is

interpreted by the earlier appeal, the Letter thus opening :
'Sir, I dare no longer be silent, lest while I think I am
modest, I wrong both myself and also the confidence my
friends have in me ; wherefore I will open my case unto
you, which I think deserves the reading at the least ; *you
know, sir, how I am now setting foot into Divinity, to lay
the platform of my future life,* and shall I then be fain al-
ways to borrow books, and build on another's foundation?
What tradesman is there who will set up without his tools ?
Pardon my boldness, sir, it is a most serious case ; nor can
I write coldly on that wherein consisteth the making good
of my former education, of obeying the spirit which hath
guided me hitherto, and of achieving my (I dare say) holy
ends.' This was written on March 18, 1617. In 1619 he
is in hot pursuit of the office of Public Orator, as looking
to tread in the footsteps of its previous occupants, Sir
Robert Naunton and Sir Francis Nethersole. As we say
in our Memorial-Introduction, he used all means to in-
terest any likely to be influential. A hint from Sir Francis
Nethersole reveals at once the political aspiration and the
underlying and still unforsaken resolution as to the Church.
Here is his message to his friend, again through his step-
father : ' I understand by Sir Francis Nethersole's Letter,
that he fears I have not fully resolved of the matter, since
this place, being civil, may divert me too much from Di-
vinity, at which, not without cause, he thinks I aim ; but
I have wrote him back that this dignity hath no such earth-
liness in it, but it may very well be joined with Heaven ;
or if it had to others, yet to me it should not, for aught I
yet knew ; and therefore I desire him to send me a direct
answer in his next Letter.' There spoke an uneasy con-
science.   The parenthetic reservations, 'not without
cause' (even taken as merely an asseveration) and 'for
aught I yet knew,' are significant. And so it was through-
out. The intention was to give himself to the Church ;
but again and again he swerved from it, again and again

swayed between intention and resolve. Many of his Poems
take a new and vivid meaning when read in the light of
this Conflict ; so true, so lowly, so wistful, so inestimable
are their confessions—worth a cartload of such unrealities
as those of Rousseau (John Morley notwithstanding).

Weighing and reweighing what I have thus far written,
I have striven to convince myself that I might withdraw
my accusation (if it be accusation) of 'a lofty self-estimate'
on GEORGE HERBERT'S part. I cannot do so. But I do
not wish to be misunderstood, or to have the fact exag-
gerated. I have no idea that, like Donne, he was of those
who, as Carlyle puts it, 'go through a mud bath in youth
in order to come out clean.' But I may not forget the
apostolic warning that we must cleanse ourselves from all
filthiness of 'the spirit' as well as of the flesh (2 Corin-
thians vii. 1). I am also satisfied of his humility in other
directions later, even of his humility by fits and starts earlier,
and that he really had dedicated all his powers to their
highest uses, whatever his way of life might be, at Court,
or in the University, or in the world. What I must recog-
nise is, that in his 'fierce youth,' while 'eager, hot, and
undertaking,' as he himself describes it, he did ' turn aside,'
did 'neglect,' and was moved thereto by ambition in not
a whit different from his eldest brother Edward's, and a
self-estimate in not a whit less pronounced. Of course it
was impossible that a man of HERBERT'S brain should
not have known himself to be superior to the mass of
those with whom he came into contact, i.e. the mass
of those of the same education and opportunities with
himself. His humility therefore inevitably consisted, not
in an undue depreciation of himself in this respect (for
that had been falsehood, false-witness to what God had
made him), but in his judgment of others whenever others
were in other qualities superior to him, and in his judg-
ment of those really greater than himself and of himself
as compared to them, and finally of his low state as com-

pared with the ideal and the infinite. Accordingly, in the closing years, and after his 'many spiritual conflicts,' GEORGE HERBERT, with all his high estimate of his own intellect *quoad* others, was indubitably lowly, even pathetically humble. But do not let us hide the conflict, and victory so resulting. Summarily, I find in his death-bed sayings and in various of his Poems a true humility and a deep-felt sense of what he was in comparison with what he would be and ought to be. His sense of unworthiness is infinitely affecting, as revealed in his reluctance to accept Orders and Bemerton, and in his prostration when ringing himself in there.

Subsidiary to, or parallel with, this is my representation of his natural temperament. I am aware that while the child is father of the man, the father is not the man. Neither do I forget that the period of puberty is a time of change inwardly as well as in the body, *i.e.* morally and physically. Consequently, I might have been persuaded that the 'native' gentleness which Walton claims for HERBERT as a youth was not impossible in combination with the narrow-mindedness or inherited belief of boyhood that made him stand up against the venerable Melville for what he believed to be the only truth, and that while as a boy naturally gentle, the stronger passions came later, and were then more hardly mastered. But again I must confess, that his whole bearing and the tone of the Epigrams-Apologetical compel me to accept his own description of himself as 'fierce' in youth and impetuous, and that the gentleness was also ultimate, not primary.

(*b*) *The contemporaneous paying court to the Court, and shouldering it with rivals to win political place.* This is simple matter-of-fact. So far from the office of Public Orator proving to be higher and heavenlier in his hands as compared with what it had been in the hands of others, the most fervent admirer of the GEORGE HERBERT we all love and revere must sorrowfully admit, that the public Letters and

Orations of his predecessors and successors compare favourably with his. Even Sir Francis Nethersole stood forth in defence of ' the Truth,' as he weened, against John Goodwin, the theological controversialist. The public occasions —historical—whereon he was called to exercise his office gave him splendid opportunities for speaking ' the truth ;' but he was dumb. His Letter to the king, on receiving that most ignorant and worthless book, 'Basilicon Doron,' is a piece of contemptible flattery where flattery was treason to the King of Kings — such as of old drew forth the smiting question to Hezekiah, ' What have they seen in thine house ?' (Isaiah xxxix. 4.) His ' Orations' are mere elegant nothings, without one gleam of the ' heaven' he named, and they are weighted with earthliness. Then there is the twofold fact of his desertion of Cambridge and delegation of his office as Public Orator to good Herbert Thorndike—wherefore? Because King James and the Court were at neighbouring Royston, and he must be there too! Walton's admirably honest words place this beyond doubt : ' With this [the sinecure], and his Annuity, and the advantage of his College and of his Oratorship, he enjoyed his genteel humour for clothes and Court-like company, and seldom looked towards Cambridge, *unless the King were there, but then he never failed;* and at other times left the manage of his Orator's place to his learned friend Mr. Herbert Thorndike, who is now Prebendary of Westminster.'[1]

Even this is not all, nor the worst. In Bishop Hacket's 'Life of the great Archbishop Williams' we find this instance of what might be called flunkeyism, and was certainly deplorable sycophancy when the sycophant was

---

[1] *En passant* it may be noted that in Dean Duport's Epicedia (Musae Subsecivae seu Poetica, 1676) is a Lament headed 'In obitum Viri omnifaria eruditione instructissimi, Herberti Thorndiki, Canonici Westmonasteriensis et Collegii SS. Trinitatis Cantab. non ita pridem Socii' (p. 494).

GEORGE HERBERT: 'Mr. George Herbert, being Prelector in the Rhetorique School in Cambridge, anno 1618, passed by those fluent orators that domineered in the pulpits of Athens and Rome, and insisted to read upon an oration of King James, which he analysed, showed the concinnity of the parts, the propriety of the phrase, the height and power of it to move the affections, the style utterly unknown to the ancients, who could not conceive what kingly eloquence was, in respect of which these noted demagogi were but hirelings and triobolary rhetoricians' (Hacket's Life of Archbishop Williams, part i. p. 175).[1]

[1] The adulation illustrated in the text is confirmed by HERBERT's royal poems. I add here another version of his epigram-Lines (of the present volume, page 169) from Amos' 'Gems of Latin Poetry:'

> ' While Prince to Spain and King to Cambridge goes,
> The question is, whose love the greater shows ?
> Ours, like himself, o'ercomes, for his wit 's more
> Remote from ours than Spain from Britain's shore.'

On this Dodd annotates as follows: 'Herbert was Public Orator when he presented this flattery to James. If his name were substituted for that of Bacon in the following epigram by Whaley, entitled "Verses occasioned by reading Lord Bacon's flattery to King James I.," the reproof would be most applicable' (Whaley's Poems, 1745):

> ' Ye, to whom Heaven imparts its special fires,
> Whose breasts the wond'rous quickening beam inspires.
> That sheds strong eloquence's melting rays,
> Or scatters forth the bright poetic blaze ;
> Look here, and learn those gifts how low a light
> If conscious dignity guides not their flight ;
> How mean, when human pride their service claims,
> And { Bacon / Herbert } condescends to flatter James.'

But it was the fashion to flatter in those days, and King James had abundance of such incense offered to him, though, according to Ben Jonson, it was impossible to *flatter* so perfect a monarch. The dramatist addressed the following epigram 'To the Ghost of Martial' (Ep. 36) :

> ' Martial, thou gav'st far nobler epigrams
> To thy Domitian than I can my James:

Eheu ! eheu ! In connection with this I had hoped to be
the possessor of GEORGE HERBERT'S copy of King James's
collective Works. A copy of the folio of 1616, with a
'George Herbert' written underneath other HERBERT au-
tographs on back of the portrait, was kindly forwarded to
me by Mr. Thomas Kerslake, of Bristol ; but it seemed to
me so comparatively eighteenth-century-like, and so utterly
unlike any one of his known autographs, that I felt com-
pelled to return it. I have rarely met with so keen a dis-
appointment ; for many years having sought in vain to
secure a specimen of HERBERT'S handwriting.

It is no pleasure to me to bring out these facts ; it is
a sorrow, a pain ; nor do they abate my veneration for
our Worthy ; neither do they, in my apprehension, go
to lessen the potentiality and blessedness of the example
of his after-Life as it grew beautiful beneath the divine
touch. Contrariwise this double matter-of-fact is fitted
to yield at once encouragement to such as are fighting to-
day the same ' spiritual conflicts,' and admonition that the
best man is but a man at the best, and the Christian just
what the grace of God creatively makes him ; while be-
yond is greater glory to that grace which out of such
earthly and base elements fashioned so lovely and lov-
able a nature. Lord Cherbury had sounded his younger
brother's character when he wrote of him in his Auto-
biography : ' His Life was most holy and exemplary ; in-
asmuch that about Salisbury, where he lived beneficed for
many years [three only], he was little less than sainted.
He was not exempt from passion and choler, being infirmi-

But in my royal subject I pass thee,
Thou flatteredst thine, mine cannot flatter'd be.'
(Dodd's Epigrammatists, p. 233.)

Verily, in Scott's words (though he himself paid like unworthy
homage to the ' Fourth George') all this was 'the immortal bowing
down to the mortal.'

ties to which all our race is subject ; *but, that excepted, without reproach in his actions.*' Izaak Walton also penetrated to the heart of the matter, when, having told of the ' conflict,' he added : ' These were such conflicts as they only can know that have endured them ; for ambitious desires and the outward glory of this world are not easily laid aside ; but *at last* God inclined him to put on a resolution to serve at His altar.' Even so. There was ' passion,' there was ' choler,' there were ' ambitious desires,' there were attractions even to seductiveness in ' the outward glory' of the world, and these born of a very lofty self-estimate ; so that not of nature, but of divine masterdom, was the final conquest gained. *En passant,* his ennobled Brother perchance had experienced the ' passion' and ' choler' which he noted from GEORGE in his remonstrances with him about his speculative theological-philosophical opinions. These words, in The Thanksgiving, seem to me to point to his sceptical brother :

> ' My bosom-friend, if he blaspheme Thy name,
> *I will tear thence his love and fame.*'

The sharp discipline of frequent bodily ailments, solitary retirements, loss of friends and patrons (if any dared patronise him) on whom he leaned, disappointment at the eleventh hour of ' painted' expectations, premonitions of a short life on earth, and the inrush of The Spirit of God upon his soul, in the last years, ' changed,' self-revealed, abased, mellowed him. That deep lovingness of his nature, which rises like incense from his private letters to his Mother and of his ' sick sister' Elizabeth—comparable with Gregory of Nyssa's wistful affection for Macrina— and to others, was dilitated and sanctified by the supreme love ; and henceforward GEORGE HERBERT remained an example and a trophy of the transforming grace of God. No need of ecclesiastical canonisation. The ' three years' at Bemerton put better than a nimbus around all.

I have dwelt thus on the story of the Life as revealing his original and ultimate character, public and private, because the Life cannot be understood in what of deepest and grandest was in it apart from the Facts, and neither can the Poems, in what is finest, tenderest, truest, be understood unless studied in the light and shadow of the Life. Let the Reader read and read again and muse over the heart-revelations of the Poems, that the music and subtle imaginativeness of them may the more touch. I bring together a few scattered stanzas that seem to me infinitely precious :

'How should I praise Thee, Lord ? how should my rymes
    Gladly engrave Thy love in steel,
      If, what my soul doth feel sometimes,
        My soul might ever feel !'   (23. The Temper.)

.   .   .   .

'Were it not better to bestow
    Some place and power on me?
Then should Thy praises with me grow,
    And share in my degree.
But when I thus *dispute and grieve,*
    I do resume my sight;
And pilfring what I once did give,
    Disseize Thee of Thy right.
How know I, if Thou shouldst me raise,
    That I should then raise Thee ?
Perhaps great places and Thy praise
    Do not so well agree.'   (68. Submission.)

.   .   .   .

'Joy, I did lock thee up, but some bad man
      Hath let thee out again ;
And now, methinks, I am where I began
      Sev'n years ago : one vogue and vein,
      One aire of thoughts usurps my brain.
I did toward Canaan draw, but now I am
Brought back to the Red Sea, the sea of shame.'
        (98. The Bunch of Grapes.)

.   .   .   .   .

> '*things sort not to my will*
> *Ev'n when my will doth studie Thy renown:*
> Thou turnest th' edge of all things on me still,
>   *Taking me up to throw me down;*
> So that, *ev'n when my hopes seem to be sped,*
> I am to grief alive, to them as dead.'   (131. The Crosse.)

> '*O that I once past changing were,*
> *Fast in Thy Paradise, where no flower can wither!*'
>   (132. The Flower.)

> 'When I had forgot my birth,
>   And on Earth
> In delights of Earth was drown'd,
> God took bloud, and needs would be
>   Spilt with me,
> And so found me on the ground.'   (151. The Banquet.)

His first poem of '16. Affliction' is faithfully auto-biographic throughout. So, too, '62. The Pearl,' with its proud yet humbling recollection of the ways of learning, and the ways of pleasure, and the ways of honour, of love, of wit, of music, which he 'knew.' Equally noticeable also is '82. The Quip,' where, personifying Beauty, Money, Glory, and Wit as successively assailing him with raillery for his neglect of their fascinations, he replies to each and all by turning to his heavenly Master: 'But Thou shalt answer, Lord, for me.'

These and other poems of The Temple belong to different years. Some probably were composed contemporaneously with the double Sonnet to his Mother; others during his retirement in Kent; most, in all likelihood, at Bemerton; the whole profoundly and blessedly real. They refer mainly to his inner or spiritual life, and thus are of rare experimental worth, and must so abide.

Looked at from either the human or the divine side, the Life of GEORGE HERBERT seems to mo of inestimable value. He was thoroughly human; no cloistered recluse, no visionary, no sentimental bookworm, but 'a man who combined

with the devotion and self-discipline of Thomas à Kempis
the accomplishments of a perfect gentleman, the genial
humour and shrewd practical sense of a thorough man of
the world.'[1] More than this; for even in his ultimate sanc-
tity he was whole-souled, whole-hearted, genial, and plea-
sant; and so 'far from being a mere devotee, planted on
his solitary column in unnatural isolation, inaccessible to
his fellow-men, he was emphatically a man of social sym-
pathies, sustained and directed upwards by the entire de-
votion of his heart to heaven, as the tendrils of a vine are
taught to ascend by the elm round which it clings.'[2] He
loved to watch the 'quidquid agunt' of men, their busi-
ness and pleasures, not with the contemptuous indifference
of a Stoic or Epicurean, but as being all, if duly regulated,
component parts in the order and beauty of the universe.
Gifted himself with rare natural advantages, he neither
neglected nor misused them. He was at home with the
humblest, and equally at home with the highest; he could
soothe the temporal anxieties and minister to the spiritual
yearnings of his lowliest parishioners, and at the same time
with all mannerly courtesy 'rebuke' the most eminent.
Walton tells us of the poor widow who touched his heart
with her little simple story; while Oley writes, ' There was
not a man in his way, be he of what rank he would, that
spoke awry in order to God, but HERBERT would wipe his
mouth [!] with a modest, grave, and Christian reproof.'
As we think, perhaps, there was a leaven of superstitious
clinging to mere ecclesiasticism; yet were his 'Friday, as
a day of mortification and humiliation,' and ' Saints' bell
[Sanctus-bell] ringing to daily prayers ' at the canonical
hours of ten and four,' whereby men 'would leave their
plough to rest awhile, that they might offer their devo-
tions to God with him and then return to their work,' and
habitual ' Fasting,' transfigured by their genuineness to

---

[1] The Christian Remembrancer, July 1862, pp. 104, 105.
[2] Ibid. p. 111.

him. Moreover, as we are anxious should be remembered, notwithstanding his intensity of disciplined devotion, he was on all sides human and a 'good citizen.' It does one good —like a full-inhaled draught of sea-air after the exhaustion of a thronged drawing-room—to read and re-read the genial, frank, plain-spoken, thoroughly fresh and real moralisings of HERBERT. Thus, has he to rebuke the young nobility for ' idleness' as the 'great national sin of the times,' how does he set about it? By no mere sentimentalisms, but by prescribing manly occupations. He recommends them to learn farming; to act as magistrates; to study civil law; the bases of international relations, and therefore especially useful to statesmen and diplomatists; to improve themselves by travelling abroad, with all their wits about them; 'to ride the great horse,' that is, to acquire the accomplishments of the tilt-yard—the last assuring us that he would have added the rifle corps to his roll. His wisdom is not of a monastical order. On the other hand, it is far removed from the sharp practice of mere worldlings. It is like the prudential maxims of the Book of Proverbs and Ecclesiastes (and Ecclesiasticus), the parallelism of duty with expediency. The Church Porch reminds us of the best parts of Horace's Satires, not less by its ' pedestrian muse' than by its shrewd wit and gracious pleasantry. It abounds in pithy sayings, such as may give a man not the manners only, but the principles and feelings of a true gentleman — meet follower of Him ' the first true gentleman that ever breathed.' Beneath the lighter raillery too, lies a deep vein of sentiment, the utterances of which sound like the voice of that great and wise king, who tried all things under the sun (not above the sun) and found them vanity. This Shakespearian element, found in Hamlet and Henry of Agincourt, whereby the utter nothingness of even the greatest affairs of this life, in one point of view, does not the less affirm the immeasurable importance of even the most insignificant, as

formative of the moral destiny, well deserves thinking-out.
'It is characteristic of him,' says The Christian Remem-
brancer (as before, p. 121),' that he translated the sensible
little treatise on " Temperance and Sobriety" of Ludovicus
Cornarus, known to Italian scholars as Luigi Cornaro, of
Padua ; a delightful sketch of a hale and hearty old age,
with rules for attaining it.' Further : ' HERBERT seems to
have had a peculiar aptness, both by nature and education,
for casuistry ; not for hair-splitting and sophistries, but for
the " noble art," as he rightly calls it, of solving the per-
plexing cases of conscience which occur every day. His
way of cutting these knots, or rather of disentangling
them, is thoroughly English. It is the evidence of a
healthy moral sense, practised in logic, but with its own
unerring instincts unblunted.' . . . . ' His " proverbs," some
apparently his own, others merely collected by him, which
the reader will find among his greater works, under the
title of " Jacula Prudentum," leave hardly anything in
life untouched.'

But while HERBERT's humanness lies as well in the
innermost of him as on the surface, the divine side of
his Life is very notable. If he mingled with his fellow-
men, as recognising that the work and excellence of man
lies *in* the world and not *out* of it, and has a fruition in
this life, though not only in this life, his supremest hours
were those passed under the shadow of the Divine Pre-
sence in his praying-chamber Study. Whether playing
his lute alone or for a gathered company of his parishioners
—as finely told by Walton—or footing it to Salisbury to
be rapt heavenward by the cathedral music—as also told
by Walton—he was still the ' man of God.' Certainly a
Life like this is worthy of the deepest and most earnest
study—a life ' in which work and rest, self-discipline and
natural impulse, secular duties and heavenly aspirations,
are blended into harmonious unity, as in one of those
rich strains of music. now grave, now joyous, but always

duly measured, which he loved to follow ; a life in which the coarser threads of existence are inextricably intertwined with and transfigured by the radiance of the more ethereal filaments ; in which the calmness and equanimity which the Roman poet vainly longed for seems attained ; as the highest and most complete development of human nature possible on earth. Monastic seclusion may secure peace by eliminating the elements of discord. "They make desolation and call it peace." A life like HERBERT'S calls into action all the component parts of our organisation, and consecrates them severally to their appointed use.[1] In nothing does the soundness and wholesomeness of our Worthy's religion more delightfully reveal itself than in his ' Sunday ;' so radiant and joyous, equally free from the intrusion of worldly cares and occupations and the vacuity and sombreness of literal sabbatarianism. Similarly noticeable is his freedom from mere pious phrases and conventionalisms of theology.

Turn we next to

III. *The Anti-Tami-Cami-Categoria controversy, and its significance, and bearings.*

From the historic memorableness of the Petition of the Puritans which Melville defended ; from the prominence and praise given to the Epigrams-apologetical of HERBERT in answer, and the censure of the illustrious Scotchman stereotyped in Walton's ' Life'—his ' praise' of the first edition being cancelled in the after ones, and so continued ; and from the important place among HERBERT'S Poems which the originals and our translations must henceforth hold—it is laid upon us to discuss this matter thoroughly, especially as it must be remembered that in his latest poem (' The Church Militant') HERBERT flouts the Puritans and The Reformation, thus linking on his earlier with his later opinions, as we shall see.

[1] The Christian Remembrancer, as before, p. 119.

Walton thus narrates the Facts—as he cared to know them—of the controversy with Andrew Melville,—whose Latinised name was 'Melvinus' (or Melvin) : 'The next occasion he had and took to shew his great abilities was with them, to show also his great affection to that Church in which he received his baptism, and of which he professed himself a member ; and the occasion was this : there was one Andrew Melvin [be it intercalated that '*one* John Miltou' was so spoken of], a minister of the Scotch Church and rector of St. Andrews, who, by a long and constant converse with a discontented part of that clergy which opposed episcopacy, became at last to be a chief leader of that faction ; and had proudly appeared to be so to King James when he was but king of that nation ; who, the second year after his coronation in England, convened a part of the bishops and other learned divines of his Church to attend him at Hampton Court, in order to a friendly conference with some dissenting brethren, both of this and the Church of Scotland : of which Scotch party Andrew Melvin was one ; and he being a man of learning, and inclined to satirical poetry, had scattered many malicious bitter verses against our Liturgy, our Ceremonies, and our Church Government ; which were by some of that party so magnified for the wit, that they were therefore brought into Westminster School, where Mr. GEORGE HERBERT then, and often after, made such answers to them, and such reflections on him and his Kirk, as might unbeguile any man that was not too deeply preëngaged in such a quarrel. But to return to Mr. Melvin at Hampton Court conference : he there appeared to be a man of an unruly wit, of a strange confidence, of so furious a zeal, and of so ungoverned passions, that his insolence to the king and others at this conference lost him both his rectorship of St. Andrews and his liberty too ; for his former verses and his present reproaches there used against the Church and State caused him to be committed prisoner to the Tower

of London, where he remained very angry for three years.
At which time of his commitment he found the Lady
Arabella Stuart an innocent prisoner there ; and he pleased
himself much in sending the next day after his commit-
ment there two verses to the good lady, which I will
under-write, because they may give the reader a taste of
his others, which were like these :

"Causa tibi mecum est communis casceris ; Ara-
    Bella tibi causa est, Araque sacra mihi."

I shall not trouble my reader with an account of his en-
largement from that prison, or his death ; but tell how
Mr. HERBERT's verses were thought so worthy to be pre-
served, that Dr. Duport, the learned Dean of Peterborough,
hath lately collected and caused many of them to be
printed, as an honourable memorial of his friend Mr.
GEORGE HERBERT and the cause he undertook.' Further :
' I have but this to say more of him, that if Andrew Mel-
vin died before him, then GEORGE HERBERT died without
an enemy.'

Dear as are ' meek' Walton's name and memory, the
truth must at long-last be told, and this mingle-mangle
of unhistoric statement and mendacious zeal exposed.
There are nearly as many blunders as sentences in the
Narrative, and the *animus* is as base as the supercilious
ignorance is discreditable. Alas that I must say these
' hard things' of anything from the pen of one I so revere
(substantially) ! Alas that they should be true !

To begin with, the Facts are jumbled, and I shall call
one to give them accurately who will not be appealed from
by any capable reader,—the preëminently judicial and
candid Dr. Thomas M'Crie, in his incomparable ' Life of
Andrew Melville' (1856 : Works, vol. ii.). In c. viii. 1603-8
he thus writes : ' The ministers of Scotland waited with
anxiety to see how James would act towards that nume-
rous and respectable body of his new subjects who had all

along pleaded for *a farther reformation in the English Church*. From this they could form a pretty correct estimate of the line of conduct which he intended to pursue with themselves. Before the death of Elizabeth he had sounded the dispositions of the Puritans. They were universally in favour of his title; and there is no reason to doubt that he gave them hopes in the event of his accession. When he was on his way to London they presented to him a petition, commonly called, from the number of names affixed to it, the *Millenary Petition;* stating their grievances, and requesting that measures might be adopted for redressing them, and for removing corruptions which had long been complained of by the soundest Protestants. No sooner was this Petition presented than the two Universities took the alarm. The University of Cambridge passed *a grace*, " that whosoever opposed, by word, or writing, or any other way, the doctrine or discipline of the Church of England, or any part of it, should be suspended, *ipso facto*, from any degree already taken; and be disabled from taking any degree for the future." The University of Oxford published a formal answer to the Petition, in which they accused those who subscribed it of a spirit of faction and hostility to monarchy, abused the Scottish Reformation, lauded the government of the Church of England as the great support of the Crown, and concluded with this very modest declaration : " There are at this day more learned men in this kingdom than are to be found among all the ministers of religion in all Europe besides." These proceedings were not only injurious to several respectable members of both Universities, who were known to have taken part in the Petition, but disrespectful to the king, who had received it, and promised to inquire into the abuses of which it complained. Melville felt indignant at this prostitution of academical authority, and attacked the resolutions of the English University in a satirical poem which he wrote in defence of the Petition-

ers. The poem was extensively circulated in England,
and galled the ruling party in the Church no less than it
gratified their opponents.'

The 'satirical poem' was the ' Anti-Tami-Cami-Cate-
goria,' which was published in 1604; so that as it came
to Westminster School, ' where Mr. GEORGE HERBERT
then was,' on publication, we have the most illustrious
scholar of his age, the coequal of Causabon and the
associate of every man of mark on the continent of
Europe, assailed by this stripling of eleven or twelve
(b. 1593); and not him alone, but the venerable minis-
ters of the Church of England, headed by the great and
good Arthur Hildersam and Stephen Egerton, and in
the roll of 750, really including the flower of the Church,
with tens of thousands of the people at their back. Dr.
Busby had had something very different from '*praise*' for
Master GEORGE if his Epigrams, ' THEN *and often after*,'
had come under *his* eyes. Nor may it be alleged as ob-
viating criticism and condemnation, that HERBERT was
young, and as yet a believer in what he had been brought
up, and a believer, therefore, in the falsehood of every-
thing opposed to his belief. Neither will it do to claim
that HERBERT was not answering Melville as a theologian,
but simply answering a satirical poem by satire. With
reference to the former, his Epigrams-Apologetical was
no boyish episode, but of the very substance of his life-
long beliefs. Moreover, it is plain that he left behind him
a carefully prepared manuscript of the whole; for Dean
Duport's text (1662) is of special accuracy, and complete.
With reference to the latter, the reader will at once dis-
cern that the churchman (if not the theologian) domi-
nates the satirist. The satire is toothless and mild; the
dogma absolute and narrow; charity absent utterly, and
equally so that respect for others' convictions which is
based on self-respect. Be it remembered likewise that
(1) The Petition of the ' Evangelical Ministers' was not

the petition of later Nonconformity (or Dissent), but of
the most venerable men of his own Church ; (2) That in
'The Church Militant'—as noted in the outset—he has a
fling at 'The Reformation,' as thus :

> 'The late Reformation never durst
> Compare with ancient times and purer yeares,
> But in the Jews and us deserveth tears.'

' Tears' !

Turning to 'Anti-Tami-Cami-Categoria' itself, it is
very much a pungent and memorable putting of the ob-
jections and reforms of the 'Petition.' The humble suit
to the king was that 'of these offences following, some may
be removed, some amended, some qualified.' I limit my-
self to those 'in the Church-service': 'That the cross in
Baptism, interrogatories ministered to infants, confirma-
tions, as superfluous, may be taken away. Baptism not
to be ministered by women [midwives], and so explained.
The cap and surplice not urged. That examination go
before the communion. That it be ministered with a ser-
mon. That divers terms of priests, and absolution, and
some other used, with the ring in marriage, and other
such like in the book, may be corrected. The longsome-
ness of service abridged. Church songs and music mode-
rated to better edification. That the Lord's Day be not
profaned. The rest upon holidays not so strictly urged.
That there may be an uniformity of doctrine prescribed.
No Popish opinion to be any more taught or defended.
No ministers charged to teach their people to bow at the
name of Jesus. That the canonical Scriptures only be
read in the church.' I add only, 'for Church discipline'
—'That the oath, *ex officio*, whereby men are forced to
accuse themselves, be more sparingly used:' of which
Lord Burghley thus wrote to Archbishop Whitgift : ' Now,
my good lord, by chance I have come to the sight of an
instrument of twenty-four articles of great length and
curiosity, formed in a Romish style, to examine all manner

of ministers in this time, without distinction of persons, to be exacted *ex officio mero* . . . . These I have read, and found so curiously penned, so full of branches and circumstances, that I think the Inquisitions of Spain use not so many questions to comprehend and intrap their preys' (Fuller, Church History).

With the knowledge that all these things were in the Petition, it is an outrage and an impertinence that HERBERT should systematically conceal the fact, and throughout answer ' Anti-Tami-Cami-Categoria,' as if its objections and demands for ' Reformation' were the crotchets of an individual, and that individual an exceptionally bigoted and blind opponent of Episcopacy. But the thing grows blacker and unworthier still when the Petition, with Melville's defence of it, is examined in the light of contemporary events and circumstances. HERBERT found it easy to raise the loud laugh against the (imagined) morbid narrowness that took exception to the sign of the cross, to the sacerdotal distinction between clergy and laity, to the claim of a ' priesthood,' to the accompanying vestures of cap and surplice, the substitution of singing (=intoning, I imagine) for articulate speech that all could hear and know, and all the rest of it, on to sacramentarianism in acts that were not sacramental. It was easy also to crack small jests on the ' *parity*' of the membership of The Church or Kirk (*Kappa* in Scotland preferred to *Chi*, as Drummond of Hawthornden played on), and the conscientious protest against law-made offices and officials of which the Word of God made no mention. I am free to concede that there was a certain narrowness, just as I must believe that ' narrow' (strait) is the Gate and the Way. I am free, too, to admit that at this late day, cap of college and surplice and other episcopal vestures and vestments are inoffensive. I am free even to allow that in the mouth of GEORGE HERBERT ultimately the name ' Priest' meant no derogation to Him the One Priest. Let these be granted ; yet let us strenuously and in charity try to *get at the motives and the conscience of the Petitioners and of such a man as Andrew Melville.*

What, then, was their standing-ground ? It was this, that they were brought face-to-face every day, all over England, with so absolute an ignorance among the great bulk of the people of what really Christianity was, as to 'constrain' them by every means available to teach and preach the simple Gospel. The reader must get away behind the mists of intervening centuries, and actualise to himself how utter was the darkness of England, and how very little the recent and relatively brief ascendancy of Protestantism had as yet served to disperse that darkness. Everywhere the masses were sunk in superstition. Witch-craft was still a terror ; fairies real existences ; moor and mountain peopled with unearthly mythology. Going with their sheep over the downs, or with their wool to market, they appealed to the tutelar saints of their several parish churches. 'Good St. Catherine, stay my oxen !' would a farmer cry, when in chase of his straying cattle over Salisbury Plain. The drover prayed to St. Anthony. As the pack-horses came sliding and stumbling with obstreperous jingle down the chalk hill-side, the men in charge would invoke the aid of St. Loy. Not only did they appeal to dead saints, but to graven images. In HERBERT'S own Wiltshire, while he was entering his vicarage of Bemerton (in 1631), Mr. Sherfield (a friend of Joseph Alleine) having long observed 'many people' pause and bow before a window in the parish church at Salisbury, asked them why they did so : ' Because the Lord our God is there,' was the reply. On looking more closely into the glass, ' all diamonded with quaint device,' he found that it contained seven representations of God the Father, in the form of a little old man with a blue and red coat, with a pouch on his side (Rushworth's Collections, vol. ii. p. 153). This

was in the diocese which had so long been illumined with
the presidency of men like Jewell and Davenant ; and if
here so much ignorance prevailed, how great would be
the darkness elsewhere ! If only we will do by others as
we would have others do by us, a thoughtful consideration
of FACTS like these, will reveal to us a spiritual meaning
and dignity, and allegiance to the Lord, and an awful
sense of responsibility to Him, in most of the opinions of
the Puritans, which wear to-day a look of the merest fan-
tastique of scrupulosity. A living historian, not a theo-
logian or ecclesiastic-official, has said on this : ' The sur-
plice was the recognised symbol of the priestly character,
and might have a tendency to recall the doctrine of a
morely human intercessor standing between God and man.
The cross in baptism and the consecrated font might,
they said, easily bring back with them the exorcisims accom-
panying the rite of baptism in Roman Catholic churches.
The observance of saints' days might suggest the adora-
tion held to be due to those saints. Kneeling at the Com-
munion had its tacit reference to the conversion of the
consecrated wafer. To retain these ceremonies, it was
agreed, even were they innocent in themselves, was ex-
tremely dangerous to the English Church, which had so
recently emerged from Romanism' (J. L. Sanford's Studies
of the Great Rebellion, p. 67). It suggests much that
is sorrowful and bewildering, that only a few miles off
GEORGE HERBERT had no sympathy with such intensity
of conviction, such ' holy fear ;' nothing but admiration
for the Church, and flouting and scorn for the Puritans.
All the more saddening is this in our knowledge that in
part from the misfortune of circumstances, but in part
also from proclaimed and enforced usages, ' the Flock' of
God went uncared for—the under-shepherds largely actu-
alising the mournful prophetic-portraitures of Ezekiel—
albeit it is the glory of GEORGE HERBERT that he was com-
petent amid abounding incompetence, and faithful amid

mere officialism. A 'preaching ministry' was an exception. Elizabeth had said, 'It is good for the world to have few preachers—three or four may suffice for a county, and the reading of the Homilies is enough.' The calm-judging Selden, speaking of the clergy, says, 'they were ignorant and indolent, and had nothing to support their credit but beard, title, and habit' (History of Titles, Preface, p. i.; 1618). Milton, in 'Lycidas,' utters a like complaint (1637). Richard Baxter, writing of Shropshire in the days of his boyhood—that is, about 1620 and ten years after—says, 'There was little preaching of any kind, and that little was rather calculated to injure than to benefit. In High Ercall there were four readers in the course of six years; all of them ignorant, and two of them immoral men. At Eaton Constantine there was a reader of eighty years of age, Sir William Rogers, who never preached; yet he had two livings, twenty miles apart from each other. His sight failing, he repeated the prayers without the book; but to read the lessons he employed a common labourer one year, a tailor another; and at last his own son, the best stage-player and gamester in all the country, got Orders, and supplied one of his places. Within a few miles round were nearly a dozen ministers of the same description; poor ignorant readers, and most of them of dissolute lives' (Orme's Life of Baxter, vol. ii. p. 3; Fuller, sub anno 1630; Rushworth, vol. i. part ii. p. 150). George Wither was roused to denounce these 'unprofitable servants :'

> 'In their poverty they will not stick
> For catechising, visiting the sick,
> With suchlike duteous works of piety
> As do belong to their society;
> But if they once but reach a vicarage,
> Or be inducted to some parsonage,
> Men must content themselves, and think it well
> If once a month they hear the sermon bell.'
>   (Britaine's Remembrancer, 1628.)

Such was the RULE, and it is of rule we are now speaking, not of a few, a very few, brilliant exceptions.[1]

Looking now into ‘ Anti-Tami-Cami-Categoria’ as first made to ‘ speak English,’ and into HERBERT’s ‘Epigrams-Apologetical’—also for the first time translated—one is almost stung into indignation, were it not for sorrow that the offender should be GEORGE HERBERT. There are incidental acknowledgments by him of the weight and worth of Andrew Melville, a sense of the impudence of such frivolous smartness, as addressed to one white-haired and renowned over Europe, a twinge of conscience as aware of misrepresentation of good and true men, and a tacit plea of necessity laid upon him to defend the Church at all hazards. The reader will judge : but for my part it broadens out what grace did for GEORGE HERBERT to find epigram on epigram and classic verse on verse, without almost one articulate word for the Master he later so served and loved. There is superfluous laudation of the Bride, but what of the Bridegroom? Insinuation and invective against the Puritans, but not a ‘ jot or tittle’ for the grand work they had done and were doing ! Clever hits, innuendoes, puns, contemptuousness ; but nothing of the ‘ charity that thinketh no evil.’ ‘ Cap and bell’ jingling ; little of the hush of reverence and awe before Spirit-born convictions. Homage to ideal bishops, but ignoble silence on that ‘ pride of prelates’ which made so many of them at the period scornful of a bishop’s true work—a pride and scorn that roused our own William Wordsworth

---

[1] Many authorities have been consulted in preparing this section of our Essay : besides those adduced I name Rev. G. G. Perry’s ‘ History of the Church of England’ and Hopkins’s ‘ History of the Puritans’ (Boston, U.S. 1860) ; George Roberts’s ‘ Social History of the Southern Counties.’ I have drawn much, and often in his own choice words, from my dearly beloved friend, Rev. Charles Stanford’s ‘ Joseph Alleine, his Companions and Times’ (London, 1861, Hodder). See especially pp. 8 seq., 108 seq.

to pronounce the same verdict with ' Anti-Tami-Cami-Categoria,' as witness in his great Ecclesiastical Sonnets (xviii.) :

CORRUPTIONS OF THE HIGHER CLERGY.

' Woe to you, Prelates! rioting in ease
And cumbrous wealth—the shame of your estate ;
You on whose progress dazzling trains await
Of pompous houses ; whom vain titles please ;
·Who will be served by others on their knees,
Yet will yourselves to God no service pay ;
Pastors who neither take nor point the way
To Heaven ; for either lost in vanities
Ye have no skill to teach, or if ye know
And speak the word— Alas! of fearful things
'Tis the most fearful when the people's eye
Abuse hath clear'd from vain imaginings ;
And taught the general voice to prophesy
Of Justice arm'd, and Pride to be laid low.'

Andrew Melville probably never read a line of the Epigrams of GEORGE HERBERT ; for he died in 1622, and they did not appear in print until 1662 ; but if he had, how the noble old man, with that high genius and scholarly culture of his, would have crushed as a limpet in the shut palm, the elegant trifles of his assailant ! Nay, rather let us say, if they had met Below, as beyond all doubt they met Above, the ' young disciple' should have been drawn to the patriarch. For, once met, how soon should a living poet's words have been fulfilled :

' We have one God, one Christ, one home,
One love ; and lighter than the foam
Is the one element of strife
That separates our way of life ;
And O, I love you still
Through all the good and ill.'

The closing address to Melville (present Volume, pp. 147-151) warrants this ' Pleasure of Imagination.'

The headings and margin-references of HERBERT's successive pieces show that he intended to reply *seriatim* to Anti-Tami-Cami-Categoria. It can scarcely be required that I examine all; but a few central truths must be brought out as against the epigram-play on them.

The Petitioners and Melville, and the Puritans generally, never called their 'pastors,' in distinction from other Christians, 'priests' or 'clergymen.' 'A priest,' said Latimer, 'importeth a sacrifice.' It was a commonplace with the Puritans. In their opinion, the only sacrifices accepted under the Gospel are the sacrifices offered by all believers: so, amongst the followers of Christ, the people are the priests (1 Peter ii. 5). Even 'clergyman,' if used at all, had, by the same Scripture rule, the same wide meaning. 'Poor men,' said Henry Jessey (Preface to Life, 1672), addressing Episcopalian ministers in reference to the members of their communion, 'are you the clergy, and not *they?* Read 1 Peter v. 3; "not as lords over God's clergy" (κλήρων). Are they the laity, and not *you?* Read Romans ix. 25, "I will call them my laity" (λαόν μου).' Out of such interpretations of texts—and who may controvert them? —relating to the priesthood, sprang that dislike of priestly vestments which sometimes startles us by its force. Mitre, crosses, hood, surplice, cap, were all denounced as 'instruments of a foolish shepherd,' *only* because they were the symbols of a priestly caste (Vavasor Powel). Similarly they had much to say as to no fixed forms of prayer, as to non-observance of saints' days, as to legal rites and ceremonies and symbolisms,—however lovely in themselves,—and even for their refusal of religious reverence for the mere fabric in which worship was offered. In regard to the last, few among them would or could have carried these principles farther than was taught in the Homily 'Against peril of idolatry, and superfluous decking of churches,' nor than Bishop Jewell, who wrote, 'My little children, saith St. John, deeply considering the matter, keep yourselves from images or idols. He saith not now, keep yourselves from idolatry, as it were from the service and worshipping of them, but from the very shape and likeness of them. . . . Think you the persons who place images or idols in churches and temples take good heed to St. John's counsel ?'

How poor are the shifts of HERBERT, as of Dean Duport, may be seen by this, that the former in 'answering' Melville's enumeration of illustrious worthies and scholars who adhered to the Reformation, can only name the Apostles Peter and Paul, Constantine, St. Augustine, St. Ambrose, Duns Scotus and King James ! ! ! while Duport (as well as HERBERT) actually deems it a clever and a wise thing to retort 'wantonness' and insinuate wickedness, because Melville's 'Anti-Tami-Cami-Categoria' was composed in Sapphics ; as though the (imagined) character of Sappho transmitted itself to the verse named after her, and while a school boy could recall Sapphics by masters of all verse. Duport's ' In Andream Melvinum Scotum de sua Anti-tami cami-categoria, Sapphico versu conscripta,' is given in his Sylvarum (lib. i. p. 70), and ' In Andream Melvinum Scotum in Ecclesiam Anglicanam Sapphico carmine debacchantem' (lib. ii. p. 226).   The latter must suffice here :

> ' Mome Anglicanam vellicans Ecclesiam,
> Cur Lesbium, Melvine, tendis barbiton,
> Satyramque versu scribis acrem Sapphico ?
> Lascivi hoc annon carmen index ingeni ?
> Meretricione proteri hoc ergo pede
> Matrona casta sponsaque haec meruit Dei ?
> Decimane Musa nunc tibi, invitis novem,
> Succurrit, apta tam protervo scommati,
> Dignum patella operculum, Sappho procax ?'
>
> (Musae Subsecivae, 1676.)

I must add here that Dean Duport furnishes much better and worthier parallels with HERBERT.

Walton's further references, with the couplet to Lady Arabella Stuart and Melville's imprisonment in the Tower,

must not tempt us to ' turn aside' to discuss them.[1] All I
ask is, that the Reader will give some thought to what
has been submitted by us, and bring knowledge and self-
knowledge, not ignorance ; and candour, not prejudice ; and
Christianhood, not ecclesiasticism, to the study of the
Anti-Tami-Cami-Categoria of Andrew Melville and to
the Epigrams-Apologetical of GEORGE HERBERT and of
Dean Duport. I as well as my good friend Rev. RICHARD
WILTON have translated all without bias and partiality.

Once more, the problem of GEORGE HERBERT'S Life
will not be mastered unless his attitude in such a historical-
ecclesiastical crisis be mastered. For my part, familiar as
I am, from special lines of research, with the Lives and
Writings of the Petitioners for whom Melville dared to
speak, when those who ought to have spoken were recreant
and dumb, I stand amazed that such an one could so over-
value a mythical Apostolic 'continuity,' and so under-
value The Reformation, as to range himself against the
true and good, and range himself with those who cared
not a straw for the vital ends of the Church of Christ.
The secret with HERBERT, as with Leighton, is, that he
regarded the Church (his 'Mother Church') as the ideal
of Perfection ; his

> ' subtle fancy sped
> Far back unto its youth, and read,
> In sculptured forms and texts and rhymes,
> The secret of the ancient times,
>   And their divinest sense
>   Of mystic reverence.
> And in its Cross the Christ he saw;
> And in its pillars stedfast law ;
> Its dim light bade with awe admire ;
> And thought soar'd heavenward on the spire,
>   Urged onwards by the chime
>   That told the fleeting time.'

There is this apology for Leighton, that he had mixed

---

[1] See annotation to Walton's Life of Herbert, in Vol. III.

little with the world, and was instinctively a Recluse and
given to contemplation ; while HERBERT knew the men—
from the king downward—who were dealing out con-
tumely and persecution, the great hearts that were break-
ing over the still superstition-haunted Church, and the
perishing multitudes who went unshepherded. One would
have rejoiced over just one cry from Bemerton like this :

'I thought
'Twere well indeed if we were brought
From our lax ways and sects and hate,
To primitive episcopate,
   And prayers lisp'd of old
   By infants in the fold.

Yet reck I not of forms ; full well
I know the pearl gives to the shell
Some beauty and virtue like its own,
And shining hue and gorgeous tone ;
   And the old forms to me
   Gleam with old sanctity.

Yet what boot they ? and what boots all
Our garb ecclesiastical,
The white-stoled priest, the altar high,
If we do err from charity ?
   O God, all gods above,
   Knit us with cords of love.

.   .   .   .   .   .

Alas ! and is it thus the State
Rewards the wise and good and great ;
That brute dragoon should quench the life
Which might have ruled our civil strife,
   Alone in royal might
   Of wisdom and high right ?
No trial held—no sifted proof—
No justice sitting calm, aloof
From human passion, human wrong,—
No advocate against the strong,
   But by the vilest he
   Meets a hard destiny.'
       ('The Bishop's Walk,' st. 73-75, 160-1.)

I proceed now to

IV. *The characteristics of Herbert's Writings, Verse and Prose.*

These I classify thus :
1. Quaintness and nicety of workmanship.
2. Thought and mysticism.
3. Imaginativeness and originality.
4. Wit and humour.
5. Sanctity.

1. *Quaintness and nicety of workmanship.* Apart from disputed etymology, usage attaches to the word 'quaint' the meaning of a certain oddness and fantasticalness; and it is thus I use it, adding the (in part) co-relative 'nicety,' simply in order to bring out more clearly an element of HERBERT'S quaintness. Here it is very much with the Poetry and in some of the Prose of our Worthy as it is with those antique great-walled Gardens, that are still to be found in our England and even in bleaker Scotland, as in France and Holland, and which, for myself, excite imagination and actualise the Past, when one is fortuned to read therein an Elizabethan or early Jacobean book ; viz. that as the grotesque shapes, clipped and trimmed and restrained yews and hollies and laurels, draw attention, first of all, to the neglect of their grand bolls and blood-spot berries and splendours of 'greene leves,' so a casual Reader of The Temple and even a Priest to the Temple is struck most of all with this thing of oddness in the form given to the thinking and fancies and teaching. To begin with, there are such Poems as, 1. The Altar ; 11. Easter Wings ; 58. Coloss. iii. 3 ; 92. Sinne's Round ; and the like. These were the playthings of a Scholar in reminiscence of Theocritus, or Simmias of Rhodes, or Dosiades of the ' Poetae Minores Graeci,' or of the marvellous ' De Laudibus S. Crucis' of Rhbanus Maurus ; or after the later Italian style, formed on the verse and thought

models from the Continent rather than of other ‘Literary Follies’ which are given a place in D'Israeli's Curiosities of Literature. In passing mood, one can enter into the *lusus* of even such artificial trifles, and mark the skill of the Artist and the devotional feeling which informs them, so that a toy grows in the hand into a portent. To have a measure of difference between the poet-writer of such things and the mere mechanic of words, let the Student turn to 1. The Altar and to 102. Paradise, and contrast them with a later imitator, and more, Samuel Speed, in his ‘Prison Pietie’ (1677), as follows :

‘¶ THE ALTAR.

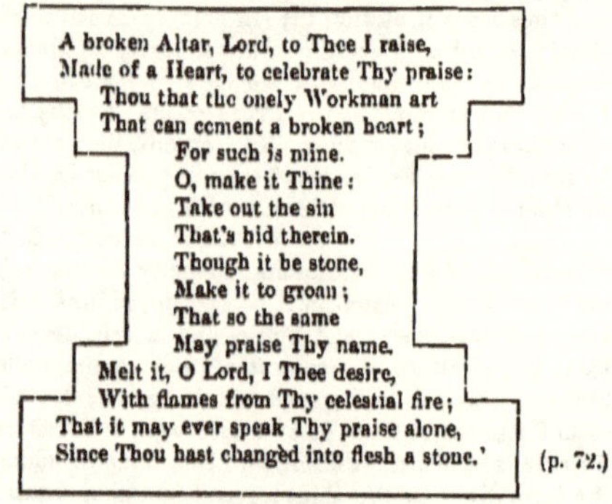

A broken Altar, Lord, to Thee I raise,
Made of a Heart, to celebrate Thy praise:
Thou that the onely Workman art
That can cement a broken heart ;
For such is mine.
O, make it Thine :
Take out the sin
That's hid therein.
Though it be stone,
Make it to groan ;
That so the same
May praise Thy name.
Melt it, O Lord, I Thee desire,
With flames from Thy celestial fire ;
That it may ever speak Thy praise alone,
Since Thou hast changèd into flesh a stone.’

(p. 72.)

‘¶ THE PETITION.

Stand by me, Lord, when dangers STARE ;
Keep from my fruit such choaking TARE
That on confusion grounded ARE.

Thou that from bondage hast me BROUGHT,
And my deliverance hast ROUGHT,
'Tis Thee that I will praise for OUGHT.

> O Lord, to evil make me CHILL,
> Be Thou my Rock and holy HILL,
> So shall I need to fear no ILL.'

En passant two things must be admitted to old Speed, spite of his plagiarisms from HERBERT and Jeremy Taylor and others : (1) That he returns finely on HERBERT his wish to be ' a weed' in his 131. The Crosse :

> 'To make my hopes my torture, and the foe
>> Of all my woes another wo,
> Is in the midst of delicates to need,
> *And ev'n in Paradise to be a weed.'*

thus :

> '¶ THE FLOWER.
> O that I were a lovely Flower
>> In Christ His Bower ;
> Or that I were a weed, to fade
>> Under His shade.
> But how can I a weed become
> If I am shadow'd with the *Son ?*[1]   = *Sun.*   (p. 150.)

and (2) that he had a chord of ' sweet-singing' of his own ; *e.g.* On Contentation (in Prison) :

> ''Tis not the largeness of the cage doth bring
> Notes to the bird, instructing him to sing.
> Moreover, though a bird hath little eye,
> Yet he hath wings by which he soars on high :
> Can see far wider and abundance better
> Than many an ox, although his eye be greater.'   (p. 30.)

Again, in Nature's Delight :

> 'Though their voices lower be,
>> Streams too have their melody ;

---

[1] ' *Son and Sun.*'   The play upon the word son—sun, repeated in HERBERT (see Glossarial Index, *s.v.*), occurs in GILES FLETCHER (Ch. Vict. on Earth, st. 18 ; our edition) :

> ' Ay me, quoth he, how many yeares have beene,
> Since these old eyes the Sunne of heav'n have seene !
> Certes the Sonne of Heav'n they now behold, I weene.'

There was nothing irreverent in this kind of serious punning, nor in Thomas Fuller.

> Night and day they warbling run,
>   Never pause, but still sing on.'[1]   (p. 74.)

Passing from mere outward quaintness, I must dispute Dr. G. L. Craik's *dictum* in respect of it. He observes: 'HERBERT was an intimate friend of Donne, and no doubt a great admirer of his poetry; but his own has been to a great extent preserved from the imitation of Donne's peculiar style, into which it might in other circumstances have fallen, in all probability, by its having been composed with little effort or elaboration, and chiefly to relieve and amuse his own mind by the melodious expression of his favourite fancies and contemplations. His quaintness lies in his thoughts rather than in their expression, which is in general sufficiently simple and luminous.'[2] This is surely hasty and superficial; for the intricacy and variety of metres in The Temple, as well as the careful and nice Various Readings and corrections of the Williams and Bodleian MSS., evidence 'elaboration' and daintiness and persistence of art of a very remarkable type; as are found

---

[1] The following is the full title-page: 'Prison Pietie, or Meditations Divine and Moral. Digested into Poetical Heads, on Mixt and Various Subjects. Whereunto is added a Panegyrick to the right Reverend and most nobly descended Henry [King] Lord Bishop of London. By Samuel Speed, Prisoner in Ludgate, London. 1677, 12mo.' In this volume, on pp. 102, 103 (*bis*), 104, 108, 110, 131, 137, 141 (*bis*), 142, and 143, are Poems by Bp. Taylor, bodily, or with very slight verbal changes: of HERBERT there are appropriation-imitations on pp. 72, 73, 93, 96, 97, and elsewhere. In mitigation, be it remembered (1) that John Speed was his grandfather; (2) that in the Epistle To the Devout he says: 'Some Creditors, severe as well as covetous, forced me to a confinement in Ludgate; where, the better to employ my time, I have *compiled* and composed this Manual of Meditations, which consists of Psalms, Hymns, and Divine Poems.' The sorrow is, that there are no marks to show what are 'compiled' and what 'composed.'

[2] 'A Compendious History of English Literature and of the English Language from the Norman Conquest.' 2 vols. 8vo, 1866 (Griffin). A sound book substantially.

also with Sir Philip Sidney, and as indeed must be with
any genuine Workman with poetic words.[1] There is a
degree of truth, perhaps, as to the quaintness being in the
thought rather than in expression, but only in degree; for
thought and expression alike bear the insignia of quaint
thoughtfulness, swift and flashing o' times, but laboured
on with fine after-patience, even when the form is as a
cathedral gargoyle.

There is this also to be borne in mind, that while the
Age's character influenced Donne and HERBERT, their own
minds were by nature adapted to the style of their Age.
The Age fed and nourished their peculiarities, but did not
create them.   Their peculiar inborn characters—as later in
Thomas Fuller—were in harmony with those of the Age.
Hence, where there was no field for these peculiarities HER-
BERT and Donne failed; as the former in his ' Psalms,' and
the latter in his ' Lamentations of Jeremiah.'   By the way,
with reference here to a quotation onward, from 'Antiphon,'
as to Shakespeare having ' cast off his Age's faults,' there
is surely need for qualification.   His mind too was in cha-
racter with that of his Age, in the matter both of subtlety
of thought and expression, and it was his excess of these

---

[1] See our Essays in editions of DONNE and SIDNEY. In reference
to the Various Readings of the Williams MS. (as given in detail in
Vol. I. pp. 219-231, and as utilised in Notes and Illustrations occa-
sionally), I should have liked space for a critical examination of
them; but this I am compelled to leave to each student-Reader on
the strength of the ample materials furnished by us. See especially
the opening stanzas of The Church Porch (Vol. I. p. 219, 220), where
surely the new lines commencing 'it is a rodd, Whose twigs are
pleasures,' &c. (to notice no others) are very memorable. They may
bear comparison with even Shakespeare's Lear (v. 3):

> ' The gods are just, and of our pleasant vices
> Make instruments to scourge us.'

The Various Readings and erasures of particles and epithets are very
noticeable.

and his genius that elevated what would in others have been faults into graces.[1]

Dr. George Macdonald (in ' Antiphon') saw deeper than Dr. Craik, and with characteristic insight puts the quaintness and nicety, as thus : '[GEORGE HERBERT] has an exquisite feeling of lyrical art. Not only does he keep to one idea in it, but he finishes the poem like a cameo. Here is an instance wherein he outdoes the elaboration of a Norman trouvère ; for not merely does each line in each stanza end with the same sound as the corresponding line in every other stanza, but it ends with the very same word. I shall hardly care to defend this if my reader chooses to call it a whim; but I do say that a large degree of the peculiar musical effect of the poem—subservient to the thought, keeping it dimly chiming in the head until it breaks out clear and triumphant like a silver bell in the last—is owing to this use of the same column of words at the line-ends of every stanza. Let him who doubts it read the poem aloud :

> " 144. AARON.
> Holinesse on the head,
> Light and perfections on the breast,
> Harmonious bells below, raising the dead
> To leade them unto life and rest :
> Thus are true Aarons drest.
>
> Profanenesse in my head,
> Defects and darknesse in my breast,

---

[1] Mr. Edward Farr, in his ' Select Poetry, chiefly Sacred, of the Reign of King James the First' (Cambridge, 1847), gives the following notice of GEORGE HERBERT in relation to Psalm v. : ' " The divine HERBERT" published his principal poetical work, entitled " The Temple," in the reign of King Charles, but in Playford's Music Book there are seven Psalms attributed to him which appear to have been written in the period to which this volume refers' (p. xvi.). It will be noted that Mr. Farr forgets that ' The Temple' was posthumously published, and that his reference to ' Playford's Music Book,' with so many issued by those of the name, is blameably vague.

> A noise of passions ringing me for dead
>   Unto a place where is no rest :
>   Poore priest, thus am I drest.
>
>   Onely another head
>   I have, another heart and breast,
> Another musick, making live, not dead,
>   Without Whom I could have no rest :
>   In Him I am well drest.
>
>   Christ is my onely head,
>   My alone-onely heart and breast,
> My onely musick, striking me ev'n dead,
>   That to the old man I may rest,
>   And be in Him new-drest.
>
>   So, holy in my head,
>   Perfect and light in my deare breast,
> My doctrine tun'd by Christ, Who is not dead,
>   But lives in me while I do rest,
>   Come, people ; Aaron's drest."

Note the flow and the ebb of the lines of each stanza
—from six to eight to ten syllables, and back through
eight to six, the number of stanzas corresponding to the
number of lines in each ; only the poem itself begins with
the ebb, and ends with a full spring-flow of energy.
Note also the perfect antithesis in their parts between
the first and second stanzas, and how the last lines of the
poem clenches the whole in revealing its idea—that for the
sake of which it was written. In a word, note the *unity*.'
I intercalate that ' 124. Clasping of Hands,' with ' mine'
and ' thine' ringing through it, is another instance of ex-
quisite art in combination with quaintness. Further, and
again much more penetratively than Craik in his Donne
reference : ' Born in 1593, notwithstanding his exquisite
art, he could not escape being influenced by the faulty
tendencies of his age, borne in upon his youth by the ex-
ample of his mother's friend, Dr. Donne. A man must
be a giant like Shakespeare or Milton to cast off his age's
faults. Indeed no man has more of the " quips and cranks

and wanton wiles" of the poetic spirit of his time than
GEORGE HERBERT, but with this difference from the rest of
Dr. Donne's school, that such is the indwelling potency
that it causes even these to shine with a radiance such
that we wish them still to burn and not be consumed.
His muse is seldom other than graceful, even when her
motions are grotesque, and he is always a gentleman,
which cannot be said of his master.   We could not bear to
part with his most fantastic oddities, they are so inter-
penetrated with his genius as well as his art.'   Lovingly
and admirably said.   Again :

'In relation to the use he makes of these faulty forms, and to
show that even herein he has exercised a refraining judgment,
though indeed fancying he has quite discarded in only somewhat
reforming it, I recommend the study of two poems, each of which he
calls *Jordan*, though why I have not yet with certainty discovered.

It is possible that not many of his readers have observed
the following instances of the freakish in his rhyming art, which
however result well.   When I say so, I would not be supposed to
approve of the freak, but only to acknowledge' the success of the
poet in his immediate intent.   They are related to a certain tendency
to mechanical contrivance not seldom associated with a love of art :
it is art operating in the physical understanding.   In the poem
called *Home*, every stanza is perfectly finished till the last: in it,
with an access of art or artfulness, he destroys the rhyme.   I shall
not quarrel with my reader if he calls it the latter, and regards it as
art run to seed.   And yet—and yet—I confess I have a latent liking
for the trick.   I shall give one or two stanzas out of the rather long
poem, to lead up to the change in the last.

"Come, Lord ; my head doth burn, my heart is sick,
　　While Thou dost ever, ever stay ;
　Thy long deferrings wound me to the quick ;
　　My spirit gaspeth night and day.
　　　　O show Thyself to me,
　　　　Or take me up to Thee.

　Nothing but drought and dearth, but bush and brake,
　　Which way soe're I look, I see :
　Some may dream merrily, but when they wake
　　They dresse themselves and come to Thee.
　　　　O show Thyself to me,
　　　　Or take me up to Thee.

> Come, dearest Lord, passe not this holy season,
>   My flesh and bones and joynts do pray ;
> And ev'n my verse, when by the ryme and reason
>   The word is *stay*,[1] says ever *come*.
>   O show Thyself to me,
>   Or take me up to Thee."

Balancing this, my second instance is of the converse. In all the stanzas but the last, the last line in each hangs unrhymed : in the last the rhyming is fulfilled. The poem is called *Denial*. I give only a part of it.

> " When my devotions could not pierce
>   Thy silent eares,
>   Then was my heart broken, as was my verse ;
>   My breast was full of fears
>   And disorder.
>
>   O that Thou shouldst give dust a tongue
>   To cry to Thee,
>   And then not hear it crying ! All day long
>   My heart was in my knee :
>   But no hearing !
>
>   Therefore my soul lay out of sight,
>   Untun'd, unstrung ;
>   My feeble spirit, unable to look right,
>   Like a nipt blossome, hung
>   Discontented.
>
>   O cheer and tune my heartlesse breast—
>   Deferre no time ;
>   That so Thy favours granting my request,
>   They and my soule may chime,
>   And mend my ryme."

It had been hardly worth the space to point out these, were not the matter itself precious.

Before making further remark on GEORGE HERBERT, let me present one of his poems in which the oddity of the visual fancy is only equalled by the beauty of the result.

> " THE PULLEY.
>
> When God at first made man,
> Having a glasse of blessings standing by,
> ' Let us,' said He, ' poure on him all we can :
> Let the world's riches, which dispersèd lie,
>   Contract into a span.'

' 1 To rhyme with *pray* in the second line.'

> So strength first made a way;
> Then beautie flow'd; then wisdome, honour, pleasure,
> When almost all was out, God made a stay,
> Perceiving that, alone of all His treasure,
> *Rest* in the bottome lay.
>
> 'For if I should,' said He,
> ' Bestow this jewell also on My creature,
> He would adore My gifts instead of Me,
> And rest in Nature, not the God of Nature :
> So both should losers be.
>
> Yet let him keep the rest—
> But keep them with repining restlesnesse :
> Let him be rich and wearie, that, at least,
> If goodnesse lead him not, yet wearinesse
> May tosse him to My breast.'"

Is it not the story of the world written with the point of a diamond ?

There can hardly be a doubt that his tendency to unnatural forms was encouraged by the increase of respect to symbol and ceremony shown at this period by some of the external powers of the Church—Bishop Laud in particular. Had all, however, who delight in symbols a power, like GEORGE HERBERT's, of setting even within the horn-lanterns of the more arbitrary of them, such a light of poetry and devotion that their dull sides vanish in its piercing shine, and we forget the symbol utterly in the truth which it cannot obscure, then indeed our part would be to take and be thankful. But there never has been even a living true symbol which the dulness of those who will see the truth only in the symbol has not degraded into the very cockatrice-egg of sectarianism. The symbol is by such always more or less idolised, and the light within more or less patronised. If the truth, for the sake of which all symbols exist, were indeed the delight of those who claim it, the sectarianism of the Church would vanish. But men on all sides call that *the truth* which is but its form or outward sign—material or verbal, true or arbitrary, it matters not which—and hence come strifes and divisions.

Although GEORGE HERBERT, however, could thus illumine all with his divine inspiration, we cannot help wondering whether, if he had betaken himself yet more to vital and less to half-artificial symbols, the change would not have been a breaking of the pitcher and an outshining of the lamp. For a symbol may remind us of the truth, and at the same time obscure it—present it, and dull its effect. It is the temple of nature and not the temple of the Church, the things made by the hands of God and not the things made by the hands of man, that afford the truest symbols of truth.

I am anxious to be understood. The chief symbol of our faith, *the Cross*, it may be said, is not one of these natural symbols. I answer—No; but neither is it an arbitrary symbol. It is not a symbol of *a truth* at all, but of *a fact*, of the infinitely grandest fact in the universe, which is itself the outcome and symbol of the grandest Truth. *The Cross* is an historical *sign*, not properly *a symbol*, except through the facts it reminds us of. On the other hand, *Baptism* and the *Eucharist* are symbols of the loftiest and profoundest kind, true to nature and all its meanings, as well as to the facts of which they remind us. They are in themselves symbols of the truths involved in the facts they commemorate.

Of Nature's symbols GEORGE HERBERT has made large use; but he would have been yet a greater poet if he had made a larger use of them still. Then at least we might have got rid of such oddities as the stanzas for steps up to the church-door, the first at the bottom of the page; of the lines shaped into ugly altar-form; and of the absurd Easter wings, made of ever-lengthening lines. This would not have been much, I confess, nor the gain by their loss great; but not to mention the larger supply of images graceful with the grace of God, Who when He had made them said they were good, it would have led to the further purification of his taste, perhaps even to the casting out of all that could untimely move our mirth; until possibly (for illustration), instead of this lovely stanza, he would have given us even a lovelier:

> " Listen, sweet Dove, unto my song,
> 　And spread Thy golden wings on me;
> Hatching my tender heart so long,
> 　Till it get wing with Thee, and fly away."

The stanza is indeed lovely, and true and tender and clever as well; yet who can help smiling at the notion of the incubation of the heart-egg, although what the poet means is so good that the smile almost vanishes in a sigh?

There is no doubt that the works of man's hands will also afford many true symbols; but I do think that, in proportion as a man gives himself to those instead of studying Truth's wardrobe of forms in nature, so will he decline from the high calling of the poet. GEORGE HERBERT was too great to be himself much injured by the narrowness of the field whence he gathered his symbols; but his song will be the worse for it in the ears of all but those who, having lost sight of or having never beheld the oneness of the God

Whose creation exists in virtue of his redemption, feel safer in a low-browed crypt than under "the high embowed roof."

When the desire after system or order degenerates from a need into a passion, or ruling idea, it closes, as may be seen in many women who are especial housekeepers, like an unyielding skin over the mind, to the death of all development from impulse and aspiration. The same thing holds in the Church : anxiety about order and system will kill the life. This did not go near to being the result with GEORGE HERBERT : his life was hid with Christ in God ; but the influence of his *profession*, as distinguished from his work, was hurtful to his calling as a poet. He of all men would scorn to claim social rank for spiritual service ; he of all men would not commit the blunder of supposing that prayer and praise are that service of God : they are *prayer* and *praise*, not *service;* he knew that God can be served only through loving ministration to His sons and daughters, all needy of commonest human help : but, as the most devout of clergymen will be the readiest to confess, there is even a danger to their souls in the unvarying recurrence of the outward obligations of their service ; and, in like manner, the poet will fare ill if the conventions from which the holiest system is not free send him soaring with seeled eyes. GEORGE HERBERT's were but a little blinded thus ; yet something, we must allow, his poetry was injured by his profession. All that I say on this point, however, so far from diminishing his praise, adds thereto, setting forth only that he was such a poet as might have been greater · yet, had the divine gift had free course. But again I rebuke myself, and say, "Thank God for GEORGE HER-BERT." '

Very gladly and gratefully have I given way to one so appreciative and reverent, and nevertheless critical, as George Macdonald ; and I must also close this section of HERBERT's quaintness and nicety of workmanship from him. Earlier he looks beneath all the *fantastique* and oddity, and catches, as all who listen and have souls must catch, that music and melody which, while genius · born, is art-matured : ' Let me speak first of that which first in time or order of appearance we demand of a poet, namely music. For inasmuch as verse is for the ear, not for the eye, we demand a good hearing first. Let no one under-value it. The heart of poetry is indeed truth, but its garments are music, and the garments come first in the process of revelation. The music of a poem is its meaning in sound as distinguished from word—its meaning in solution, as it were, uncrystallised by articulation. The music goes before the fuller revelation, preparing its way. The sound of a verse is the harbinger of the truth contained therein. If it be a right poem, this will be true. Herein HERBERT excels. It will be found impossible to separate the music of his words from the music of the thought which takes shape in their sound.

> "I got me flowers to straw Thy way,
>   I got me boughs off many a tree;
> But Thou wast up by break of day,
>   And broughtst Thy sweets along with Thee."

And the gift it enwraps at once and reveals is, I have said, truth of the deepest. Hear this song of divine service. In every song he sings a spiritual fact will be found its fundamental life, although I may quote this or that merely to illustrate some peculiarity of mode' (pp. 174-5). Summarily, then, the quaintness of HERBERT in thought and wording, must not be allowed to hide from the Reader the exquisite nicety of workmanship spent on it. To those unfamiliar with the contemporary literature, it may at first repel, but a closer study will draw out full and abiding admiration and gratitude. The most odd outward forms will prove to hide in them precious things; as I found the other day a glorious eastern shell, purple-lipped, passion-flower stained, carrying within murmurous memories of its far-off sea, notwithstanding that it was cut and shaped into a very humble use; or as one marks in the old gardens, of which mention was made earlier, the clipped and trimmed boughs, bursting into a glory of blossom and odour beneath the breath of the returning season. It is very noticeable how the Poet asserts himself against the somewhat ultra-correct Artist in many of the quaintest of HERBERT'S Poems. The careless lines, the lines that have not been worked and re-worked, are few and far between. Moreover, the quaintness and *fantastique* of some of the poems—the thinking taking such shape inevitably—hide a secret that good James Montgomery did not discern when in his 'Christian Poet' he hastily described 'The Temple' as 'devotion itself turned into masquerade.' If he had reversed it, it had been truer; for HERBERT turns even masquerade into devotion. He fulfilled the Bible-vision of 'Holiness to the Lord,' graven on the very bells of the horses.

2. *Thought and mysticism.* While agreeing in part with 'Antiphon's' aphoristic judgment, that 'as verse is for the ear, not for the eye, we demand a good hearing first,' I must nevertheless reiterate a former opinion (in relation to Fulke Greville, Lord Brooke[1]) that 'music' (or rhyme and rhythm in perfection), if the 'first,' is not the 'last' or supremest thing. Or, to put it in another way, unless the 'music' inform great and noble thought, and be thrilled by that subtlety of emotion which I call here mysticism, it may be of the poorest and emptiest Poetry *qua* Poetry : *e.g.* Thomas Moore is all but faultless in his rhyme and melody; but one yearns for the roughness of a grand idea or fancy—just as one likes the break of the flowing stream through the obstacle of some great stone or dipping branch, anything rather than the Dutch-dyke smoothness and mere flow. The quantity and quality of the thinking, and that as intensified by feeling, must ever determine the quantity and quality of a Poet's genius— must, in truth, decide us whether or no it be genius and the results poetry. Where genius is, the Thinking and the Feeling send out their own 'music,' and that far beyond such as is put above the Thinking and the Feeling, instead of within them. William Cartwright, in his verse-

[1] See Essay on his Poetry in our edition of his Complete Works (4 vols.), where the traditionalism of criticism has been, I hope, thoroughly dealt with.

tribute to John Fletcher, has very vividly expressed this, *e.g.*

> ' Fletcher, though some call it thy fault that wit
> So overflow'd thy scenes, that ere 'twas fit
> To come upon the stage, Beaumont was fain
> To bid thee be more dull, *that's write again*
> *And bate some of thy fire*, which from thee came
> In a clear, bright, full, but too large a flame ;
> And after all (finding thy genius such)
> That, blunted and allay'd, 'twas yet too much ;
> Added his sober spunge, *and did contract*
> *Thy plenty to less wit* to make't exact :
> *Yet we through his correcting could see*
> *Much treasure in thy superfluity,*
> *Which was so fil'd away, as when we do*
> *Cut jewels, that that's lost is jewell too ;*
> Or, as men use to wash gold, which we know
> By losing makes the stream thence wealthy grow.'[1]

Of GEORGE HERBERT in kind this holds. With all his nicety of workmanship, or even his quaintness (one of many things), there is underneath it, as the matter of his workmanship all through, substantive Thought of a high order. His art was fine and subtle, but it ceased when further use of

> ' the file would not make smooth, but wear.'[2]

Hence, as true of HERBERRT as of Jonson is it :

> ' Thy *thought's* so order'd, so express'd, that we
> Conclude that *thou didst not discourse, but see ;*
> *Language so master'd, that thy numerous feet,*
> *Laden with genuine words, do alwaies meet*
> *Each in his art*, nothing unfit doth fall ;
> Showing the Poet—like the wise men—all.'[3]

That word ' see,' as I take it, goes critically deep, and is very much superior (with all respect) to Dr. George Macdonald's test of the ' ear.' Music is for the ear, must satisfy

[1] Comedies, Tragi-Comedies, with other Poems, 1651, p. 271.
[2] Ibid. To the Memory of Ben Jonson ; Lament, p. 314.
[3] Ibid. p. 312.

it to be music. Poetry is also for the ear; yet is it also for the eye, that the spirit may take in the altitudes and depths from the printed and read page. I claim for 'The Temple,' and for GEORGE HERBERT, this *peculium* of the true poet, that his poetry is high thought and his high thought poetry. Here I accept 'Antiphon's' welcome to him: 'With my hand on the lock, I shrink from opening the door. Here comes a poet indeed! and how am I to show him due honour? With his book humbly, doubtfully offered; with the ashes of the poems of his youth fluttering in the wind of his priestly garments, he crosses the threshold. Or rather, for I had forgotten the symbol of my book, let us all go from our chapel to the choir, and humbly ask him to sing, that he may make us worthy of his song. In GEORGE HERBERT there is poetry enough and to spare; it is the household bread of his being. If I begin with that which first in the nature of things ought to be demanded of a poet—namely, Truth, Revelation—GEORGE HERBERT offers us measure pressed down and running over' (p. 174). 'Truth,' 'Revelation,' are other synonyms for my 'Thought' and 'Mysticism.' I find in the Writings of HERBERT profound, meditative, slow-patient Thought in the very cathedrals of Thinking, *i.e.* on the most ultimate problems of Fact and destiny. I find in it all, or in nearly all, that emotional element which I designate by Mysticism, or Thought trembling into feeling, feeling deepening into passion, passion laying hold of the Eternal and the True. There is a delicate mist (not haze) of the mystical (as in Henry Vaughan, the Silurist) over 'The Temple,' from Porch to L'Envoy—comparable with the amethyst edgings of cloud-land, or the purples, opal-streaked, that fill Italian and Swiss hill-hollows. You come on a grand Thought, either naked or clad in a metaphor or symbol, and as you dwell upon it, lo! not the brain only but the heart is led captive. Let Dr. Samuel Brown cull for us instances in his charming Essay on

GEORGE HERBERT,[1] as thus: 'There is a tradition that, on the occasion of the birth of Christ, there flitted over sea and land, like an awestruck aurora of sound, a voice that murmured, "Great Pan is dead;" but Pan is made alive again with Christianity by the rural scholar of Bemerton, in this exquisite stanza:

> "Now I am here, what Thou wilt do with me
>   None of my books will show:
> I read, and sigh, and wish I were a tree;
>   For sure then I should grow
> To fruit or shade; at least some bird would trust
> Her household to me, *and I should be just*."

But could the gentle Dryad have written down the quality of prayer in such a precious, though fantastic, string of similes as we have here?—

> "19. PRAYER.
>
> Prayer, the Churche's banquet, Angels' age,
>   God's breath in man returning to his birth,
>   The soul in paraphrase, heart in pilgrimage,
> The Christian plummet sounding heav'n and earth;
>
> Engine against th' Almightie, sinner's towre,
>   Reversèd thunder, Christ-side-piercing spear,
>   The six-daies-world transposing in an houre,
> A kinde of tune which all things heare and fear;
>
> Softnesse, and peace, and joy, and love, and blisse,
>   Exalted manna, gladnesse of the best,
>   Heaven in ordinarie, man well drest,
> The milkie way, the bird of Paradise,
>
>   Church-bels beyond the stars heard, the soul's bloud,
>   The land of spices, something understood."

Nor would not the delicate poet, like another and more blessed Ariel, have soon enough languished to be free from rind and leaves, even though musical with nightingales and bees, if for no other purpose than to inscribe this wise and witty couplet on the flyleaf of his study-Bible,

---

[1] 'Lectures on the Atomic Theory and Essays Scientific and Literary,' 2 vols. 8vo, 1858, vol. ii. pp. 119, 120.

before becoming the permanent captive of a hundred
sheltering years :

> " Stars are poor books, and oftentimes do miss ;
> This book of stars lights to eternal bliss."

Alas, he could not have lived the oaken, or ashen, or
any other vegetable life, one day in peace. His ardent
spirit would have burned itself to death long before the
first browning of the foliage, bringing in a premature
autumn !

> " O raise me then! poor bees, that work all day,
>   *Sting my delay,*
> Who have a work as well as they,
>   And much, much more." '

Finer yet is Dr. Brown's estimate of the utmost utter-
ance of GEORGE HERBERT in Thought and Feeling, Ima-
gination and Fancy, and word-painting and solemn me-
lody—his poem of MAN, especially read in the light of
' Man's Medley' and ' Providence.' ' Then there is,' says
he, ' a wonderful statue of Man erected about the middle
of the Church, which the sculptor, we shall not say has
hardly dared, but has scarcely been able, to deface with
one wayward stroke of the heaven-taught chisel that cut
it out of the pure block of thought.' The wisdom, the real
new insight, the revelation, so to speak, expressed in this
striking production, are so great, that the language
draws no part of the student's attention ; he only con-
siders its mighty burden of remote truth, and wonders
how it has been brought so near' (p. 123).

> ' My God, I heard this day
> That none doth build a stately habitation
>   But he that means to dwell therein.
>   What house more stately hath there been,
> Or can be, then is Man? *to whose creation*
>   *All things are in decay.*

>   .   .   .   .   .   .

---

¹ Yet see the Various Readings from the Williams MS.

Man is all symmetrie,
Full of proportions, one limbe to another,
And all to all the world besides ;
Each part may call the farthest brother,
For head with foot hath private amitie,
And both with moons and tides.

Nothing hath got so farre
But Man hath caught and kept it as his prey ;
His eyes dismount the highest starre ;
He is in little all the sphere ;
Herbs gladly cure our flesh, because that they
Finde their acquaintance there.

. . . .

The starres have us to bed,
Night draws the curtain, which the sunne withdraws ;
Musick and light attend our head,
All things unto our flesh are kinde
In their descent and being ; to our minde
In their ascent and cause.

. . . .

More servants wait on Man
Than he'l take notice of : in ev'ry path
He treads down that which doth befriend him
When sicknesse makes him pale and wan.
Oh mightie love ! Man is one world, and hath
Another to attend him.'

Professor Nichol has later pronounced the same verdict, as thus : 'HERBERT'S poem on "Man" is his masterpiece. The most philosophic as well as the most comprehensive of his writings, it stands by itself, and has enlisted the admiration even of those furthest removed from him in creed, and cast, and time. Embodying his recognition of the mysterious relationship of the chief of created beings to his Creator and to the universe, it seems to anticipate centuries of discovery. The faculty which can range from heaven to earth, from earth to heaven, discerns the hidden links by which the world is woven together, and poetry prophesies what science proves. In the microcosm of man :

> " East and west touch,—the poles do kiss,
>   And parallels meet."

Man, with HERBERT, is everything—" a tree," " a beast, yet is, or should be, more ;" he is

> " all symmetry,
> Full of proportions, one limb to another,
> And all to all the world besides."

Claiming brotherhood with moons and tides, " in little all the sphere," everything ministers to his service :

> " For us the winds do blow,
> The earth doth rest, heaven move, and fountains flow."

Clenching the whole into one grand line, the poet ex-claims :

> "Man is one world, and hath
> Another to attend him."

And then, from the open vault of day, he turns again reverently towards the temple, crying :

> " Since then, my God, Thou hast
> So brave a palace built, oh, dwell in it."

This, which was the prayer and effort of his life, was surely in full measure granted to GEORGE HERBERT. Nothing arrests us more than his perfect honesty. There is no writing for effect in his pages ; as we turn them we feel ourselves in the presence of a man speaking out of the fulness of his heart, and carried away into a higher air by the sustaining power of his own incessant aspirations.[1] With kindred insight and eloquent statement the Rev. George Gilfillan, of Dundee, also selecting 'Man' (and ' Providence'), has set forth the Thought and Mysticism of HERBERT. I feel assured every Reader will thank me for a long quotation : ' We have spoken of the philosophy of " The Temple." We do not mean by this, that

---

[1] The Poetical Works of GEORGE HERBERT, ... with Introduction by John Nichol, B.A. Oxon., Professor of English Literature, University of Glasgow ; London : 1863 (Bickers and Bush), pp. xxiv.-v.

it contains any elaborately constructed, distinctly defined,
or logically defended system, but simply that it abounds
in *glimpses of philosophic thought of a very profound and
searching cast.* The singular earnestness of HERBERT'S
temperament was connected with—perhaps we should
rather say *created* in him—an eye which penetrated below
the surface, and looked right into the secrets of things.
In his peculiarly happy and blessed constitution, piety
and the philosophic genius were united and reconciled ;
and from those awful depths of man's mysterious na-
ture, which few have more thoroughly, although inci-
dentally, explored than he, he lifts up, not a hand of
despair, nor a curse of misanthropy, nor a cry of mere
astonishment, but a hymn of worship. We refer espe-
cially to those two striking portions of the poem en-
titled "Man" and "Providence." The first is a fine
comment on the Psalmist's words, "I am fearfully and
wonderfully made." HERBERT first saw, or at least first
expressed in poetry, the central position of man to the
universe—the fact that all its various lines find a focus in
him—that he is a microcosm to the All, and that every part
of man is, in its turn, a little microcosm of him. The
germs of some of the abstruse theories propounded by
Swedenborg, and since enlarged and illustrated by the
author of "The Human Body considered in its Relation
to Man" (a treatise written with a true Elizabethan rich-
ness of style and thought, and which often seems to ap-
proach at least great abysses of discovery), may be found
in HERBERT'S verses.' .... 'How strikingly do these
words [in 'Man'] bring before us the thought of Man the
Mystery! "What a piece of workmanship" verily he is !
He is formed as of a thousand lights and shadows. He is
compacted out of all contradictions. While his feet touch
the dust, and are of miry clay, his head is of gold, and
strikes the empyrean. He is mysteriously linked on the
one side to the beasts that perish, and has an affinity as

mysterious on the other to the angels of God.   Nay, inanimate nature itself claims "acquaintance" with this "quintessence of dust."   The periods of his life bear a striking analogy to the seasons ; his brain at times moves to the moon ; his breast, as well as cheek, is coloured by the sun ; his advancement as a species bears a distinct relation to the changes of the earth's surface, and to its place in the heavens ; he is the representative of the universe, has imbibed at once its glories and its glooms, has snatched from the star its fire and its mystery, and vibrates like the string of a harp to any breath of the great system with which he is indissolubly connected. Made in the image of God, and having notions of and expectations after absolute perfection, he is, and in some measure knows himself to be, a vile sinner.   Lord of earth, air, sea, and all their riches, he is a fretful, discontented, hating, hateful, and on the whole, so far as his present life goes, miserable wretch.   He is, in one view, a whole, and in another a yawning fragment ; and, according to the angle at which you see him, resembles, now a full moon, now a crescent, and now a waning orb.   Able to "weigh the sun," span the fields of space, acquainted with the times and seasons of the heavenly bodies, full of "thoughts that wander through eternity," he is yet doomed to sicken, to die, and to have his low grave kissed, in scorn or pity, by the orbs whose spots he has numbered and whose eclipses he has foretold.   Humboldt speaks of the Andes as including the world in their vast sweep, all climates, and seasons, and productions of earth being found between their base and their summit, between the ocean below and the hoary head of Chimborazo above. Thus man rises from his dim embryo up to his gray head in age, touching, as he ascends, all conditions of being, and rising in parallel to all gradations of the universe, and remaining in each and all a mystery, having, indeed, all mysteries compounded and compressed

in his one mysterious self. " When I consider the heavens,"
says David, " what is man ?"   But may we not, with all
reverence, invert David's statement, although not his
spirit, and say, " When we consider man, what" (in gran-
deur, incomprehensibility, and terror) " are the heavens ?"

> " For us the winds do blow,
> The earth doth rest, heaven move, and fountains flow."

Many of HERBERT'S modern admirers, while quoting the
rest of these verses on " Man," omit its last stanza, although
it seems to contain the moral of the wondrous fable he had
told, the solution of the Great Riddle he had propounded.
Man is, in a great measure, a mystery, because he has for-
saken his God ; he is a wondrous palace, untenanted by
the only Being whose presence can fill the crevices, supply
the deficiencies, occupy the vast rooms, glorify the gloomy
places, explain the mysteriousness and fulfil the destiny of
the fabric ; and whenever He shall return to it Man's con-
tradictions shall be reconciled, his controversies ended, all
that is now ambiguous about him shall be explained, and
while his microcosmal character still continues, it shall as-
sume a diviner meaning, and become as pure as it is uni-
versal.'[1]   All this is really fetched out of ' Man' and ' Pro-
vidence,' not put into it (as too many preachers do with
God's Word, to an imagined ' edification') ; and it is evi-
dence of the THOUGHT in HERBERT. One can readily under-
stand how Bacon and GEORGE HERBERT were congenial
minds. They were Thinkers, with MAN to them as the end
of the universe, and so its key in His Hands.   That the
thought ; and then there is the mysticism, the seer-gift,
which puts the small hand of man in the great hand of
God, and thus elevates and ennobles him still more, as
being fallen, yet redeemed.

[1] The Poetical Works of GEORGE HERBERT, with Life, Critical
Dissertation, and Explanatory Notes, by the Rev. George Gilfillan.
Edinburgh : 1857 (Nichol).   There is not a single ' explanatory
note.'

Perhaps sufficient has been said and suggested to vindicate a higher recognition than hitherto of the *thinking power* of GEORGE HERBERT as distinguished from his ineffable sweetness and saintliness. 'With a conscience tender as a child's,' says Dr. Macdonald on this, 'almost diseased in its tenderness, and a heart loving as a woman's, his intellect is none the less powerful. Its movements are as the sword-play of an alert, poised, well-knit, strong-wristed fencer with the rapier, in which the skill impresses one more than the force, while without the force the skill would be valueless, even hurtful, to its possessor' (Antiphon, p. 176). Even so : the gleam of the Damascus blade, lightning-edged, flames under the wreathing myrtles with which Peace has twined it ; or, unmetaphorically, the brain-strength is used gently and without display, but it is there. With reference to Dyce's little painting of GEORGE HERBERT as an angler, the writer in the Christian Remembrancer—from whom we have quoted more than once—lays stress on this intellectuality and thought of 'The Temple,' and indeed of all HERBERT'S verse and prose, as thus : 'Mr. Dyce's picture,' while representing well the serenity which HERBERT'S impetuous nature gained by rigid exercise of self-control and resignation, illustrates only too well the popular misconception, universal among those who know GEORGE HERBERT only by report. Most persons, we may venture to say, only think

[1] 'In last year's exhibition of paintings, not a few among the gazers who crowded the Royal Academy's rooms were attracted round a small but highly finished picture, which, to say nothing of its other claims to be noticed (and these are considerable with all who can appreciate the delicacy, repose, and careful execution of Mr. Dyce's manner), certainly stood out in unique contrast to its companions both in subject and colouring,' &c. (Chr. Remembr. p. 104). A. Cooper, R.A., selected the incident of HERBERT'S helping the poor man whose horse had fallen by the wayside for a kindred painting. Major engraved it for his edition of the 'Lives' (1825, p. 320). It is commonplace, save in the horse's eye.

of him as, to borrow Mr. Spurgeon's elegant designation of him, "a devout old Puseyite" of the time of the first Stuart, completely estranged from their sympathy, not by the antiquated manners of the period only, but by his own singular austerity of life and extraordinary self-abnegation. Most persons merely know his poetry by a few lines culled here and there to provoke a smile at their quaintness and want of rhythm. Even among those who cherish with loving reverence the memory of his holy and beautiful life, few are aware—for it needs patient research, undiscouraged by the archaisms of a style strangely dissonant to modern ears—*how high a place he is entitled to, purely on the ground of intellectual ability.* Among the rich legacies of literature bequeathed to us from the past, ... HERBERT'S " Remains" especially [Prose] deserve to be rescued from neglect, and restored to a place on our bookshelves and in our hearts. They are valuable, not merely or chiefly to the archæologist, but intrinsically ; and in particular, at the present time, as containing the antidote to many of the evils incidental to the tendencies of our modern literature' (pp. 104-5). Proceed we now to his

3. *Imaginativeness and originality.* Imagination is so utterly of the *stuff* of poetry, that no one may hope to retain a place among the great*est* 'Makers' (reverting to the fine old name) without it. Yet never was it more necessary than in our own day to remember that there is imagination *and* imagination ; never more necessary to test what claims our acceptance as poetry by Shakespeare's definition.   Let us recall it :

> ' Lovers and madmen have such seething brains,
> Such shaping fantasies, that apprehend
> More than cool reason ever comprehends.
> The lunatic, the lover, and the poet
> *Are of imagination all compact :*
> One sees more devils than vast hell can hold ;

> That is the madman: the lover, all as frantic,
> Sees Helen's beauty in a brow of Egypt:
> *The poet's eye, in a fine frenzy rolling,*
> *Doth glance from heaven to earth, from earth to heaven ;*
> *And as imagination bodies forth*
> *The forms of things unknown, the poet's pen*
> *Turns them to shapes, and gives to airy nothing*
> *A local habitation and a name.'*
>
> (Midsummer-Night's Dream, act v. sc. 1.)

We have many 'seething brains,' but lack the 'fine frenzy ;' abundance of 'great swelling words,' little of that 'imagination' which is '*compact*.'   The thick-coming epithets, the laborious and gaudy word - painting, the spasm and mouthing of belauded poetry, are the antithesis of what I take to be true Imaginativeness, an essential of which is that it be not diffuse but *compact*. Of this condensation and compactness of imagination I pronounce GEORGE HERBERT on his own level—level rather than altitude— to be a master ; and I regard 'The Temple' as furnishing incomparable examples of the fulfilment of the 'Midsummer-Night's Dream's' supreme requirement:

> ' As Imagination bodies forth
> The forms of things unknown, the poet's pen
> Turns them to shapes, and gives to airy nothing
> A local habitation and a name.'

Take this of the Agony of Gethsemane :

> ' Sin is that press and vice, which forceth Pain
> To hunt his cruel food through every vein ;'

and this in ' The Church Porch' (st. xv.) :

> ' Chase brave employments with a naked sword
> Throughout the world.   Fool not, for all may have,
> If they dare choose, a glorious life or grave.'

Of the former, its naked simpleness of wording is surely declarative of the highest type of the imaginative faculty —'compact' and restrained. Of the latter, had Byron it in unconscious reminiscence in the close of the last, per-

haps truest as deepest, of all his poems, ' On this day I
complete my thirty-sixth year' ?—

> ' Tread those reviving passions down,
>   Unworthy manhood—unto thee
> Indifferent should the smile or frown
>   Of beauty be.
>
> If thou regret'st thy youth, *why live !*
>   The land of honourable death
> Is here :—up to the field, and give
>   Away thy breath !
>
> Seek out—less often sought than found—
>   A soldier's grave, for thee the best :
> Then look around, and choose thy ground,
>   And take thy rest.'

' Man' and ' Man's Medley' and ' Providence' afford abun-
dant examples of the imaginativeness and originality of our
Poet.   I retain a line and a half of the penultimate stanza
of ' Man :'

> ' Man is one world, and hath
> Another to attend him.'

I know nothing more magnificent than this as a thought,
and nothing more perfect than its form.   It was only a
grotesque grandeur to make Earth (as old astronomic sci-
ence did) the centre of the universe, and the huge sun to
wheel in attendance on it ; but it is grand, without touch of
grotesqueness, to recognise thus in Man the centre of the
vastest and remotest circumference, with all the visible
world ' to attend him.'   How wide-reaching as Words-
worth at his best, is this in 90. Providence (ll. 29-32) !—

> ' We all acknowledge both Thy power and love
>   To be exact, transcendent, and divine ;
> Who dost so strongly and so sweetly move,
>   *While all things have their will, yet none but Thine.*'

Nor is this in 129. ' The Search' at all inferior :

> ' Where is my God? what hidden place
>   Conceals Thee still ?
> *What covert dare eclipse Thy face ?*
>   Is it Thy will ?

O let not that of any thing ;
    Let rather brasse,
Or steel, or mountains be Thy ring,   *ring-fence*
    And I will passe.
Thy will such an intrenching is
    As passeth thought :
To it all strength, all subtilties
    Are things of nought.
Thy will such a strange distance is
    As that to it
East and West touch, the poles do kisse,
    And parallels meet.'   (ll. 29-44.)

But perhaps the fineness of HERBERT's imagination is best seen in his eye for Nature. Purblind critics, calling themselves philosophers, have ignorantly said of HERBERT that he knew and cared little or nothing for the sights and sounds of outside Nature.[1] No genuine stu-

---

[1] An example occurs in a Paper on ' Mr. Tennyson as a Botanist' in St. Pauls Magazine (October 1873), as follows : ' Although belonging to an earlier date than the sterile period referred to, GEORGE HERBERT might also be quoted here as a case of poetic talent of a very genuine kind, yet unaccompanied by much perception of natural beauty or picturesqueness. He has sometimes been likened to Keble, a brother churchman and clergyman ; but between the two in their feeling and apprehension of the wonders of creation the difference is singular and complete. HERBERT's strong point was spiritual anatomy. His probing and exposure of the deceits and vanities of the human heart, and his setting forth of the dangers of the world to spirituality of mind, is at once quaint and incisive. But of any love or special knowledge of the physical world there is scarcely a trace. Keble's poetry, on the other hand—quite as unworldly as that of the author of " The Temple"—is redolent everywhere of the sights and sounds of Nature. The seasons with their endless changes, the motions of the heavenly bodies, the fragrance of the field, trees, rivers, mountains, and all material things, are assimilated, so to speak, into the very essence of his verse. That very world which to HERBERT was only base and utterly indifferent, seemed to Keble, to use his own words, " ennobled and glorified," and awakened in his soul poetical emotions of the highest and purest kind.' A footnote is

dent of 'The Temple' will be cheated by such hasty
generalisation. While it must be granted that his pe-
culiar poetic gifts were exercised most of all in the
uttering of those spiritual experiences which rounded his
remarkable Life, and while the penetrativeness and reve-
lation that give Wordsworth his renown belong to a later
day, I must nevertheless strenuously assert that all through,
our 'sweet singer' walks the earth as still God's Eden, the
great Gardener's Garden. If you bring insight to discern,
you come on the daintiest, quietest, tenderest, winsomest
allusions to Nature as he saw it, in simple level English
landscape, and so worked-in that you feel at once the
presence of Imagination, not mere word-painting :

> 'The consecration and the poet's dream,
> The light that never was on sea or shore.'

' Never was there,' says Dr. Samuel Brown, 'sweeter sym-

---

added : ' One of his biographers has discovered a solitary verse, on
the faith of which he complacently assumes that HERBERT " was
thoroughly alive to the sweet influences of nature"' (p. 444).
Conceding to this writer (Mr. J. Hutchison) that ' HERBERT'S
strong point was spiritual anatomy,' and pleased that he admits the
'genuine kind'of our Worthy's 'poetic talent'(albeit 'talent'is a sin-
gularly ill-chosen term), it seems a bounden duty to protest against
the serene ignorance of HERBERT'S 'Temple' herein exhibited. If
Mr. Hutchison had really given a couple of open-eyed hours to
the study of HERBERT'S Poetry, such as he has to Mr. Tennyson's,
with good results, he would have been astonished by the ' special
knowledge' of the ' sights and sounds of Nature' shown by him.
Indeed his own description of Keble (from which none will seek to
abate) is an accurate one of HERBERT. Nothing is more profoundly
false than that HERBERT regarded this present world 'as only base
and utterly indifferent.' His was too spacious a soul and he was
too whole-hearted for such sentimentalism of misanthropy. The
footnote reference to a 'solitary verse' is simply ludicrous and
blundering. Mr. Hutchison's foolish criticism was very well dis-
posed of in the same periodical for November 1873 in a Paper by
Georgiophilus, entitled ' George Herbert as a Lover of Nature;'
and our examples confirm all stated therein.

pathy with Nature half alive than our sweet-souled Pastor's : *e.g.* praying down grace, he remembers how it is said, " Come, let us reason together," and he murmurs with the veritable delicacy of a child :

> " The dew doth every morning fall :
> And shall the dew outstrip Thy Dove?
> The dew *for which grass cannot call,*
>   Drop from above."

Ay, and he is a lover of the Night, after his own dear familiar fashion ; he says :

> " I muse which shows more love,
> The day or night: that is the gale, this the harbour ;
>   That is the walk, and this the arbour ;
>   Or that the garden, this the grove."

Perhaps as good a specimen as could be shown of HERBERT'S peculiar vein is to be found in the apostrophe called " The Star." It turns on a fanciful, almost a fantastic conceit ; but the moment you admit its legitimacy —and you can do it only by an act of poetic faith—you are ravished by the infinite ingenuity and beauty with which the author turns it to the fair and sacred uses for which he snatched it down from the " heaven of imagination." Examine the subtlety and feel the real beauty of this curious rapture :

> " 47. ¶ THE STARRE.

> Bright spark, *shot from a brighter place,*
>   Where beams surround my Saviour's face,
>   Canst thou be any where
>   So well as there ?

> Yet if thou wilt from thence depart,
>   Take a bad lodging in my heart ;
>   For thou canst make a debter,
>   And make it better.

> First with thy fire-work burn to dust
> Folly, and worse then folly, lust :
>   Then with thy light refine,
>   And make it shine.

> So, disengag'd from sinne and sicknesse,
>   Touch it with thy celestial quicknesse,
>   *That it may hang and move*
>   *After thy love.*   *according to*
>
> Then with our trinitie, of light,
>   Motion, and heat, let's take our flight
>   Unto the place where thou
>   Before didst bow.
>
> Get me a standing there, and place
>   Among the beams which crown the face
>   Of Him Who dy'd to part
>   Sinne and my heart ;
>
> That so among the rest I may
>   *Glitter, and curle, and winde as they :*
>   *That winding is their fashion*
>   *Of adoration.*
>
> Sure thou wilt joy by gaining me
>   To flie home, like a laden bee,
>   Unto that hive of beams
>   And garland-streams."

This is the operation of the pure fancy ; and it is this sort of voluntary conceit that HERBERT excels and delights in. Yet it must be owned that these turns and feats of the mind, though frequently violent and against the use of nature, are not without their power and grandeur on occasion, apart from the beauty with which the lovely spirit of the author almost unfailingly illustrates them. How sublime a prank is this all but imaginative anagram of the name of the Virgin Mary, the letters of which are the same as "Army" !—

> " How well her name an Army doth present
>   In whom the Lord of Hosts did pitch His tent!"

There is also something of the identifying process, or passionate condensation of imagination-proper, in this more sober repetition of the Oreadic aspiration :

> " O that I were an orenge-tree,
>   That busy plant!

> Then I should ever laden be,
>> And never want
> Some fruit for Him that dresseth me."

'Although, however, the imagery and illustrations of HERBERT'S poems are almost entirely drawn from the storehouse of fancy, he was a man of true and penetrating imagination. All his most kindly sympathies; the overwhelming passion of his piety; his love, as universal as the sun's radiance, and as particular as its ray; *his profound insight into nature* and man, and his trembling sense of the essential unity of all thoughts and things, were all the outcomings of a most imaginative spirit. These constituted his genius; his fanciful mode of handling his expositions of himself was the result of his cultivated talent. Like Donne, he had acquired the trick, the habit of working in that manner; but in all that is within the mere manner of his works, in all that gives that mannerism its perennial worth, he was alike untaught and unlearned. Nor does he not frequently drop his manner, and sing his word like a man too inspired to be capable of a style? In what style or school can this solemn and beautiful thought be classed, unless it be in the unnameable one of human nature?—

> "What hath not man sought out and found,
>> But his dear God? Who yet His glorious law
> Embosoms in us, mellowing the ground
>> With showers and frosts, with love and awe." [1]

The Reader will note how instinctively the 'showers' and 'frosts' and the 'mellowing' of the 'ground' symbolise to HERBERT the great Father's discipline and holy striving with His prodigal son, Man. So when he would 'body forth' his own quick resolves and slow fulfilment, he thus answers all who think him 'eager, hot, and undertaking, but in his prosecutions slack and small :'

[1] Lectures and Essays, as before, pp. 120-3.

> 'As a young exhalation, newly waking,
>   Scorns his first bed of dirt, and means the sky,
> But cooling by the way, grows pursie and slow,
>   And settling to a cloud, doth live and die
> In that dark state of tears,—*to all that so*
> *Show me and set me I have one reply,*
> *Which they that know the rest know more then I.'*

The 'young exhalation' matches Byron's 'young earthquake.'

Thus is it invariably and inevitably; and hence you have in well-nigh every poem the breath of the cool rural air, the gleam of the green fields, the sparkle of rain and infinite radiance of dew, the 'dark and shadie grove' and sky beyond, the 'sweet surprise' of woodland and wayside flowers in 'momentanie bloom,' or 'green and gay,' or autumn-stained, or twined in quick-fading 'posie,' and 'tender grasse,' and bud, 'nipt blossome,' and fruit; the bird in its nest or on the wing, or lifting its little head after sipping a drink, the 'nightingale,' and 'lark,' and 'sweet Dove,' of changeful plumage; the clouds, the stars' 'noiseless spheres,' light, and lightning—God's 'golden spear,'—wind and wave, 'rolling waves,' the tossing yet straight-steered 'boat,' the limpet on the rock, the 'bubble' iridescent and fragile, the snow, the flooded meadow, the 'secret cave,' the 'ringing' woods, the sunbeam reaching up like a golden stair from earth to heaven, the rainbow, light 'watrish' or flashing; bees, the 'worm' ('griev'd for a worm on which I tread'), dogs, the horse—in fine, *bits* of nature comparable with the landscape backgrounds of our greatest portrait-painters—behind the portraits, yet cunningly and inestimably done. HERBERT indeed actualised William Blake's 'Auguries of Innocence:'

> 'To see a world in a grain of sand,
>   And a heav'n in a wild flower,
> Hold infinity in the palm of your hand,
>   And eternity in an hour.'

Only one who found 'a heav'n in a wild flower,' one to
whom his Parsonage-garden was a very Garden of Eden,
would thus have cried out :

> 'Rain, *do not hurt my flowers*, but gently spend
>> Your hony-drops : presse not to smell them here;
> When they are ripe their odour will ascend,
>> And at your lodging with their thanks appears.'
>>>>> (Providence, ll. 117-120.)

Only one, too, who was 'all eare,' as ever Shakespeare was,
could thus have 'imagined :'

> 'All must appeare,
> And be dispos'd, and dress'd, and tun'd by Thee,
> Who sweetly temper'st all. IF WE COULD HEARE
> THY SKILL AND ART, WHAT MUSICK WOULD IT BE !'
>>>>> (Ibid. ll. 37-40.)

This latter especially shows how vocal to him was the
' physical world,' to which critics have supposed he was
' utterly indifferent,' or regarded as ' only base.'   There is
within it, too, as often, a subtle doubling of the thought,
in its earthly and divine side—a subtlety that comes out
in the very first stanza of ' The Church Porch,' wherein
' delight' itself becomes consecrate with the awfulness of
' sacrifice.'

Dr. Macdonald has pointed out another element of
HERBERT'S imaginativeness and originality in his ' use of
homeliest imagery for highest thought.'   This, he justly
thinks, ' is in itself enough to class him with the highest
kind of poets.'   He proceeds : 'If my reader will refer to
" The Elixir," he will see an instance in the third stanza,
"You may look at the glass or at the sky"—"You may
regard your action only, or that action as the will of God."
Again, let him listen to the pathos and simplicity of this
one stanza from a poem he calls " The Flower."   He has
been in trouble; his times have been evil, he has felt a
spiritual old age creeping upon him ; but he is once more
awake :

> " And now in age I bud again,
> After so many deaths I live and write ;
>   I once more smell the dew and rain,
> And relish versing : O, my onely Light,
>   It cannot be
>   That I am he
> On whom Thy tempests fell at night!"

Again :

>   " Some may dream merrily, but when they wake
>   They dress themselves and come to Thee." '
>
> (Antiphon, p. 180.)

That vivid line, 'I once more smell the dew and rain,'
was the grateful sigh of one whose heart-delight was in
Nature, even beyond his 'versing,' which, be it noted,
comes after, not before, his celebration of return from
the sick-chamber to his seat on the garden-meadow facing
the Neddar.

The ORIGINALITY of HERBERT is remarkable. His Son-
net (a double one) to his Mother—the Poem to the Queen
of Bohemia by 'G. H.,' which I have reclaimed, with only
slight hesitation, for him—and 'The Parodie' bear the
impress of Donne,' and prove that he was potential over
him to the last ;² and there are cadences and pauses and
breaks of melody that tell us Shakspeare's folio was all but
certainly one of the books for which he fasted that he
might possess it. But substantially he thought and felt and
saw and sang for himself. Henry Vaughan thought more
deeply, saw more magnificent visions (as of Eternity's
'great ring' of Light), felt perhaps more passionately,
looked more widely, sang with a fuller music and a
more absolute spontaneity ; but GEORGE HERBERT was

---

¹ The 'Parody' (Vol. I. pp. 211, 212) is after Donne's Love-lyric
(vol. ii. pp. 235-6).

² The line quoted by HERBERT in the 'Church Porch' (st. xiv.
l. 2) occurs in Donne's Lines to 'Mr. Tillman on his taking Or-
ders.' It is just *the* poem of his friend that we would have expected
HERBERT to turn to and value. It must have gone home to him as
he hesitated to accept Bemerton.

autochthonal after a remarkable type, alike in his thinking and imaginativeness, and wording and art. His 'The Rose' and 'Sunday' attest this in their combined familiarity and newness.[1] I invite brief attention next to his

4. *Wit and Humour.* Wit, in present meaning, is synonymous with 'humour,' as humour is with 'wit.' Formerly it designated much more, as elsewhere is shown.[2] I use it in the old sense of Wisdom, and in that GEORGE HERBERT is affluent; while I combine it with humour, inasmuch as there is a delicate playfulness in his gravest wisdom that is to me infinitely winning. You cannot study 'The Temple,' or 'A Priest to the Temple,' or 'Jacula Prudentum' without being struck with the *fulness* of sound common-sensed counsels on everyday duties and obligations, as well as on the higher and everlasting, or without perceiving that the Parson of Bemerton could unbend, and enjoy 'pleasant laughter.' His humour we should ill have spared, so gracious is it in itself, and so much more human and near to us does it make the Saint ; for never was falser idea of Christ than the patristic legend of the Lord having wept but never laughed, as though He Who fashioned the 'fount of tears' were not He Who strung the risible nerves, and implanted in His most absolute and crowned men, a keen sense of the ludicrous, the incongruous, the odd, as 'all things are big with jest.' Yet is the 'jest' ever that of a profoundly thoughtful man, as in 'The Church Porch' (st. v. l. 2), wherein he proclaims the levelling character in saint and

---

[1] I may be permitted to refer to my Essay on the Life and Writings of HENRY VAUGHAN (Works, vol. ii. pp. lxxviii.-xcvi.) for 'His Relation to GEORGE HERBERT.' I have very little to even modify therein, except perhaps that I have allowed Vaughan's grandeur of imagination to overshadow the not less genuine imaginative faculty of HERBERT, though on a humbler plane.

[2] See Notes and Illustrations, Vol. I. pp. 255, *et alibi.*

sinner of 'strong drink'—'When once it is within.' Once
let it pass 'within,' and 'grace' as 'flesh' falls before it—
surely a living word for to-day!!¹

The wit, *id est* wisdom, of HERBERT, is most of all re-
vealed in 'the simple but substantial and ever stately
Church Porch.' Here once more I draw upon that thought-
ful Essay which has already yielded so much of value :
This ['The Church Porch'] consists of seven-and-seventy
stanzas, full of clear sense concerning the common con-
duct of life, chastened worldly wisdom, and pure Chris-
tian morality, addressed to the Laertes or young son of
the Church :

> " Thou whose sweet youth and early hopes inhance
>   Thy rate and price, and mark thee for a treasure."

The neophyte is cordially, fervently, but above all sensi-
bly, warned against lust, wine, and, especially, boastful-
ness and sensuality. It is roundly and grandly said of
the boaster,

> " He makes flat war with God, and doth defy
>   With his poor clods of earth the spacious sky."

Swearing, leasing, and idleness are next rebuked with as
much *pungency as wit*. The very soldier is adjured to use
a noble sedulity :

> " Chase brave employment with a naked sword
>   Throughout the world.   Fool not; for all may have,
>   If they dare try, a glorious life or grave."

Constancy, frugality, regularity of living, love of solitude
and thrift are all enforced with singular judgment.
Hints about dress, play, conversation, quarrel, laughter,
wit, the great, friendship, and general behaviour are spun
into as many stanzas. At length there is more seriously
inculcated the duty of respect for Sunday, the Church, the

---

¹ I searched Ryley's MS. Notes on 'The Temple' for something
quick ; but found them dreary and empty and torpid, and un-
worthy of quotation.

Minister, and the institution of Prayer ; all done with as much point as gravity ; and with a most gallant ending, which will always please the wisest best :

> " In brief, acquit thee bravely ; play the man.
>   Look not on pleasures as they come, but go.
>   Defer not the least virtue ; life's poor span
>   Make not an ell by trifling in thy woe.
>   If thou do ill the joy fades, not the pains ;
>   If well, the pain doth fade, the joy remains."

That which strikes one most forcibly in all these preliminary stanzas is the practical sense that pervades them. One had thought HERBERT a meek and innocent Church-mystic, and here one finds him a man of life and counsel. The saint approves himself a gentleman ; the scholar a man of the world ; the minister a citizen. The reader is reminded of Bacon's minor Essays ; in some of the passages there is, here and there, a touch of pawky Benjamin Franklin ; but such is the thoroughbred air of the whole "Porch," that the image of old Polonius bestowing wise and elegant advices on his son is more frequently suggested than either. These fits of easy association last only a moment now and then, however ; for the most part the individuality of GEORGE HERBERT is not to be lost sight of, for the fragrant breath of the Church is in the Porch. Besides, the style of the expression as well as the thought is remarkably idiosyncratic ; it is quite as much so in this profane portion of the piece as it is within "The Temple." It is full of felicities.' Further : ' We would hasten into the sacred and equalising enclosure, but that we wish to point out a certain hidden significance in the construction of the "Porch" before doing so. In this the prelude of the piece there is nothing set forth but manners and morality. Nothing truly sacred, nothing that is spiritual is introduced. The inner life of the Church member is hardly hinted at ; that life of Christ which is hid with God is religiously reserved for the in-

terior of " The Temple." With how much care and touch-
ing simplicity is morality, pure and undefiled, kept sepa-
rate and differentialised from Christianity by this poetic
contrivance! Ethics, and even christianised ethics, which
form " the be-all and the end-all" here of certain ancient
and modern codes, is the mere Perirrhanterium of the
religion of Jesus. Beyond the endeavours and attain-
ments of him " whose life is in the right" there is a whole
universe of higher, deeper, subtiller, tenderer, and more
glorious experiences for the Christian. Morality is no
part of Christianity proper ; it is its best and likeliest pre-
parative of the way, or it is its first and its necessary sign ;
but it is not an integral part of it, any more than health
is part and parcel of morality, although it is one of its
delightful consequences. The Christian is and must be
moral ; but he is not a Christian in virtue of his morality,
he is a moral being in consequence of his Christianity.
As it has been forcibly expressed by Coleridge, in his com-
ment upon James i. 27, morality is the mere outer service
or ceremonial of Christianity : it bears the same propor-
tion and relation to the moral essence itself as the exter-
nal services of the tabernacle and the temple sustained to
the faith and theopathic life of Moses and the fathers.
It is a mere body, capable of subsisting by itself ; but also
capable of becoming informed and glorified by the new
spirit of Christ. Now the reader of sensibility cannot
fail to perceive that all this is enfolded in, or rather poeti-
cally adumbrated by, the very subject-matter and the
treatment of the " Porch," at which we have just been glanc-
ing. Nor can any one very well escape the feeling by way
of inference that the author of so much plain good sense
is a trustworthy guide to loftier themes. The priest has
gained one's confidence on the threshold of his sacred
home ; and one advances full of trust in the candour
of the wise young minister, not overawed even by those
solemn words from the Superliminare :

> " Avoid profaneness ; come not here : .
> Nothing but holy, pure, and clear,
> Or that which groaneth to be so,
> May at his peril further go." [1]

By the way, 'Avoid profaneuess' as = a counsel to the reader is the usual way of understanding this ; but surely our reading 'Avoid' as = ' Avaunt, Profaneness !' is deeper. With all this wisdom and all his gravity there is ever and anon, as indicated, scintillation of humour. Take these among many :

> ' God gave thy soul brave wings'

is his awakening and grand clarion-call to the Sluggard in the face of the sun ; but how quaint and sly follows this !—

> ' Put not those feathers
> Into a bed, to sleep out all ill weathers.'

Again, he has been holding interview in his parish with some stupid and obese squire ; and his portrait goes into ' The Church Porch :'

> ' O England !   .   .   .   .
>   .   .   .   fill thy breast with glory !
> Thy *gentry* bleats, as if thy native cloth
> *Transfused a sheepishness* into thy story.'

Donne earlier and Cowper and Lamb later would have ' clasped hands' with warble of soft laughter over that. Again :

> ' He's *a man of pleasure,*
> A kind of *thing* that's for itself too dear.'

The scorn of ' thing' here is almost terrible, yet is there gleam of humour in it. There is a ' grave sad' humour too in this emblem-conception of death :

> ' Therefore Thou dost not show
> This fully to us, till death blow
>   The dust into our eyes ;
> For by that powder Thou wilt make us see.'

In this also, and something profounder still :

[1] Dr. Samuel Brown, as before, pp. 112-14, 115-17.

> 'If, poor soul, thou hast no tears,
> *Would thou hadst no faults*, or fears ;
> *Who hath these*, those ills forbears.'

'The Quip' brims over with humour, and so too 'Death' (personated as a skeleton). Even the grave 'Church Militant' has flashes of playful seriousness that would be greatly relished at Weston.

It were easy to cull aphorisms of wisdom, succinct and condensed so as to be almost proverbial in their form, and to multiply, by puns and quips and playings on words and varying meanings, proofs of HERBERT's humour, that inevitable element in the highest kind of Poet ; but sufficient has been said for those willing to 'search' for themselves. I have to notice

5. *Sanctity*. Our analysis and interpretation of the Life of HERBERT has demonstrated that it was out of conflict and anguish, backsliding and tears, he grew up into the holy 'divine' man he ultimately became, and is to the universal heart ; but of that ultimate holiness and consecration there is not the shadow of a doubt. Few things consequently will more reward the student of human nature than an earnest, vigilant reading and re-reading of the writings of our Worthy, so as to receive into his heart-of-hearts the sanctity of his Poetry as represented by 'The Temple' and 'A Priest to the Temple.' Turning to 'Antiphon' again, here is criticism that is not so much criticism as outpoured affection, born of that infinite debt which every true HERBERT lover feels :

'No writer before him has shown such a love to God, such a child-like confidence in Him. The love is like the love of those whose verses came first in my volume. But the nation had learned to think more, and new difficulties had consequently arisen. These, again, had to be undermined by deeper thought, and the discovery of yet deeper truth had been the reward. Hence, the love itself, if it had not strengthened, had at least grown deeper. And GEORGE HERBERT had had difficulty enough in himself ; for, born of high family, by nature fitted to shine in that society where elegance of mind, person, carriage, and utterance is most appreciated, and having indeed enjoyed something of the life of a courtier, he had forsaken all in obedience to the voice of his higher nature. Hence the struggle between his tastes and his duties would come and come again, augmented probably by such austere notions as every conscientious man must entertain in proportion to his inability to find God in that in which he might find Him. From this inability, inseparable in its varying degrees from the very nature of growth, springs all the asceticism of good men, whose love to God will be the greater as their growing insight reveals Him in His world, and their growing faith approaches to the giving of thanks in everything.

When we have discovered the truth that whatsoever is not of faith is sin, the way to meet it is not to forsake the human law, but so to obey it as to thank God for it. To leave the world and go into the desert is not thus to give thanks: it may have been the only way for this or that man, in his blameless blindness, to take. The divine mind of GEORGE HERBERT, however, was in the main bent upon discovering God everywhere.

The poem I give next powerfully sets forth the struggle between liking and duty of which I have spoken. It is at the same time an instance of wonderful art in construction, all the force of the germinal thought kept in reserve, to burst forth at the last. He calls it—meaning by the word, *God's Restraint*—

"THE COLLAR.

I struck the board, and cry'd, ' No more ;
I will abroad.'
What, shall I ever sigh and pine ?
My lines and life are free ; free as the road,
Loose as the winde, as large as store.
Shall I be still in suit ?
Have I no harvest but a thorn
To let me bloud, and not restore
What I have lost with cordiall fruit ?
Sure there was wine
Before my sighs did drie it ; there was corn
Before my tears did drown it ;
Is the yeare onely lost to me ?
Have I no bayes to crown it,
No flowers, no garlands gay ? all blasted,
All wasted ?
Not so, my heart ; but there is fruit,
And thou hast hands.
Recover all thy sigh-blown age

On double pleasures ; leave thy cold dispute
Of what is fit and not ; forsake thy cage,
    Thy rope of sands
Which pettie thoughts have made ; and made to thee
  Good cable, to enforce and draw,
    And be thy law,
  While thou didst wink and wouldst not see.
    Away! take heed ;
    I will abroad.
Call in thy death's-head there, tie up thy fears ;
    He that forbears
   To suit and serve his need
    Deserves his load.
But as I rav'd and grew more fierce and wilde
    At every word,
  Methought I heard one calling, ' Childe ;'
    And I reply'd, ' My Lord.' "'

Even more reverently and finely Dr. Macdonald con-
cludes :

' It will be observed how much GEORGE HERBERT goes beyond all
that have preceded him, in the expression of feeling as it flows from
individual conditions, in the analysis of his own moods, in the logic
of worship, if I may say so. His utterance is not merely of personal
love and grief, but of the peculiar love and grief in the heart of
GEORGE HERBERT. There may be disease in such a mind ; but, if there
be, it is a disease that will burn itself out. Such disease is, for men
constituted like him, the only path to health. By health I mean
that simple regard to the truth, to the will of God, which will turn
away a man's eyes from his own conditions, and leave God free to
work His perfection in him—free, that is, of the interference of the
man's self-consciousness and anxiety. To this perfection St. Paul
had come when he no longer cried out against the body of his death,
no more judged his own self, but left all to the Father, caring only
to do His will. It was enough to him then that God should judge
him, for His will is the one good thing securing all good things.
Amongst the keener delights of the life which is at the door, I look
for the face of GEORGE HERBERT, with whom to talk humbly would
be in bliss a higher bliss.'

I know not that I need to add more than a sentence
to these ' Good Words.' The Christian will ever find in
the Life and Writings of GEORGE HERBERT at once
motive and impulse, reproof and aspiration, and human

evidence of how an imagined impossible ideal may become
a living reality on earth, and how the grand apostolic
charge—at first sight more wasteful than to ' gild refined
gold,' to ' paint the lily,' to ' throw a perfume on the
violet'—to ' *adorn* the doctrine,' may be done by men and
women to-day.   The Sanctity of the Life, and the Sanc-
tity in the very substance of the Writings of HERBERT, is
a legacy to Christendom that arithmetic cannot estimate.
We have finally

v. *Early and later estimates.*

The ' Commendatory Verses' prefixed to some of the
early editions of ' The Temple' are very poor.   The first,
entitled ' A Memorial to the Honourable GEORGE HER-
BERT, author of the Sacred Poems, who died about anno
1635,' is anonymous, and its ' about anno 1635,' when it
would have been so easy to have given the correct year
(1632-3), is an index of its carelessness.   He sings :

'Great saint, unto thy memory and shrine
I owe all veneration, save divine,
For thy rare poems : piety and pen
Speak thee no less than miracle of men ;'

and it is pleasing to read his closing testimony that he
' lived and died without an enemy.'   ' P. D. Esq.' is
quaint and loving, but unpoetic ; his last couplet is :

'Here a divine, prophet, and poet lies,
That laid up mana for posterities.'[1]

The lines on ' The Church Militant,' by ' Adversus
Impia, anno 1670,' find their fitting place with that
poem.[2]   Paling all the verse-tributes is Richard Crashaw's
little Letter, 'sent to a gentlewoman' along with a gift-
copy of ' The Temple.'   We give them in our Memorial-

---

[1] In Appendix to our annotated Life of HERBERT by Walton
(Vol. III.) I give these Commendatory Poems, and also Daniel
Baker's.   [2] Present volume, pp. 17, 18.

Introduction.[1] They are daintily wrought. They would
have delighted the Author. Walton was appreciative
enough to add these lines to his Life.

Dean Duport, who first published the 'Epigrams-
Apologetical' in answer to Anti-Tami-Cami-Categoria,
has several Latin poems commemorative of HERBERT. I
limit myself here to the one on the Poems, reserving
that on the Life by Walton for its place therewith (in
Vol. III.) :

'ON THE DIVINE POEM (ENTITLED THE TEMPLE) OF GEORGE
HERBERT ;

*A Poet at once most witty and most devout, moreover Public Orator of
the University of Cambridge, and formerly Fellow of Trinity College
in the same place.*

> If pointed wit and pious zeal were found
> Ever in one book, with like glory crowned,
> 'Tis thine, O HERBERT: all votes dost thou carry
> Who to sweet music heavenly sense canst marry.
> No lyre e'er sang so smoothly hymns divine,
> But either it was David's or 'twas thine.
> What use then can it be my Muse to call
> To weaken mighty songs with numbers small?
> In vain such praises I should strive to write,
> Or for thy Temple's steps measures indite,
> Till from the Blest Dove's wing a pen I steal,
> Or a live coal from thine own altar feel ;
> Till I perceive, in fine, the sacred fire
> Thy heart and mine with equal vein inspire.
> Then let me thy own phrases to thee bring,
> And thus my gardens water from thy spring.
> Not better can I praise this work of thine
> Than thou the king's grand work, Poet divine.
> " Bodleian, Vatican, why, stranger, vaunt?
> One Book is all the Library we want."
> This I will say—You'll find no better book,
> Except the Bible, wheresoe'er you look,
> Since, then, on earth no holier hymn is known,
> Or song, than this same Temple of thine own,

[1] Vol. I. pp. lxv.-vi.

> To make eternal songs in heaven aspire,
> Which thou mayst sing to the angelic choir.'[1]

The versification is superior to the substance in these
as in all Duport's Latin and Greek Poems; yet is it of
interest to blow the dust from his long-shut leaves to open
on certain of them, such as these on our Worthy.[2]

The Preface-Memoir—discursive and somewhat verbose
—of Barnabas Oley (1651), and the fuller Life by Walton
(1670), are full of personal admiration, but contain little of
critical value, except as seen earlier, that the former drew
a broad line of demarcation between the sacred poems of
'The Temple' and his 'Parentalia' and 'Epigrams-Apolo-
getical.' The next noticeable mention of HERBERT as a
Poet is by Richard Baxter, in the Preface to his 'Poetical
Fragments.'[3] It runs as follows: 'But I must confess,
after all, that, next the Scripture Poems, there are none so
savoury to me as Mr. GEORGE HERBERT's. I know that
Cowley and others far excel HERBERT in wit and accurate
composure; but as Seneca takes with me above all his
contemporaries, because he speaketh things by words feel-
ingly and seriously, like a man that is past jest, so HER-
BERT speaks to God like a man that really believeth in
God, and whose business in the world is most with God:
heart-work and heaven-work make up his book.'

Baxter elsewhere incidentally works in *bits* from 'The
Temple.' He was related to the Danvers kindred, if I err
not, and was introduced to Court by Sir HENRY HERBERT.
Following Baxter comes Henry Vaughan, in his solemn
and affecting Preface to 'Silex Scintillans,' as follows:

[1] By Rev. Richard Wilton, as before: the Latin will be found
in Duport's Musae Subsecivae (1676), pp. 357-8. Duport's allusion
is to HERBERT's Letter as Public Orator to the king on the gift-copy
of 'Basilicon Doron' to the University. See it in Vol. III., in its
place, with relative Note.

[2] The full title of his collected Poems is 'Musae Subsecivae
seu Poetica Stromata. Autore J. D. Cantabrigiensi. 1676, 8vo.'

[3] 1681.

'The first that with any effectual success attempted a diversion of this foul and overflowing stream [of love-verse] was the blessed man Mr. GEORGE HERBERT, whose holy life and verse gained many converts—of whom I am the least—and gave the first check to a most flourishing and admired wit of his time.   After him followed diverse—Sed non passibus aequis : they had more of fashion than force. And the reason of their so vast distance from him, besides differing spirits and qualifications—for his measure was eminent—I suspect to be, because they aimed more at verse than perfection, as may be easily gathered by their frequent impressions and numerous pages.'   These lowly and grateful words have been pushed far beyond their meaning and intention, traditional criticism ignorantly finding in them a profession of indebtedness to HERBERT as a Poet, while it was only spiritual good the Silurist owned.   Accordingly in my edition of his Works[1] I have vindicated for Henry Vaughan not his originality merely, but his well-nigh infinite supremacy over HERBERT in all that goes to constitute the aboriginal Poet; and the more I study him the more I feel what an outrage it is to place 'Silex Scintillans,' 'Olor Iscanus,' and 'Thalia Rediviva' beneath 'The Temple.'   But while this is so, and while Henry Vaughan in almost every way bulks out a larger-souled, more nobly-dowered Poet, it is very satisfying to find how our 'sweet Singer' ministered consolation and peace to him in that ' valley of the shadow of death' from which he came up ; as earlier the same ' little volume' was a soothing companion to unhappy Charles [I.] in his Prison ;[2] and later to William Cowper, when he wrestled

[1] Our edition of HENRY VAUGHAN's complete Works, Verse and Prose, 4 vols.

[2] Dibdin, in his Library Companion, p. 702, says : 'The second and best edition of HERBERT's Poems appeared in 1633, in a slender duodecimo volume. I have seen more than one beautiful copy of the pious volume, which has brought as much as 4l. 4s., in a delicately-ruled and thickly-gilt ornamented condition ; and in some

with despair and suicide, as he himself tells us in his fragment of Autobiography, as follows:

'I was struck, not long after my settlement in the Temple, with such a dejection of spirits as none but they who have felt the same can have the least conception of. Day and night I was on the rack; lying down in horror, and rising up in despair. I presently lost all relish for those studies to which I had before been closely 'attached. The classics had no longer any charms for me; I had need of something more salutary than amusement, but I had no one to direct me where to find it. At length I met with HERBERT's Poems, and Gothic and uncouth as they were, I yet found in them a strain of piety which I could not but admire. This was the only author I had any delight in reading. I pored over him all day long; and though I found not here what I might have found—a cure for my malady—yet it never seemed so much alleviated as while I was reading him.'

The Writings of HERBERT continued to be 'in print' from generation to generation, and hence must have had a place in many homes and hearths. You come on not unfrequent citations from 'The Temple' in more especially godly Nonconformist authors. Thus, in Dr. Bryan's 'Dwelling with God, the Interest and Duty of Believers,' 1670—that book which is one of the very few known by his autograph on a copy to have been in the library of John Bunyan—page on page is brightened with 'apples of gold' from The Temple's 'basket-work of silver ;'[1] and it were not hard to multiply similar recognitions of HERBERT in the way that Dr. Samuel Johnson pronounced to be the 'highest compliment you could pay an Author,'

---

such condition there is good reason to believe that Charles I. possessed it. Indeed his own copy of it, in blue morocco with rich gold tooling, was once, I learn, in the library of Tom Martin, of Palgrave.'. Sir Thomas Herbert, in his Carolina Threnodia, or Remains of the Two Last Years of Charles the First, names 'Herbert's Poems' among the books which the monarch-prisoner read most frequently.

[1] See a Paper by us, in 'Leisure Hour' (October 1873), on 'A Book that belonged to John Bunyan' (pp. 686-88).

viz. to quote him. But you do not meet with his name in
the usual biographic and literary authorities. Far inferior
names occur and recur ; his does not. I have been spe-
cially struck with the absence of so much as one hearty
sentence about him, or quotation from him, in a Divine
of his own Church ; and, curiously enough, the thing re-
mains to-day very much the same. For while Coleridge
has shown that the competent reader of HERBERT must
not only be a Christian, devout and devotional, as well as
the subject of poetical sensib lity and culture, but further
(to give his own words) 'must be an affectionate and
dutiful child of the Church [of England], and from habit,
conviction, and a constitutional predisposition to cere-
moniousness in piety as well as in manners, find her forms
and ordinances aids to religion, not sources of formality ;
for religion is the element in which he lives and the region
in which he moves'—it is simple matter-of-fact that the
only approaches to adequate critical estimates of GEORGE
HERBERT have been from the hearts and pens of Non-
conformists. Witness the often-quoted Essays of our
own day, in Dr. Samuel Brown and Dr. George Mac-
donald, Professor Nichol and George Gilfillan, as com-
pared with the *jejune* and captious notice of even such-
an-one as Keble : of the last, more anon. The first-named
must be allowed to offer his commentary on Coleridge's
dictum: 'This is very true, if the object desired, or de-
sirable, by the reader be such total absorption in the poet
as is certainly the highest pleasure, and the most profit-
able experience, in the study of poetry or any other
sovereign art. Yet poetic merit is shed so profusely over
the pages of this peculiar work, that the most uncom-
panioned poetic taste is sure to find far more delight than
weariness and offence. On the other hand, the well-tuned
Christian mind, Episcopalian, Presbyterian, or Morellian
—we had almost said Roman or Psalanthropist—will dis-
cover such an excess of pure gold, that what may look like

dross to this reader or to that, will hardly be observed, or only kindly smiled at in passing by. The fact is, that HERBERT'S poem [The Temple] is more catholic than HERBERT'S creed, and incomparably more so than his doctrine of Church services. As surely as a man is a poet, so surely is he humane, overgrowing every pale whatever, and possessed of blessings for all men. And HERBERT the man had often been wrapt in the unconsuming flame of inspiration as well as HERBERT the priest.' Personally it may be permitted us to state that Nonconformist though the present Writer be of the old Scottish Presbyterianism, his heart yearns to GEORGE HERBERT, while there is not a section of Nonconformity almost that is not represented in his constituency in bringing out this first adequate collection of the Works.

There is a gap between Baxter and Vaughan and further noticeable mention of GEORGE HERBERT of fully a century. Headley's criticism was the first to break the long silence ; and Churchman though he was, it is an impertinence exceeded only by its characteristic shallowness ; *e. g.* '" The Temple" is a compound of enthusiasm without sublimity, and conceit without ingenuity or imagination' (Select Specimens, 2 vols. 8vo, 1810). Deplorable to say, across the Atlantic, Henry Neele is found indolently all but accepting the imbecile verdict (Lectures on English Poets).

One cannot wonder that ' The Temple' fell out of sight comparatively during the eighteenth century ; for as the Christian Remembrancer (as before, p. 106) observes : ' His style was too abrupt and unadorned for their elaborately rounded periods, his religious aspirations too glowing for their decorous conventionalities, his theology too patristic for their latitudinarianism, and, we may add, his thoughts at once too profound and too rudely chiselled for their polished but superficial philosophy.' To be read *cum grano salis*, seeing that Butler and Jonathan Edwards

belong to the century : yet relatively true. Of its criticism
the Christian Remembrancer (as before, p. 127) observes :
'Warton, in a strange confusion of metaphors, speaks of
Pope " judiciously collecting gold from the dregs of HER-
BERT, Crashaw," &c. It would be nearer the mark to say
that Pope had penetration to detect the rich unpolished
ore strewn at random in HERBERT'S poems, and skill to
give it new lustre by the charm of his elaborate workman-
ship.' Who doubts this, let him read the ' Church Porch'
and 'Essay on Man' in the light of each other.

It is not until our own time that GEORGE HERBERT
has received his due crown of praise. Hallam—as so often
—has not a line to spare for GEORGE HERBERT as a Poet,
and is wooden and unsympathetic on the one book of his
which he glances at, although he turns aside to pay prepos-
terous praise to a 'friend' bearing the name of Herbert,
for a poem yclept 'Attilla ;' others are supercilious and
ignorant ; and others feel repelled by the man's accusing
sanctity. But Coleridge stooped his broad forehead to
do honour to the Poet and to the Saint, and by sheer in-
sistence talked many, who never would have opened his
pages, into studying him, and that sufficed ; for if you
once really read ' The Temple' a spell is on you, and you
are held captive, as were his listeners by the 'Ancient
Mariner.'

I return now upon Dr. Samuel Brown for other critical
estimates, all the more that in these the Prose of HER-
BERT also comes in, and in the knowledge of which I have
only thus far incidentally noticed it. Besides what has
been already given from his Essay, take these suggestive
and finely-touched criticisms of the Life and of the Writ-
ings, the Man and the Poet. Thus of the Man : ' It was
not till after a final struggle—not with civil ambition [?],
but with his inward sense of unworthiness—that he entered
into priest's Orders, and was inducted into the parsonage
of Bemerton. It was not till after Dr. Laud, then the

Bishop of London, and subsequently the historical Arch-
bishop of Canterbury, did "so convince Mr. HERBERT
that the refusal of it was a sin, that a tailor was sent for
to come speedily from Salisbury to Wilton, to take his
measure, and make him canonical clothes against next
day: which the tailor did."

'It is a fine spectacle for the imagination to see the graceful,
elegant, accomplished, witty, learned, eloquent, courtly, and high-
born orator of Cambridge University turning meekly down one of
England's green lanes, and stepping over the threshold of a country
parsonage, of which it is said that it was "more pleasant than
healthful." Nor was it suffered by this gentle and laborious spirit
to become a rural bower for learned or poetic leisure. No sooner
had he taken up his abode in this humble and industrious home,
than he painfully elaborated his ideal-real of the country parson in
thirty-seven weighty chapters, afterwards known as *A Priest to the
Temple*. Carlyle writes with generous fire about poor Irving's de-
termination, on entering the metropolis, veritably and once for all to
be a minister of God's gospel, and not to seem it only, like the
almost infinite majority of nominal priests. But we are profoundly
impressed with the conviction, that never has that sacred resolution
been more deeply felt, nor more fully acted out, than by GEORGE
HERBERT; no, not since the peculiar days of prophets and apostles.
It is the common testimony of contemporaries that he was his own
country parson, as entirely as it is possible for mortal to realise an
ideal so exalted, so glowing, so severe. The *Priest to the Temple*
ought to be in the hands and in the heart of every young minister in
Scotland as well as in England; for it is a genuine classic. No
Scottish clergyman will agree with every particular it contains; nor
do we. Its severity borders on the austere. His notions concerning
the marriage of ministers, his preference of celibacy for them unless
marriage be necessary for some reason or other, his carefulness about
fasts and meats, his tendency to formalism (not formality) in almost
every direction, are all rather extreme. We would venture to say
he overvalues the outward act of charity, the good deed, were it not
impossible to overvalue Christian beneficence in those sad days of
suffering and sorrow among the many. On the whole, however, it
is clear that HERBERT was a genuine Anglican, setting his reverted
eye with peculiar love upon the patristic Church, abominating and
cursing the errors of Romanism, under-estimating the Reformation,
loving and inculcating the plentiful use of outward symbols or

ceremonies for the expression of inward worship, and enamoured of
charity practised within bounds. But if he was a formulist, he was
no formalist, but as sincere a heart as ever bled under the sense of
sin. In truth it is not easy to say what precise amount of symbolism
or formalism is the best; we cannot do without some, we must pray
either standing or kneeling; we cannot pray sitting with open eyes;
and certainly, if the Anglican party in the Church of England is
prone to one extreme, the Kirk of Scotland has long been an exem-
plar of the other. Deducting these things, however, there is not,
and there could not be, a better manual for our own parochial clergy,
than this Pharos of that richly-laden, toil-worn, and yearning man
of God,.GEORGE HERBERT.

Our poet was not permitted to illustrate his priestly ideal very
long, alas! for he died towards the close of his thirty-ninth year;
born in April 1593, he fell asleep in March 1632; and it is enough
to say, he died as became so noble, gifted, and gracious a man. It
was within three weeks of his death that he gave the manuscript of
the *Temple*, his great work, into the hands of a friend, saying,
" Sir, I pray deliver this little book to my dear brother Ferrar, and
tell him he shall find in it a picture of the many spiritual conflicts
that have passed betwixt God and my soul, before I could subject
mine to the will of Jesus, my Master—in Whose service I have now
found perfect freedom: desire him to read it, and then, if he can
think it may turn to the advantage of any dejected poor soul, let it
be made public; if not, let him burn it; for I and it are less than
the least of God's mercies." It is this singular combination of
poems that we wish to introduce to the affectionate admiration of
our more lyrical readers' (pp. 108-110).

Of the Poet :

'The *Temple* itself may be viewed as the fair ideal of English
churches, built up with words. It is not Canterbury, nor York, nor
Westminster, nor any one of the thousand parish churches of Eng-
land; but it is the essence of all and each of these. It is, moreover,
that inalienably English conception of a church transformed by the
creative fancy of a free poet into a poem of rare architectural
beauty. In approaching this song-temple, one must by no means
think of the Scottish kirk on one side, any more than of the Roman
Catholic cathedral on the other. The latter

> " Hath kissed so long her painted shrines,
> That e'en her face with kissing shines,
>   For her reward :"

and as for the former—

> " She in the valley is so shy
> Of dressing, that her hair doth lie
> About her ears."

Our poem is simply a numerous and vocal symbol of that fine and matronly intermediate between those extremes, an English church:

> " A fine aspect in fit array,
> Neither too mean, nor yet too gay,
> Shows who is best.
> Outlandish looks may not compare,
> For all they either painted are,
> Or else undrest." '   (pp. 111, 112.)

Again :

'Once within, it is truly a wonderful place for eye and ear. There is a "broken altar," composed of the contrite heart of the poet, which every reader may appropriate with tears; there is an elaborate altar-piece of the "sacrifice" painted immediately behind; thanksgivings, confessions, prayers, sighs, and aspirations murmur everywhere around; hymns and psalms, choruses and fugues resound throughout the fane; homilies, lessons, and sermons solemnise the intervals of orison and song; there are carved pillars uplifting the roof, full of quaint devices, anagrams, and quips; monumental inscriptions and statues are all about; painted windows let in whole passages of poetry from the heaven without; and an unknown organ never ceases to suffuse the holy place with its melodious breath, till the last anthem has been pealed forth from the sobbing depths:

GLORY BE TO GOD, AND ON EARTH PEACE, GOOD-WILL TOWARDS MEN.'
(p. 117.)

Finally :

'Such then is the sacred poetry of GEORGE HERBERT, the country parson of Bemerton. It is peculiar; it even requires a peculiar cantation to secure its due effect upon the ear; but it is resonant with genuine music, to the sense as well as to the soul. He was, indeed, a passionate lover and practitioner of music, so it were sacred; for all his passions seem to have been subordinated to the idea of Christianity with which he was overflowed. Apart from such overflowing, in truth, he had scarcely been a poet of any renown, for his few profane pieces have none of the indelible glow of immortality upon them. He was inspired by the Bible as its vati-

cinators were inspired by God.   He seems to stand in a relation to
these sacred penmen, like that of the Greek rhapsodists, of whom
Ion is our Platonic type, to the Homeric epics; or like that of the
actor of genius, a Siddons or a Kean, to the orb of Shakespeare's
many-coloured song. As has already been hinted, this secondary
relation to the original fountain of inspiration seems to be the con-
dition of the modern hymnist's very existence; and surely no man
has drunk so deeply of the old river of joy as this English priest of
the seventeenth century.

Yet when under the glow of his sacred intoxication and self-
abandonment, he sends out the most original coruscations of insight
in other directions, as we have seen. His pages teem with the
most novel conceits, and the most aboriginal images on the one
hand; and, on the other, from what book or Bible did he draw
those subtle and far-reaching intuitions in the above-quoted piece
upon Man, to signalise only one example?' (pp. 126-7.)

Professor Nichol has also other 'Good Words' of our
Worthy that may not be passed by, as these: 'No one
ever lived to whom those words of a recent singer could
more appropriately have been applied than to "holy
GEORGE HERBERT :"

> " Better to have the poet's heart than brain,
>   To feel than write; but better far than both
>   To be on earth a poem of God's making." '

Again :

'The collection of poems entitled "The Temple" .... embraces
an almost indefinite variety of theme and measure, from the slender
notes of the flute to the full tones of the organ bass; yet it is per-
vaded by a unity of thought and purpose which justifies the single
name. Those poems are a series of hymns and meditations within
the walls of an English church. They are Church music crystal-
lised. There is a speciality about them which continually recalls
the circumstances of the writer. "The Temple," as Coleridge re-
marked [I intercalate, that the remark can bear repetition for sake
of the further comment], will always be read with fullest appreci-
ation by those who share the poet's devotion to the Dear Mother
whose praises he has undertaken to celebrate. The verses on
"Easter" and "Lent," on "Baptism" and "Communion," on
"Church Monuments" and "Music" seem most directly to address
the worshippers in that flock of which he was so good a shepherd,

whose affections are entwined around his Church, who love to linger
on the associations of her festivals, the rubrics of her creed, and the
formularies of her service—to feel themselves under the shadow of
the old cathedrals—to draw allegories from the fantasies of their
fretted stone—to watch the light flicker through the painted glass
on marble tombs, and listen to the anthems throbbing through the
choir. Yet there is in the author and in his work catholicity enough
to give his volume a universal interest, and make his prayer and
praise a fit expression of Christian faith under all varieties of form'
(pp. xix, xx.).

George Gilfillan furnishes also additional memorable
things of our 'sweet Singer' and Saint, as thus : ' " Life,"
it has been said, " is a Poem." This is true, probably, of
the life of the human race as a whole, if we could see its
beginning and end as well as its middle. But it is not true
of all lives. It is only a life here and there which equals
the dignity and aspires to the completeness of a genuine
and great Poem. Most lives are fragmentary, even when
they are not foul; they disappoint even when they do
not disgust; they are volumes without a preface, an index,
or a moral. It is delightful to turn from such apologies
for life to the rare but real lives which God-gifted men
like Milton or HERBERT have been enabled to spend even
on this dark and melancholy foot-breadth for immortal
spirits, called the Earth. We class Milton and HERBERT
together for this among other reasons, that in both the
life and the poems were thoroughly correspondent and
commensurate with each other. Milton lived the " Para-
dise Lost" and the " Paradise Regained" as well as wrote
them. HERBERT was as well as built " The Temple."
Not only did the intellectual archetype of its structure
exist in his mind, but he had been able, in a great mea-
sure, to realise it in life before expressing it in poetry.
His piety was of a more evangelical cast than Milton's, his
purity was tenderer and lovelier, he had more of the Chris-
tian and less of the Jew. Milton ranks with the austere
and sin-denouncing prophets of Israel—HERBERT reminds

us of that "disciple whom Jesus loved" ' (pp. v. vi.).
Again : ' HERBERT, although his mind wrought in a super-
induced atmosphere of mysticism, and although he is
commonly classed with those whom Dr. Johnson [Dryden]
calls the metaphysical poets, was by no means naturally
or generally a mystic. The form of his writing was some-
times dark and involved, but the substance and matter of
it were generally clear. His views of religion, at least,
seem to us to have been exceedingly explicit and distinct.
He belonged neither to Paul (the metaphysical), nor alto-
gether to Cephas (the ceremonial), nor to Apollos (the
rhetorical), nor even, although he resembled him much,
to John (that lovely flower on the breast of Christ), but
to Jesus Himself, Whom he so often calls his " Master,"
and Whom he loved with a love passing the love of women.
Emphatically he was a worshipper of Jesus Christ, and all
his nature and all his genius spread out their full riches
only to the magnet of the God-Man of Nazareth. His
love to Him amounted to a personal passion. It is said of
Robert Hall that in prayer he sometimes seemed abso-
lutely to *see* Christ, and so probably it was with HERBERT.
But it was not the glorified Christ that he saw so much
as the pale Sufferer at Cavalry crowned with thorns,
bleeding, forsaken, with His eyes full of a far look of
love and sorrow, as they gazed down on His murderers,
and with His lips now uttering the awful question to His
Father, "My God, My God, why hast Thou forsaken
Me ?" and now asking heaven, earth, and hell, "*was ever
grief like Mine?*" The Atonement was his favourite doc-
trine, and how heavily does he lean all the weight of his
hope upon the Cross !' (pp. xx. xxi.) Further : ' " The
Temple," . . . . as a piece of devotion, is a Prayer-book in
verse. We find in it all the various parts of prayer. Now
like a seraph he casts his crown at God's feet, and covers
his face with his wings, in awful adoration. Now he looks
up in His face with the happy gratitude of a child, and

murmurs out his thanksgiving. Now he seems David the
penitent, although fallen from an inferior height, and into
pits not nearly so deep and darksome, confessing his sins
and shortcomings to his Heavenly Father. And now he
asks, and prays, and besieges Heaven for mercy, pardon,
peace, grace, and joy, as with " groanings that cannot be
uttered." We find in it, too, a perpetual under-song of
praise. It is a Psalter no less than a Prayer-book. And
how different its bright sparks of worship, going up with-
out effort, without noise, by mere necessity of nature
[through grace] to heaven, from the majority of hymns
which have since appeared! No namby-pambyism, no
false unction, no nonsensical raptures are to be found in
them ; their very faults and mannerisms serve to attest
their sincerity, and to show that the whole man is reflected
in them. Even although the poem [" The Temple"] had
possessed far less poetic merit, its mere devotion, in its
depth and truth, would have commended it to Christians
as, next to the Psalms, the finest collection of ardent and
holy breathings to be found in the world. But its poetical
merit is of a very rare, lofty, and original order. It is full
of that subtle perception of analogies which is competent
only to high poetical genius. All things to HERBERT
appear marvellously alike to each other. The differences,
small or great, whether they be the interspaces between
leaves or the gulf between galaxies, shrivel up and disap-
pear. The ALL becomes one vast congeries of mirrors, of
similitudes, of duplicates—

> " Star nods to star, each system has its brother,
>   And half the universe reflects the other."'

This principle, or perception, which is the real spring of
all fancy and imagination, was very strong in HERBERT'S
mind, and hence the marvellous richness, freedom, and
variety of his images. He hangs upon his "Temple" now
flowers and now stars, now blossoms and now full-grown

fruit. He gathers glories from all regions of thought—
from all gardens of beauty—from all the history, and art,
and science then accessible to him—and he wreathes them
in a garland around the bleeding brow of Immanuel.
Sometimes his style exhibits a clear massiveness like one
of the Temple pillars, sometimes a dim richness like one of
the Temple windows ; and never is there wanting the
Temple music, now wailing melodiously, now moving in
brisk, lively, and bird-like measures, and now uttering loud
pæans and crashes of victorious sound. It has been truly
said of him, that he is "inspired by the Bible, as its vatici-
nators were inspired by God." It is to him not only the
"Book of God, but the God of Books." He has hung
and brooded over its pages, like a bird for ever dipping
her wing in the sea ; he has imbibed its inmost spirit—
he has made its divine words " the men of his counsel, and
his song in the house of his pilgrimage," till they are, in
his verse, less imitated than reproduced. In this, as in
other qualities, such as high imagination, burning zeal,
quaint fancy, and deep simplicity of character, he resem-
bles that " Child-Angel," John Bunyan, who was proud to
be a babe of the Bible, although his genius might have
made him without it a gigantic original' (pp. xxi. xxii.).
Once more : ' Altogether there are few places on earth
nearer heaven filled with a richer and holier light, ad-
orned with chaster and nobler ornaments, or where our
souls can worship with a more entire forgetfulness of self,
and a more thorough realisation of the things unseen and
eternal, than in " The Temple" of GEORGE HERBERT.
You say, as you stand breathless below its solemn arches,
"This is none other than the house of God ; it is the
gate of heaven. How dreadful, and yet how dear, is this
place !" ' (p. xxvi.)

    The 'Christian Remembrancer' (as before)—the solitary
adequate Anglican estimate of our Worthy—thus sums
up his conception of HERBERT as man and writer : ' We

have been reluctant to quit a subject so fascinating. Men like GEORGE HERBERT are rare. It is not his wide learning, nor his refined taste, nor his high spirit, nor his amiability, nor even his strictness of life ; it is not any of these qualities singly that distinguishes him, but the rare combination in one person of qualities so diversely beautiful. He was " master of all learning, human and divine." So writes his brother, Lord Herbert of Cherbury, and his Remains, few as they are, confirm this eulogy ; yet his learning is not what strikes the reader most, it is so thoroughly controlled and subordinated by his lively wit and practical wisdom. He was exemplary in the domestic relations of life, " tender and true," as son, husband, friend : yet he seems to have lived as a " home-missionary" among his parishioners. He was a man of letters, yet ever condescending to the petty concerns of his poor ignorant clients ; an ambitious man, yet he relinquished all worldly objects for the humble work of the ministry. He was, in a word, a man of extraordinary endowments, both personal and such as belonged to his rank—not lost in indolence nor wasted in trivialities, but all disciplined and cultivated to the utmost, and then devoted to the highest purposes. Men of a less evenly-balanced genius may create a greater sensation in the world ; as the eccentric course of a comet may attract more notice than steadier and less startling luminaries. But it may be questioned whether the influence of men like GEORGE HERBERT is not wider and deeper, though less perceptible, in the end. From them come the hidden watercourses of thought and action that irrigate the world with ever fresh supplies of life and vigour by innumerable unnoticeable rills, preserving its morality from corruption and stagnation. The influence of those who possess HERBERT's natural ability, combined with his solidity of character, cannot be measured by what we see. It is to men of this metal that England owes her greatness—men. like him, of high spirit, strict principle, genial practical energy—men who, over and above other fine qualities, are strong in that reality and earnestness on which we are apt to pride ourselves as peculiarly English' (p. 137). This also might have been added, that, while thoroughly a man of his Age, GEORGE HERBERT, even when at Court, partook of none of its stains. He would fain have won high place there; was not conscience-driven from it, as was Richard Baxter later when introduced by Sir Henry Herbert; yet was he pure and true :

'not mixt

> With th' Age's torrent, but still clear and fixt;
> As gentle oyl upon the streams doth glide,
> Not mingling with them, though it smooth the tide ;'[1]

so that, as William Bell sang of William Cartwright, 'The Priest may own all that the Poet writ.' Thus is it that these odd antique books hold their own amid all ebbing and flowing of opinion and circumstance :

'though dumb

> Thy picturesque old language, long outworn,
> And spoken now by none of woman born,
> . . . Thy work, like some naive early fresco, keeps
> Its first quaint charm—its feelings fresh as morn:
> Its mythic flowers, whose roots are in the deeps
> Of Truth; and from which, though they seem t' adorn
> Alone, deep inward meanings Wisdom reaps.'[2]

One could as soon conceive the Skylark's singing or the Primrose's beauty to pall, as one stone of 'The Temple' to be suffered to moss over or to go to decay. Their very modesty and unpretence secure the undyingness of HERBERT'S Writings, and especially his Verse :

'like the ivy, it grows

> Around neglected things : to beautify
> The commonplace, and touch with poesy

---

[1] Cartwright: 'To the memory of Sir Henry Spelman,' p. 310.
[2] Henry Ellison: To Herodotus, p. 161.

> The Daily and the Homely—and it throws
> Its large affections, tendril-like and close,
> Round the familiar hopes and fears whereby
> The household bosom of Humanity
> Is touched, *as round the cottage-porch the rose.*[1]

I would draw these Estimates to a close with (*a*) 'The Christian Remembrancer's' comparison of HERBERT and Keble; (*b*) Archbishop Leighton's notes on his copy of 'The Temple;' (*c*) Coleridge's notes on HERBERT—gathering up the little all as we do filings of gold.

(*a*) GEORGE HERBERT, JOHN KEBLE, AND COWPER.

'To compare HERBERT with the colossal genius of Milton would be preposterous. He is more nearly on a par with the others whom we have mentioned. If he wants their polished and musical diction, and is comparatively deficient in the variety of natural imagery and the tenderness of domestic pathos which belong to the poets of Olney and Hursley, he may be ranked above Keble in terseness and vigour, while his manly cheerfulness is a delightful contrast to the morbid gloom which throws its chilling shade over many of Cowper's most beautiful passages. In the general characteristics of profound and reflective philosophy, HERBERT and Trench [Archbishop of Dublin] may be classed together. Between HERBERT and Keble the resemblance is still more striking. The influence of the older poet is very perceptible throughout the "Christian Year,"—here and there in the very words of it. It is interesting to trace the coincidences[?] of these kindred minds. In the "Flower," which Coleridge calls "a delicious poem," HERBERT rejoices in the return of Spring to the earth, and of Spring-like feelings to his own heart, and proceeds:

> "These are Thy wonders, Lord of power,
> Killing and quickning, bringing down to hell

---

[1] Henry Ellison, 'My Poetry.'

> And up to heaven in an houre.
>   We say amisse
>   This or that is ;
> Thy Word is all, if we could spell."

In almost the same words, Keble exclaims :

> " These are Thy wonders hourly wrought,
>   Thou Lord of time and thought ;
>   Lifting and lowering souls at will,
>   Crowding a world of good or ill
>   Into a moment's vision."   (Sixth S. after Trinity.)

In another place Keble expresses the longing, such as even
heathen philosophers felt, for the glorious emancipation
of the immortal nature of man from its earthly elements :

> " Till every limb obey the mounting soul,
>   The mounting soul the call by Jesus given :
> He, Who the stormy heart can so control,
>   The laggard body soon will waft to Heaven."
>   (Twenty-third S. after Trinity.)

The same thought occurs in HERBERT :

> " Give me my captive soul, or take
>   My body also thither !
> Another lift like this will make
>   Them both to be together."

In both poets alike we see a natural inclination towards
the attractions of the world checked by self-discipline :

> " I thought it scorn with Thee to dwell,
>   A hermit in a silent cell,
>   While, gaily sweeping by,
>   Wild Fancy blew his bugle strain,
>   And marshalled all his gallant train
>   In the world's wondering eye.
>   I would have joined him, but as oft
>   Thy whispered warnings kind and soft
>   My better soul confest.
>   ' My servant, leave the world alone ;
>   Safe on the steps of Jesus' throne
>   Be tranquil and be blest.' "   (First S. after Trinity.)

So in " The Quip," which we have already referred to :

> " The merrie World did on a day
> With his train-bands and mates agree
> To meet together where I lay,
> And all in sport to jeer at me."

And the " merrie World," in the person of his representatives, " Beautie," " Money," " Wit," tries all his allurements, but in vain. HERBERT writes, in his poem on " Giddinesse :"

> " Surely, if each one saw another's heart,
> There would be no commerce,
> No sale and bargain passe : all would disperse
> And live apart."

Keble has expressed the same idea more fully in his beautiful lines for the Twenty-fourth Sunday after Trinity :

> " Or, what if Heaven for once its searching light
> Sent to some partial eye, disclosing all
> The rude bad thoughts that in our bosoms might
> Wander at large, nor heed love's gentle thrall,
> Who would not shun the dreary uncouth place ?
> As if, fond leaning where her infant slept,
> A mother's arm a serpent should embrace ;
> So might we friendless live, and die unwept."

In both Poets the consecutiveness of the ideas is often far from obvious, and must be sought beneath the surface. In HERBERT there is less periphrasis in the expression of devotional feelings.   Such outbursts as—

> " Oh ! my dear God, though I am clean forgot,
> Let me not love Thee, if I love Thee not,"

cannot be paralleled in Keble ; they are characteristic of HERBERT and of his age.

' These parallel passages are interesting as marking the similarity of character which subsists in great and good men, even of very distinct individualities.   The admirers of the " Christian Year" will find much in " The Temple" to remind them of their favourite passages. If " The Temple"

is never likely to exercise the extraordinary influence of
the " Christian Year"—an influence on the religious mind
of England greater than has ever been exercised by any
book of the kind,—an influence extending itself imper-
ceptibly even to quarters seemingly most alien—still it is
a book to make a deep impression, when it impresses at
all ; and its influence is of a kind to percolate through the
few to the many.

'The resemblance between HERBERT and Cowper is
fainter ; or rather, a strong resemblance is qualified by
equally strong traits of difference. Both poets have much
in common with Horace, strange as any comparison may
appear at first sight between them and the pagan poet of
the licentious court of Augustus. They have no small
share of his lyrical fervour, his adroitness in the choice of
words, and in the adaptation of metres ; and in satire,
the same light touch, the same suppressed humour, the
same half-sportive, half-pensive strictures on the anomalies
of life. Both HERBERT and Cowper love to dwell on the
transitoriness of earthly pleasures ; but there is this differ-
ence : HERBERT oftener adds that man may enjoy them
in moderation while they last :

<blockquote>
"Not that he may not here
  Taste of the cheer;
But as birds drink, and straight lift up their head,
  So must he sip, and think
  Of better drink
He may attain to after he is dead."
</blockquote>

' Both poets complain alike of times of religious depres-
sion ; but HERBERT'S lyre is more often tuned to joy and
thankfulness for refreshment and relief. He was natur-
ally of a more hopeful temperament. But there are
other causes to account for the difference. That distrust-
ful dread of alienation from the favour of Heaven, which,
in religious minds of Cowper's school, seems even to over-
cloud the sense of reconciliation through the Cross, was no

part of HERBERT's creed. On the contrary, it was the very essence of his faith, a source of unfailing strength, to regard himself and his fellow-Christians as having all the privileges of adoption within reach freely to enjoy. Again, while poor Cowper's mental vision was for ever introverted on himself, and busied with that dissection of transient phases of feeling which paralyses the healthy action of the soul, HERBERT's glance was oftener turned to the great objective truths of Christianity, deriving from them support in the consciousness of infirmity. Here is the secret of the cheerfulness of his poetry. The vivid realisation of the great external facts of Christianity is what distinguishes him from the " erotic school" of Germany. But for this, he might be classed with many of the poets of the " Lyra Germanica." But his poetry, though instinct with the same glow of seraphic love, is more definite, more practical, less sentimental. There is in it more substance for the mind to take hold of, more suggestiveness of something beyond, less evaporation into mere transports of emotion. His expressions of devout love, however eager and impulsive, are always (as in a short poem called " Artillerie") profoundly reverential. Love and obedience, faith and duty, are with him inseparable. This habitual attitude of mind toward the Deity, this filial feeling of love tempered by awe, is beautifully apparent in the closing lines of another poem :

<blockquote>
" But as I grew more fierce and wild,
  At every word
 Methought I heard one calling ' Childe !'
  And I replied, ' My Lord !' " ' (pp. 131-134.)
</blockquote>

I venture to add, that in the ending of one of the hitherto unprinted poems from the Williams MS. there is a fine parallel with the last quotation, as thus :

<blockquote>
'. . . . Tandem prehensa comiter lacernula
 Susurrat aure quispiam,
Haec fuerat olim potio Domini tui
 Gusto proboque dolium.' (Present vol. p. 71.)
</blockquote>

With reference to Cowper and Keble, it is very satisfying to have the former's almost adoring expression of indebtedness to 'The Temple'—as given onward; while it is disappointing, if not more, with all our veneration for the latter, that he had nothing more to say of HERBERT than to transfer to him his own pervading fault of ' a constant flutter of his fancy for ever hovering round and round the theme' (Prælectiones Academicæ, xx. 12)—a fault instinctively dealt with by the Church everywhere, by excision,—as of the 'flutter of fancy' in opening his truly sweet and beautiful hymn, instead of bursting out at once as HERBERT would have done—' Sun of my soul !' The 'Christian Year' is infinitely indebted within and on the surface, in its thinking and emotion and wording, to ' The Temple ;' and one reads the poor criticism of the ' Prælectiones' with a pain correspondent to that with which one reads Campbell's condemnation of Henry Vaughan— while pilfering from him. I must also be permitted to demur to the closing remarks on the imagined non-objective character of Cowper's poetry in relation to the *Cross* and cognate doctrines. Personally, the dark shadow of insanity held him in subjective misery and hopelessness certainly ; but the peculiarity is, that through all, his eye saw clearly the grand outstanding Facts. Be it remembered that, as Cowper wrote it (not as Hymn-book compilers mutilate), ' There is a fountain filled with blood' reads gloriously and gratefully thus :

> ' The dying thief rejoiced to see
> That Fountain in his day ;
> And there *have I*, though vile as he,
> Wash'd all *my* sins away.'

His subjective anguish Cowper kept to himself. His poetry is all radiant with the light of the objective, and is as definite and articulate as HERBERT's, or any of our Poets.

(b) Archbishop Leighton's Notes on his Copy of 'The Temple.'

Dr. Burgon, in his 'Life of Patrick Fraser Tytler,' in giving an account of that Historian's visit to the Leighton Library at Dunblane, makes the following statement: 'This visit, I remember, delighted him much; and he brought away an interesting memorial of it by transcribing the abundant notes with which Leighton has enriched his copy of HERBERT'S Poems' (The Portrait of a Christian Gentleman: a Memoir of P. F. Tytler, 1859; p. 250). It is not to be wondered at that such an intimation as '*abundant notes*' by so preëminent and like-minded a man as Leighton on so congenial a 'little book' excited interest in all Christian and literary circles. Investigation very soon dispelled the pleasing hope of a real addition to that most covetable of our book-treasures, 'Marginalia,' after the type of Selden long ago, and Coleridge recently. Memory ('I remember' is the Biographer's phrase) must have given a larger meaning to Tytler's spoken words than those warranted. At least Leighton's copy of 'The Temple' (the edition of 1634, and the only early one that ever belonged to the Library) does not contain a single note in the proper sense of the term, *id est*, on GEORGE HERBERT. Yet are his jottings of patristic quotations and references, suggested to the good bishop as he read, worthy of permanent record; the more especially as, after a first loss and recovery of the volume, it has again disappeared—surely through culpable negligence of the trustees of the Leightonian Library.[1] The

---

[1] The Letters referred to are from the Rev. James Boe, of the Kirk of Scotland, Dunblane, and are dated 24th November and 24th December 1859; and to the *Times*, December 24th, 1859. The volume was then in the Library, and the Notes were transcribed by the late Mr. Boe (who died in 1860), with praiseworthy carefulness, indeed in facsimile so as to authenticate the handwriting as Leighton's own. Now, on repeated inquiries, the volume is not to be found.

following details are derived from private letters and public addressed to B. H. Beedham, Esq., Ashfield House, Kimbolton, and to the *Times*, with which I have been favoured. As stated above, the edition was that of 1634 ('the Third'), and on the blank page, fronting the first verses of 'The Church Porch,' are these two quotations in Greek from Gregory Nazianzen :

τέχνῃ γλυκάζων τὸ πικρὸν τῶν ἐντολῶν. ΝΑΖ.

τὸ τερπνὸν οἶμαι τοῦ καλοῦ ποιούμενοι ὄχημα καὶ τυποῦντες ἐκ μελῶν τρόπους. ΝΑΖ.

These are connected with stanza i. ll. 5, 6, by a cross mark in each case :

> 'A verse may finde him who a sermon flies,
> And turn delight into a sacrifice.'

In the former it will be seen that the old Father, having previously spoken of the persuasive influence of verse over certain classes of persons, in leading them to the practice of what is worthy and profitable, represents the versifier

---

Surely the representatives of Mr. Boe ought to be communicated with. In all likelihood it was inadvertently retained among his own books. Dr. Walter C. Smith of Glasgow, in ignorance of Mr. Boe's letter to the *Times*, has this pungent note to 'The Bishop's Walk:' 'Mr. Burgon states in his Life of P. F. Tytler, that a copy of HERBERT's Poems, with notes by Leighton, once existed in the Library at Dunblane. It certainly is not there now; and I take this opportunity of again advertising all whom it may concern, that if they do not return it, all literature will *persecute* them' (p. 138). The loss of HERBERT's Poems recalls a wish of Mr. Allen of Prees, Shrewsbury, 'that those volumes which contain Leighton's notes (not, as I believe, a very large number) could be carefully catalogued by themselves, and put under closer restrictions as to loan than the other volumes that could be easily replaced.' Certainly the Trustees of the Leightonian Library owe it to themselves —(1) to spare no effort to recover Leighton's HERBERT's Poems; (2) to show a more adequate appreciation of the inestimableness of the Leighton-noted books in their custody.

as ' skilfully sweetening the bitter or unacceptable parts of his moral precepts by presenting them in an agreeable or attractive form.' In the latter, having adduced the example of the ancients and of even not a few of the authors of the books of Holy Scripture, who composed their writings in verse, he suggests the following reason : ' Those persons, as I imagine, making that which is pleasant the vehicle of that which is excellent, and teaching morals by means of verses or of acceptable songs.' The apostolic words, ' being crafty I caught you with guile' (2 Cor. iv. 16), and that he 'might by all means save some' (1 Cor. ix. 22), adumbrate the principle. Other jottings are on the fly-leaves, without mark or reference, as follow :

(1) μικρὸν καὶ πάντα λέλασται.

(2) οἴκοι γενοίμην.

(3) Eripe me his, invicte, malis.

The last of these, which is found in several of Leighton's books, was suggested no doubt by the ' evil days' on which his meek spirit was fallen. Others have been scratched out and are illegible. Besides these small notes, round pencil-marks (dots) abound ; but it is impossible to say whether they were made by Leighton. If it be disappointing that for ' abundant notes' we must be content with these very slight things, it is satisfactory to have all that really exists (or existed). But the published works of Archbishop Leighton contain a number of allusive quotations from HERBERT that it seems well to bring together. There are these from the Commentary upon the First Epistle of St. Peter. (1) ' This is the form and life of actions, that by which they are earthly or heavenly. Whatsoever be the matter of them, the spiritual mind hath that alchemy indeed of turning base metals into gold, earthly employments into heavenly' (c. ii. 18-20). The tacit reference is to ' The Elixir :'

> ' This is the famous stone
>   That turneth all to gold ;
> For that which God doth touch and own
>   Cannot for less be told.'

(2) ' What is all knowledge but painted folly in comparison of this ? Hadst thou Solomon's faculty to discourse of all plants, and hadst not the right knowledge of this Root of Jesse ; wert thou singular in the knowledge of the stars and of the course of the heavens, and couldst walk through the spheres with a Jacob's staff [== Cross Staff], but ignorant of this Star of Jacob ; if thou knewest the histories of all time, and the life and death of all the most famous princes, and could rehearse them all, but dost not spiritually know and apply to thyself the death of Jesus as thy life,—thou art still a wretched fool, and all thy knowledge with thee shall quickly perish' (c. ii. 24).   The entire passage recalls the opening of ' The Agony :'

> ' Philosophers have measured mountains,
>   Fathomed the depths of seas, of states and kings,
> Walked with a staff to Heaven, and tracèd fountains:
>   But there are two vast, spacious things
>   The which to measure it doth more behove,
>   Yet few there are that sound them,—Sin and Love.'

(3) ' He who sends oftenest out those " ships of desire," who makes the most voyages to that land of spices and pearls, shall be sure to improve his stock most, and have most of heaven upon earth' (c. iv. 7).   So HERBERT calls prayer itself ' the land of spices' (19. Prayer).   (4) ' In this lower world it is man alone that is made capable of showing the glory of God, and of offering Him praises. He expresses it well who calls man " the World's High-Priest ;" all the creatures bring their oblations of praise to him, to offer up for them and for himself, for whose use and comfort they are made' (c. v. 11).   Leighton had thus singled out HERBERT's ' Providence,' where we read :

> ' Man is the world's High-Priest; he doth present
>   The sacrifice for all; while they below
> Unto the service mutter an assent,
>   Such as springs use that fall, and winds that blow.'

The Sermons and Lectures also give these : (5) ' This He does infallibly and uncontrollably, yet in such a way as there is nothing distorted or violenced. *Fortiter et suaviter*—strongly and sweetly, all is so done' (on Jeremiah x. 23-25).   So HERBERT apostrophises ' Providence :'

> ' O sacred Providence, who from end to end
>   Strongly and sweetly movest.'

Both followed the Vulgate (Sap. viii. 1) : 'Attingit a fine usque ad finem *fortiter*, et disponit omnia *suaviter*.'   (6) ' He is admirable in all : the very lowest and smallest creatures have their wonders of Divine wisdom in their frame more than we are able to think.   *Magnus in minimis*—He is great in the least of His works' (Exp. Lect. on Psalm viii.).   So again in ' Providence :'

> ' Thou art in small things great, not small in any ;
>   Thy even praise can neither rise nor fall ;
> Thou art in all things One, in each thing many ;
>   For Thou art infinite in one and all.'

(7) ' The sea fitted for navigation . . . and the impetuousness of it, yet confined and forced to roll in its channel so that it cannot go forth ; the small sands giving check to the great waters' (ibid.).   So once more in ' Providence :'

> ' Thou hast made poor sand
> Check the proud sea, even when it swells and gathers.'

(8) ' Thou mindest him in all these things ; the works above him, even in the framing of these heavens, the moon and the stars, designing his good ; Thou makest all attend and serve him' (ibid.).   So in ' Man :'

> ' Man is one world, and hath
> Another to attend him.'

(9) ' The Church of Rome hate it for their common shift ;

they have shut out the heart from this employment, where it hath most interest, by praying in an unknown tongue ; and this defect they make up with long continuance and repetition of *Pater-nosters*, with a devotion as cold and dead as the beads they drop' (Exp. of the Lord's Prayer). This reminds of HERBERT's "only beads" (Glossary, *s.v.*). (10) 'This [Sunday] is the loveliest, brightest day in all the week to a spiritual mind. These *rests* refresh the soul in God, that finds nothing but turmoil in the creature. Should not this day be welcome to the soul, that sets it free to mind its own business, which is on other days to attend the business of its servant, the body? And these are a certain pledge to it of that expected freedom, when it shall enter into an eternal sabbath, and rest in Him for ever, Who is the only rest of the soul' (Exp. of the Ten Commandments). This was inspired by

'O Day most calm, most bright!'

With these jottings and references before us, it will be felt that most fitting it is that in 'The Bishop's Walk' Leighton should be introduced as reading (among others) GEORGE HERBERT, thus :

'Two hundred years have come and gone
Since that fine spirit mused alone
On the dim walk, with faint green shade
By the light-quivering ash-leaves made,
  And saw the sun go down
  Beyond the mountains brown.

Slow-pacing, with a lowly look,
Or gazing on the lettered book
Of Taylor, or a-Kempis, or
Meek HERBERT with his dulcimer,
  In quaintly pious vein
  Rehearsing a deep strain.'[1]   (p. 13.)

---

[1] There are other tacit reminiscences of HERBERT in Leighton's Works ; but both read in the same line and were of kindred head and heart. It was to the present Writer a sad stern duty to expose

(*e*) NOTES BY S. T. COLERIDGE ON HERBERT'S POEMS.
From Pickering's edition of 1835.

G. HERBERT is a true poet, but a poet *sui generis*, the merits of whose poems will never be felt without a sympathy with the mind and character of the man. To appreciate this volume, it is not enough that the reader possesses a cultivated judgment, classical taste, or even poetic sensibility, unless he be likewise a *Christian*, and both a zealous and an orthodox, both a devout and a *devotional* Christian. But even this will not quite suffice. He must be an affectionate and dutiful child of the Church, and from habit, conviction, and a constitutional predisposition to ceremoniousness, in piety as in manners, find her forms and ordinances aids of religion, not sources of formality; for religion is the element in which he lives, and the region in which he moves.

The Church—say, rather, the Churchmen of England under the two first Stuarts—has been charged with a yearning after the Romish fopperies and even the papistic usurpations; but we shall decide more correctly, as well as more charitably, if for the Romish and papistic we substitute the *patristic* leaven. There even was (natural enough, from their distinguished learning and knowledge of eclesiastical antiquities) an overrating of the Church and of the Fathers for the first five or even six centuries; these lines on the Egyptian monks, 'Holy Macarius and great Anthony' [Vol. II. p. 4, l. 42], supply a striking instance and illustration of this.

Vol. I. p. 21, st. xlviii. I do not understand this stanza.

P. 52, l. 25. 'My flesh begun unto my soul in pain.' Either a misprint, or a noticeable idiom of the word 'began'? Yes! and a very beautiful idiom it is;—the first colloquy or address of the flesh.

P. 57, l. 43. 'With an exact and most particular trust.' I find few historical facts so difficult of solution as the continuance, in Protestantism, of this anti-scriptural superstition.

P. 65, l. 19. 'This verse marks that,' &c. The spiritual unity of the Bible==the order and connexion of organic forms, in which

---

the well-meant but absolutely worthless edition of Archbishop Leighton's Writings, edited by the Rev. William West of Nairn. His laboriousness and enthusiasm are neutralised by the pervading corruption of his author's text, under a delusion of 'improvement.'

the unity of life is shown, though as widely dispersed in the world of the mere sight ; as the text.

P. 65, l. 21. 'Then, as dispersed herbs do *watch* a potion.' Some misprint. [See our Notes and Illustrations.]

P. 90, l. 10. 'A *box* where,' &c. Neat.

P. 103, l. 39. ' Distinguished.' I understand this but imperfectly. Dist. they form an island ? and the next lines refer perhaps to the then belief that all fruits grow and are nourished by water ? but then how is the ascending sap ' our cleanliness'? Perhaps, therefore, the ruins.

P. 154, l. 21. ' But He doth bid us take His blood for wine.' Nay, the contrary ; take wine to be blood, and *the* blood of a man who died 1800 years ago. This is the faith which even the Church of England demands ; for Consubstantiation only *adds* a mystery to that of Transubstantiation, which it implies.

Pp. 190-2. 'The Flower.' *A delicious poem.*

P. 190, l. 4. 'The late-past frosts tributes of pleasure bring.'

$\breve{\cup}\ -\ -\ -\quad -\ \cup\ \cup\quad -\ \cup$

Epitritus primus + Dactyl + Trochee + a long word − syllable, which together with the pause intervening between it and the word — trochee, equals $\cup\ \cup\ \cup\ -$ form a pleasing variety in the Pentameter Iambic with rhymes. Ex. gr.

Thĕ lātĕ pāst frŏsts | trībutĕs ŏf | pleasure | brīng.

N.B. First, the difference between $-\ \cup\ |\ -$ and an amphimacer $-\ \cup\ -\ |$ and this not always or necessarily arising out of the latter being one word. It may even consist of three words : yet the effect be the same. It is the pause that makes the difference. Secondly, the expediency, if not necessity, that the first syllable both of the Dactyl and the Trochee should be short by quantity, and only = — by force of accent or position — the Epitrite being true *lengths.* Whether the last syllable be — or = —, the force of the rhymes renders indifferent. Thus : . . .

P. 190, l. 7. 'As if there *were no such cold thing.*' Had been no such thing.

P. 190, l. 5. '*That* choice,' &c. Their.

P. 190, l. 18. ' E'en in my *enemies*' sight.' Foemen's.

P. 216, l. 7. 'That they in *merit* shall excel.' I should not have expected from HERBERT so open an avowal of Romanism in the article of *merit.* [A misprint ' here' for ' hear' misled Coleridge. See our Notes and Illustrations *in loco.*] In the same spirit is *holy* Macarius and great Anthony, Vol. II. p. 4. l. 42.

Besides these Notes-proper, Coleridge has passing tributes elsewhere to HERBERT as Poet as well as Man : *e.g.* in 'The Friend' (vol. i. p. 53) : ' Let me add, that the quaintness of some of his thoughts, not of his diction, than which nothing can be more pure, manly, and unaffected, has blinded modern readers to the general merits of his poems, which are for the most part exquisite in their kind.' Similarly in 'Biographia Literaria,' he speaks of the ' weight, number, and compression of HERBERT'S thoughts, and the simple dignity of the language :' and he wrote to his friend Collins the Painter : ' Read " The Temple," if you have not read it.'   Again : ' The characteristic of our elder poets is the reverse of that which distinguishes more recent versifiers ; the one (HERBERT and his school) conveying the most fantastic thoughts in the most correct and natural language ; the other, in the most fantastic language conveying the most trivial thoughts.   The latter is a riddle of words, the former an enigma of thoughts.'

Finally : I envy not the man who can read the story of GEORGE HERBERT'S Life, as told by Izaak Walton and Barnabas Oley and ourselves, and as interwoven with his Verse and Prose, without thankfulness to the Great Giver for such a Life and such Writings.   The Church of England has had many illustrious Sons, who hold a permanent place in the Theological Literature of Europe ; but I do not know that she has had a finer intellect, a nobler spirit, a more lovable nature, a truer ' Maker' than the 'Country Parson' of Bemerton.[1]   'Two years and

[1] In the Christian Remembrancer we read : ' The Poems seem to have been written before the " Country Parson." His preface to the latter is dated 1632, the year of his death ; and its other name, by which it was more usually known at first, " A Priest to the Temple," seems to indicate that it was conceived in its Author's mind as a companion volume to the already existing, though unpublished, collection of poems entitled " The Temple"' (p. 105).   I suspect that

three months may seem a disproportionate space of time
for his work in the ministry, after so long and so careful
preparation for it.   But it is not for us to call his death
premature.   To himself the old adage may safely be ap-
plied—"his wings were grown;" and, as for his work, it
was ended.   "Non diu sed multum vixit."   His contem-
poraries complained that "he lost himself in that humble
way," while devoting his energies to that obscure little
parish.   But his influence in forming the highest type of
Christian character for laity as well as clergy, has been
extended, by his example and writings, far beyond the
narrow limits of that little parish on Salisbury Plain, with
its "twenty cottages" and "less than a hundred and twenty
souls," far beyond the age in which he lived.[1]   Our own
generation has witnessed an Augustus Hare, in his little
sequestered parish (also in Wilts), sustaining the Her-
bertian type of Life.

Such, then, is what we wished to say and furnish on
the Life and Writings of GEORGE HERBERT.   Now that
our Essay is finished, and we go back on it, its inadequate-
ness pains us ; yet there is this consolation, that perhaps
our words may suggest and allure Readers ; and above all
it is our priceless privilege to present FOR THE FIRST TIME
fully and worthily the Works of one of the uncanonised
Saints of the Church Catholic.   For Leighton, of 'The
Bishop's Walk,' I substitute the 'Parson' of Bemerton ;
and as I turn and return on the Face, as reproduced in
integrity from that of 1674 (in the Quarto form), I find in
its vivid portraiture our very own GEORGE HERBERT.   I

---

the 'other name' was given by Oley in order to relate it to 'The
Temple,' and that as not 'The Temple' but 'The Church' was HER-
BERT's own title, so the 'Country Parson' was probably his own.
See account of the Williams MS.

[1] Christian Remembrancer, as before, p. 115.

cannot more fitly close our Essay than with it (slightly adapted) :

> 'Slow-pacing with a downcast eye,
> Which yet, in rapt devotion high,
> Sometimes its great dark orb would lift,
> And pierced the veil, and caught the swift
> > Glance of an angel's wing,
> > That of the Lamb did sing;
>
> And with the fine pale shadow, wrought
> Upon his cheek by years of thought,
> And lines of weariness and pain,
> And looks that long for home again;
> > So went he to and fro,
> > With step infirm and slow.
>
> A frail slight form—no temple he
> Grand for abode of Deity;
> Rather a bush inflamed with grace,
> And trembling in a desert place,
> > And unconsumed with fire,
> > Though burning high and higher.
>
> A frail slight form, and pale with care,
> And paler from the raven hair
> That folded from a forehead free,
> Godlike of height and majesty—
> > A brow of thought supreme,
> > And mystic glorious dream.'   (pp. 14, 15.)

ALEXANDER B. GROSART.

I.

THE CHURCH MILITANT.

NOTE.

'The Church Militant' is Herbert's heading in the Williams MS., and is in agreement with his title of 'The Church Porch' and 'The Church' for the other two portions of the volume of 1632-3, published by Nicholas Ferrar as 'The Temple.' It occupies pp. 184-192 of the original edition, and ever since has been regarded as a third division of one set of poems. It is independent; and I have deemed it better to disjoin it from the minor pieces of 'The Temple,' differing as it does from them alike in substance and form.

At the close of this Poem will be found various-readings and additions from the Williams MS.; some of the latter inserted in the text (ll. 17, 61-3, and 162-4). For more on it, see our Essay in the present volume.   G.

THE CHURCH MILITANT.

Almightie Lord, Who from Thy glorious throne
Seest and rulest all things ev'n as one;
The smallest ant or atome knows Thy power,
Known also to each minute of an houre:
Much more do common-weals acknowledge Thee,   5
And wrap their policies in Thy decree,
Complying with Thy counsels, doing nought
Which doth not meet with an eternall thought.
But above all, Thy Church and Spouse doth prove,
Not the decrees of power, but bands of love.   10
Early didst Thou arise to plant this vine,
Which might the more indeare it to be Thine.
Spices come from the East, so did Thy Spouse,
Trimme as the light, sweet as the laden boughs
Of Noah's shadie vine, chaste as the dove,   15
Prepar'd and fitted to receive Thy love,—
All emblems which Thy darling doth improve.—
The course was westward, that the sunne might light
As well our understanding as our sight.
Where th' Ark did rest, there Abraham began   20
To bring the other Ark from Canaan.

Moses pursu'd this; but King Solomon
Finisht and fixt the old religion.
When it grew loose, the Jews did hope in vain
By nailing Christ to fasten it again;   25
But to the Gentiles He bore Crosse and all,
Rending with earthquakes the partition-wall.
Onely whereas the Ark in glorie shone,
Now with the Crosse, as with a staffe, alone,
Religion, like a pilgrime, Westward bent,   30
Knocking at all doores ever as She went.
Yet as the sunne, though forward be his flight,
Listens behinde him, and allows some light
Till all depart; so went the Church her way,
Letting, while one foot stept, the other stay   35
Among the Eastern nations for a time,
Till both removèd to the Western clime.
To Egypt first she came, where they did prove
Wonders of Anger once, but now of Love;
The Ten Commandments there did flourish more   40
Then the ten bitter plagues had done before;
Holy Macarius and great Anthonie
Made Pharaoh Moses, changing th' historie;
Goshen was darknesse, Egypt full of lights,
Nilus for monsters brought forth Israelites.   45
Such power hath mightie Baptisme to produce,
For things misshapen, things of highest use.
How deare to me, O God, Thy counsels are!
               Who may with Thee compare?

Religion thence fled into Greece, where arts   50
Gave her the highest place in all men's hearts;
Learning was pos'd, Philosophie was set,   puzzled
Sophisters taken in a fisher's net.
Plato and Aristotle were at a losse,
And wheel'd about again to spell Christ-Crosse.   55
Prayers chas'd syllogismes into their den,
And Ergo was transform'd into Amen.
Though Greece took horse as soon as Egypt did,
And Rome as both, yet Egypt faster rid,
And spent her period and prefixèd time   60
Before the other two were in their prime;
From Greece to Rome she went, subduing those
Who had subduèd all the world for foes.
The Warrier his deere skarres no more resounds,
But seems to yeeld Christ hath the greater wounds;   65
Wounds willingly endur'd to work his blisse,
Who by an ambush lost his Paradise.
The great heart stoops, and taketh from the dust,
A sad repentance, not the spoils of lust ;
Quitting his spear, lest it should pierce again   70
Him in His members, Who for him was slain.
The Shepherd's hook grew to a scepter here,
Giving new names and numbers to the yeare;
But th' Empire dwelt in Greece, to comfort them
Who were cut short in Alexander's stemme.   75
In both of these Prowesse and Arts did tame
And tune men's hearts against the Gospel came ;

Which using, and not fearing skill in th' one
Or strength in th' other, did erect her throne.
Many a rent and struggling th' Empire knew— 80
As dying things are wont—untill it flew
At length to Germanie, still Westward bending,
And there the Churche's festivall attending;
That as before Empire and Arts made way—
For no lesse Harbingers would serve then they— 85
So they might still, and point us out the place
Where first the Church should raise her downcast face.
Strength levels grounds, Art makes a garden there;
Then showres Religion, and makes all to bear.
Spain in the Empire shar'd with Germanie,   90
But England in the higher victorie,
Giving the Church a crown to keep her state,
And not go lesse then she had done of late.
Constantine's British line meant this of old,
And did this mysterie wrap up and fold   95
Within a sheet of paper, which was rent
From Time's great Chronicle, and hither sent.
Thus both the Church and sunne together ran
Unto the farthest old meridian.
How deare to me, O God, Thy counsels are ! 100
     Who may with Thee compare?
 Much about one and the same time and place,
Both where and when the Church began her race,
Sinne did set out of Eastern Babylon,
And travell'd Westward also : journeying on 105

He chid the Church away where e're he came,
Breaking her peace and tainting her good name.
At first he got to Egypt, and did sow
Gardens of gods, which ev'ry yeare did grow
Fresh and fine deities.   They were at great cost,   110
Who for a god clearely a sallet lost.
Ah, what a thing is man devoid of grace,
Adoring garlick with an humble face,
Begging his food of that which he may eat,
Starving the while he worshippeth his meat!   115
Who makes a root his god, how low is he,
If God and man be sever'd infinitely!
What wretchednesse can give him any room,
Whose house is foul, while he adores his broom?
None will beleeve this now, though money be   120
In us the same transplanted fooleric.
Thus Sinne in Egypt sneakèd for a while;
His highest was an ox or crocodile,
And such poore game. Thence he to Greece doth passe,
And being craftier much then Goodnesse was,   125
He left behinde him garrisons of sinnes,
To make good that which ev'ry day he winnes.
Here Sinne took heart, and for a garden-bed   =instead of
Rich shrines and oracles he purchasèd;
He grew a gallant, and would needs foretell   130
As well what should befall as what befell;
Nay, he became a poet, and would serve
His pills of sublimate in that conserve.

The world came both with hands and purses full
To this great lotterie, and all would pull.   draw   135
But all was glorious cheating, brave deceit,
Where some poore truths were shuffl'd for a bait
To credit him, and so discredit those
Who after him should braver truths disclose.
From Greece he went to Rome; and as before   140
He was a god, now he's an emperour;
Nero and others lodg'd him bravely there,
Put him in trust to rule the Romane sphere.
Glorie was his chief instrument of old;
Pleasure succeeded straight when that grew cold,   145
Which soon was blown to such a mightie flame,
That though our Saviour did destroy the game,
Disparking oracles and all their treasure,
Setting affliction to encounter pleasure;
Yet did a rogue, with hope of carnall joy, Mahomet 150
Cheat the most subtill nations.   Who so coy,
So trimme, as Greece and Egypt? Yet their hearts
Are given over, for their curious arts,
To such Mahometan stupidities
As the old heathen would deem prodigies.   155
How deare to me, O God, Thy counsels are!
                Who may with Thee compare?
   Onely the West and Rome do keep them free
From this contagious infidelitie;   160
And this is all the Rock whereof they boast,
As Rome will one day finde unto her cost;

Traditions are accounts without our host;
They who rely on them must reckon twice,
When written Truths shall censure man's devise.
Sinne being not able to extirpate quite   165
The Churches here, bravely resolv'd one night
To be a Churchman too, and wear a mitre;
The old debauchèd ruffian would turn writer.
I saw him in his studie, where he sate
Busie in controversies sprung of late: 170
A gown and pen became him wondrous well;
His grave aspect had more of heav'n then hell;
Onely there was a handsome picture by,
To which he lent a corner of his eye.
As Sinne in Greece a prophet was before,   175
And in old Rome a mightie emperour;
So now, being priest, he plainly did professe
To make a jest of Christ's three offices;
The rather since his scatter'd jugglings were
United now in one, both time and sphere.   180
From Egypt he took pettie deities,
From Greece oracular infallibilities,
And from old Rome the libertie of pleasure,
By free dispensings of the Churche's treasure;
Then, in memoriall of his ancient throne,   185
He did surname his palace Babylon.
Yet that he might the better gain all nations,
And make that name good by their transmigrations,
From all these places, but at divers times,

He took fine vizards to conceal his crimes—   190
From Egypt anchorisme and retirednesse,
Learning from Greece, from old Rome statelinesse;
And blending these, he carri'd all men's eyes,—
While Truth sat by, counting his victories;
Whereby he grew apace, and scorn'd to use   195
Such force as once did captivate the Jews,
But did bewitch, and finally work each nation
Into a voluntarie transmigration.
All poste to Rome; princes submit their necks
Either t' his publick foot or private tricks.   200
It did not fit his gravitie to stirre,
Nor his long journey, nor his gout and furre;
Therefore he sent out able ministers,
Statesmen within, without doores cloisterers;
Who, without spear, or sword, or other drumme   205
Then what was in their tongue, did overcome;   than
And having conquer'd, did so strangely rule,
That the whole world did seem but the Pope's mule.
As new and old Rome did one Empire twist,
So both together are one Antichrist;   210
Yet with two faces, as their Janus was,
Being in this their old crackt looking-glasse.
How deare to me, O God, Thy counsels are !
                    Who may with Thee compare?
    Thus Sinne triumphs in Western Babylon;   215
Yet not as Sinne, but as Religion.
Of his two thrones he made the latter best,

And to defray his journey from the East.
Old and new Babylon are to hell and night
As is the moon and sunne to heav'n and light.   220
When th' one did set, the other did take place,
Confronting equally the Law and Grace.
They are hell's landmarks, Satan's double crest;
They are Sinne's nipples, feeding th' East and West.
But as in vice the copie still exceeds   225
The pattern, but not so in virtuous deeds;
So, though Sinne made his latter seat the better,
The latter Church is to the first a debter.
The second Temple could not reach the first;
And the late Reformation never durst   230
Compare with ancient times and purer yeares,
But in the Jews and us deserveth tears.
Nay, it shall ev'ry yeare decrease and fade,
Till such a darknesse do the world invade
At Christ's last coming as His first did finde ;   235
Yet must there such proportions be assign'd
To these diminishings as is between
The spacious world and Jury to be seen.
Religion stands on tiptoe in our land,
Readie to passe to the American strand.   240
When height of malice and prodigious lusts,
Impudent sinning, witchcrafts, and distrusts—
The marks of future bane—shall fill our cup
Unto the brimme, and make our measure up ;
When Sein shall swallow Tiber, and the Thames, 245

By letting-in them both, pollutes her streams;
When Italie of us shall have her will,
And all her calendar of sinnes fulfill,
Whereby one may foretell what sinnes next yeare
Shall both in France and England domineer—   250
Then shall Religion to America flee;
They have their times of Gospel ev'n as we.
My God, Thou dost prepare for them a way,
By carrying first their gold from them away;
For gold and grace did never yet agree,   255
Religion alwaies sides with povertie.
We think we rob them, but we think amisse;
We are more poore, and they more rich by this.
Thou wilt revenge their quarrell, making grace
To pay our debts, and leave our ancient place   260
To go to them, while that which now their nation
But lends to us shall be our desolation.
Yet as the Church shall thither Westward flie,
So Sinne shall trace and dog her instantly;
They have their period also and set times,   265
Both for their vertuous actions and their crimes.
And where of old the Empire and the Arts   =whereas
Usher'd the Gospel ever in men's hearts,
Spain hath done one; when Arts perform the other,
The Church shall come, and Sinne the Church shall
                smother ;   270
That when they have accomplishèd the round,
And met in th' East their first and ancient sound,   =haven

Judgement may meet them both and search them round.
Thus do both lights, as well in Church as sunne,
Light one another and together runne ;   275
Thus also Sinne and Darknesse follow still
The Church and sunne with all their power and skill.
But as the sunne still goes both West and East,
So also did the Church by going West
Still Eastward go ; because it drew more neare   280
To time and place where judgement shall appeare.
How deare to me, O God, Thy counsels are!
     Who may with Thee compare?

¶ L'ENVOY.

King of glorie, King of peace,
With the one make warre to cease;
With the other blesse Thy sheep,
Thee to love, in Thee to sleep.
Let not Sinne devoure Thy fold,
Bragging that Thy bloud is cold;
That Thy death is also dead,
While his conquests dayly spread ;
That Thy flesh hath lost his food,
And Thy Crosse is common wood.
Choke him, let him say no more,
But reserve his breath in store.
Till Thy conquest and his fall
Make his sighs to use it all;

And then bargain with the winde
To discharge what is behind.

𝕭𝖑𝖊𝖘𝖘𝖊𝖉 𝖇𝖊 𝕲𝖔𝖉 𝖆𝖑𝖔𝖓𝖊,
𝕿𝖍𝖗𝖎𝖈𝖊 𝖇𝖑𝖊𝖘𝖘𝖊𝖉 𝕿𝖍𝖗𝖊𝖊 𝖎𝖓 𝕺𝖓𝖊.

NOTES AND ILLUSTRATIONS.

Line 14, ' *trimme*'=spruce or sprucely adorned. See its use again in l. 152.

Line 16. I insert this line from the Williams ms., but mark it as a kind of parenthetical glance back on the similes or ' emblems' of the Church, the Spouse, as 'Light,' 'Vine,' ' Dove.' By ' improve' Herbert seems to mean set forth fittingly in the old sermon-sense of ' improve.' It was probably struck out by Ferrar as not very well agreeing with ' trimme as—sweet as, chaste as.'

Line 26, ' *bore Crosse and all.*' Cf. Passio Discerpta.

„ 33, '*Listens behinde him:*' a metaphor drawn from field-sports.

Line 34, ' *depart:*' the Williams ms. reads ' begone': the reference being to ' light' and ' twilight.' I have deemed it better to retain the printed text, ' depart.'

Line 50. In Williams ms. it is

' Thence into Greece she fled, where curious Arts.'

' Her' is=Religion. Cf. ll. 84-5 and 267-9. The liberal arts, which *emolliunt mores*, and the habit of philosophic thought, prepared them for the reception of the truth.

Line 55, ' *Christ-Crosse:*' colloquially criss-cross, the alphabet in a horn-book or primer; called so, either because a cross was prefixed to the alphabet row, or because the alphabet was arranged to form a cross.

Lines 61-3. I adopt the Williams ms. readings here. They are much more vivid and striking than the usual text, which runs:

' Before the other. Greece being past her prime,
Religion went to Rome, subduing those
Who, that they might subdue, made all their foes.'

Line 64, ' *Warrier:*' Williams ms. spells ' Warriour.'

„ 65, ' *hath:*' Williams ms. reads ' had ;' but ' hath,' in its ' present for all time,' gives the finer sense.

Line 73, '*new names*'=the change of Pagan holy days to Christian: the 'new numbers;' and perhaps the whole line, may refer to the change of style introduced by Pope Gregory in 1582.

Line 77, '*tune :*' Williams ms. 'clense'—inferior, if indeed it be not untrue.

Line 79, '*did erect her throne :*' Williams ms. 'took possession'—again inferior.

Line 85, '*Harbingers :*' see full Note on 147. The Forerunners, l. 1, in Vol. I.

Line 89, '*Then showres Religion*'=Then Religion showers.

„ 92, '*a crown :*' the reference is, as in the next note, to the Reformation.

Line 93, '*Constantine's British line.*' The thought is here obscure and probably far-fetched. When Constantius Chlorus Cæsar, in Britain, died at York, his son Constantine was proclaimed and eventually became emperor, and on his conversion gave, so to speak, a crown to the Church. Thus his rise in Britain, and his giving a crown to the Church, foreshadowed, says Herbert, or was a type, that hereafter Britain should give the Church a crown; meaning that at the Reformation Henry VIII. would put down the usurped authority of the Church, and make it a national Church, and the State's head its supreme head. This is the more probable interpretation of 'giving the Church a crown to keep her state,' inasmuch as Herbert afterwards distinctly dissociates the Church from the Papacy and Papal polity, calling the latter 'the reign of Sin.' The mode of giving also corresponds, the action of Henry being more like that of Constantine than that of John in his giving up of his crown to the Pope, which otherwise we might have supposed to be the reference.

Line 124, '*poore :*' Williams ms. 'small,' inferior in relation to 'ox' and 'crocodile.'

Lines 132-3. The oracular responses being in verse, Herbert says they hide their poison in the sweetness of verse.

Line 134, '*both :*' Williams ms. 'in.'

„ 135, '*pull :*' another proof that 'pulling prime' consisted in drawing from the pack. See Glossarial Index *s.v.*

Line 138, '*so :*' from Williams ms. for 'to' of printed text.

„ 148, '*disparking.*' On 'disparking' in connection with destroying game, see Glossarial Index *s.v.*

Line 152, '*trimme.*' See Note on l. 14.

Line 158. In Williams MS. originally 'Europe alone and Rome:' but Herbert erases, and writes 'Onely the West.'

Lines 162-4. I insert these lines from the Williams MS. They are too characteristic to be lost. Line 162: to reckon without one's host is to reckon mistakenly; and that Herbert was here thinking of the saying is clear by the next line, and the use in it of 'reckon.' Traditions, says he, are accounts at second, third, or other hand, not verified by the personal or written word of the host; and those who rely on them must reckon twice, consider well when they are not only so verified, but differ from the written truths, the host's own words.

Line 172, '*had more of:*' Williams MS. 'was liker.'

,,   173, '*Onely there was a handsome picture by:*' I fear the allusion is to certain Popes' 'lust' after pictures of 'fair women,' their concubines and mistresses, semi-nude—the scandals of the Church.

Line 184, '*dispensings:*' Williams MS. 'dispensations,' which has a somewhat ambiguous sound.

Lines 193-4. I punctuate parenthetically ' While Truth sat by.' Hitherto it has not been so done. Of course it may be said that Truth is represented as having nothing else to do; but is that counting of Sin's victories an occupation for Truth? I prefer considering ' While Truth sat by' *i. e.* aside and idly —as parenthetical, and that it is Sin that counts or reckons up her victories, and, glorying therein, grows apace, &c.

Line 197. Williams MS. 'bewitch both kings and many a.'

,,   198, '*Into:*' Williams MS. 'Vnto;' but we transmigrate ' into,' not ' unto,' for the soul transmigrates, not the body.

Line 202, '*and:*' Williams MS. ' or.'

,,   205-8. Not in the Williams MS., but the following come after line 204:

> ' Who brought his doctrines and his deeds from Rome ;
> But when they were vnto the Sorbon come,
> The waight was such they left the doctrines there,
> Shipping the Vices onely for our sphere.'

Line 218, '*defray*'=and made [from line above] [it] the latter to defray; an irregular ellipsis.

Line 232=But [the second Temple] in the Jews and [the late Reformation] in us [each or each part] deserveth tears. Again very elliptical.

Line 233, '*yeares:*' Williams MS. ' days,' which less accords with a progress reckoned by centuries than 'yeares.'

Lines 239-40. On these famous lines, see our Essay in present volume.

Line 252, '*times :*' Williams MS. ' time.'

„   262, '*lends to :*' Williams MS. ' lendeth.'

„   265, '*period*'==termination.

„   272, '*sound:*' an expanse of sea or kind of sea-lake, with a narrow outlet, giving, therefore, a land-locked haven or harbour.

Line 275. In Williams MS. ' Like Comick Lovers euer one way runn.'

Lines 276-7. In Williams MS. these read as follows :

<blockquote>
' Darknesse constantly
Follow the Church and Sunn where ere they fly.'
</blockquote>

¶ *L'Envoy.* In the Williams MS. Herbert himself has written this as a heading.

On a Latin verse-translation of The Church Militant, with a specimen, see our Essay as before. The following verse-tribute to ' The Church Militant' appeared in 1674 and after editions of The Temple :

THE CHURCH MILITANT.

The Churche's progress is a master-piece,
Limn'd to the life, of Egypt, Rome, and Greece ;
Wherein he gives the Conclave such a blow,
They nere receiv'd from either friend or foe.
England and France do bear an equal share
In his predictions ; which Time will declare.
Here's height of malice, here's prodigious lust,
Impudent sinning, cruelty, distrust ;
Here's black ingratitude, here's pride and scorn ;
Here's damnèd oaths, that cause the land to mourn ;
And here's oppression, marks of future bane,
And here's hypocrisie, the counter-pane ;
Here's love of Gininies—curs'd root of all—
And here's religion turn'd up to the wall ;
And could we see with Herbert's eagle eyes,
Without checkmate Religion westward flies.
A most sad sacrifice was made of late
Of God's poor lambs by Pharisaique hate :
For discipline with doctrine so to jarr,
Was just like bringing Justice to the barr.
Was it the will, or judgment, or commands
Of the great Pilot for to pass the Sands ?
Well may we hope that our quick-fited State
Will take God's grievance into a debate.
Cathedrall priests long since have laid about
Hammer and tongs, to drive Religion out ;
Her grace and majesty makes them so 'frald
They cry content, and so espouse her maid.
Shee's decent, lovely, chaste, divine, they say ;
She loves their sons that sing our sins away.

Could we but count the thousands every year
These dreams consume, the musick is too dear.
When Elie's sons made luxury their god,
Their widows nam'd their posthumes Icabod.
They both were slain, God's sacred ark was lost,
Though they had with it a most mighty hoast.
Well may ingratitude make us all mourn ;
Pearls we receive, poor pebles wo return.
Now Sein is swallowing Tiber, if the Thames,
By letting in them both, pollute her streams ;
Or if the Seeres shall connive or wink,
Beware the thunderbolt : *migremus hinc.*
O, let me die, and not survive to see,
Before my death, Religion's obseqnie.
Religion and dear Truth will prove at length
The Alpha and Omega of our strength ;
Our Boaz, our Jakine, our Great Britain's glory,
Look'd on by owls as a romantick story.
Our CLOUD that comes behind us in the day,
Night's fiery pillar, to direct our way ;
Our chariots, ships, and horsemen to withstand
The fury of our foes by sea or land ;
Our eyes may see, as hath been seen before,
Religion's foes lye floating on the shore.
The head of England's Church, proud Babel's, but
Will Faith defend, and Peace will Janus shut.

Adversus Impia, Anno 1670.   G.

II.

LILIES OF THE TEMPLE.

FROM UNPUBLISHED MSS.

NOTE.

The first six pieces in this section were published by us
from the Williams MS. in the 'Leisure Hour' of the Religious
Tract Society. See our Preface and Memorial-Introduction in
Vol. I., and Essay in present volume. The last piece is from
'Miscellanea Sacra, or Poems on Divine and Moral Subjects,'
collected by N. Tate. 2d edition, 1698, p. 51, where it is headed
'The Convert. An Ode written by Mr. George Herbert.' It is
to be regretted that Tate does not inform us whence he derived
this Ode. But as he was well-circumstanced to procure MSS.,
and as others of eminent names first published by him have been
authenticated, there is every probability that he had an auto-
graph of this poem. It has touches of Herbert in it. I am not
aware that any one until now has reprinted it. I gladly entwine
it with the six Lilies. G.

I. THE HOLY COMMUNION.

O Gratious Lord, how shall I know
Whether in these gifts Thou bee so
    As Thou art everywhere ?
Or rather so, as Thou alone
Tak'st all y^e Lodging, leaving none   5
    For Thy poore creature there.

First I am sure, whether bread stay,
Or whether Bread doe fly away,
    Concerneth Bread, not mee;
But y^t both Thou and all Thy traine   10
Bee there, to Thy truth and my gaine
    Concerneth mee and Thee.

And if in comming to Thy foes,
Thou dost come first to them, y^t showes
    The hast of Thy good will;   15
Or if that Thou two stations makest,
In Bread and mee, the way Thou takest
    Is more, but for mee still.

Then of this also I am sure,
That Thou didst all these pains endure   20
    T' abolish Sinn, not Wheat;

Creatures are good, and have their place;
Sinn onely, wch did all deface,
      Thou drivest from his seat.

I could beleeve an Impanation   25
At the rate of an Incarnation,
      If Thou hadst dyde for Bread;
But that wch made my soule to dye,
My flesh and fleshy villany,
      That allso made Thee dead.   30

That flesh is there mine eyes deny:
And what shold flesh but flesh discry—
      The noblest sence of five?
If glorious bodies pass the sight,
Shall they be food and strength and might,   35
      Euen there where they deceiue?

Into my soule this cannot pass;
Flesh, though exalted, keeps his grass,
      And cannot turn to soule.
Bodyes and Minds are different spheres;   40
Nor can they change their bounds and meres,
      But keep a constant Pole.

This gift of all gifts is the best,
Thy flesh the least y^t I request;
      Thou took'st that pledg from mee: 45
Give me not that I had before,
Or give me that so I have more;
      My God, give mee all Thee.   (Fol. 81.)

II. LOVE.

Thou art too hard for me in Love;
There is no dealing wth Thee in that Art,
    That is Thy Masterpeece, I see.
    When I contrive and plott to prove
Something that may be conquest on my part,   5
    Thou still, O Lord, outstrippest mee.

    Sometimes, when as I wash, I say,
And shrodely as I think, 'Lord, wash my soule,
    More spotted then my Flesh can bee.'
    But then there comes into my way   10
Thy ancient baptism, wch when I was foule
    And knew it not, yet cleansèd mee.

    I took a time when Thou didst sleep,
Great waves of trouble combating my brest:
    I thought it braue to praise Thee then;   15
    Yet then I found that Thou didst creep
Into my hart wth ioye, giving more rest
    Than flesh did Lend Thee back agen.

    Let mee but once the conquest have
Vpon ye matter, 'twill Thy conquest prove: 20
    If Thou subdue mortalitie,
    Thou dost no more than doth ye graue;
Whereas if I orecome Thee and Thy love,
    Hell, Death, and Divel come short of mee.
(Fols. 38, 39.)

III. TRINITY SUNDAY.

<pre>
He that is one
                Is none;
Two reacheth Thee
In some degree:
Nature and Grace   5
W^th Glory may attaine Thy Face.
    Steele and a flint strike fire;
    Witt and desire
    Never to Thee aspire,
Except life catch and hold those fast.   10
    That wch beleefe
Did not confess in ye first Theefe   Satan
    His fall can tell
From Heaven through Earth to Hell.
    Lett two of those alone   15
    To them that fall,
Who God and Saints and Angels loose at last :   lose
    Hee that has one
            Has all.   (Fol. 40.)
</pre>

IV. EUEN-SONG.

The Day is spent, and hath his will on mee :
    I and ye Sunn haue runn our races :
    I went ye slower, yet more paces ;
For I decay, not hee.

Lord, make my Loss vp, and sett mee free,   5
    That I, who cannot now by day
    Look on his daring brightnes, may
Shine then more bright then hee.

If Thou deferr this light, then shadow mee,
    Least that the Night, earth's gloomy shade,   10
    Fouling her nest, my earth invade,
As if shades knew not Thee.

But Thou art Light and darkness both togeather:
    If that bee dark we cannot see,
    The sunn is darker then a Tree,   15
And Thou more dark then either.

Yet Thou art not so dark since I know this,
    But that my darknes may touch Thine;
    And hope that may teach it to shine,
Since Light Thy darknes is.   20

O lett my Soule, whose keyes I must deliver
    Into the hands of senceles dreames,
    W^{ch} know not Thee, suck in Thy beames,
And wake wth Thee for ever.   (Fol. 41.)

V. THE KNELL.

The Bell doth tolle:
Lord, help Thy servant, whose perplexèd Soule
    Doth wishly look   wistfully
    On either hand,

And sometimes offers, sometimes makes a stand,   5
       Strugling on th' hook.
       Now is the season,
Now ye great combat of our flesh and reason :
       O help, my God ;
       See, they break in,   10
Disbanded humours, sorrows, troops of Sinn,
       Each wth his rodd.
       Lord, make Thy Blood
Convert and colour all the other flood
       And streams of grief,   15
       That they may bee
Julips and cordials when we call on Thee
       For some relief.   (Fol. 75.)

VI. PERSEVERANCE.

My God, ye poore expressions of my Love,
W^{ch} warme these lines and serve them vp to Thee,
Are so as for the present I did moue,
       Or rather as Thou mouèdst mee.

But what shall issue, whether these my words   5
Shal help another, but my iudgment bee ;
As a burst fouling-peece doth saue ye birds,
       But kill the man, is scald wth Thee.

For who can tell, though Thou hast dyde to winn
And wedd my soule in glorious paradise,   10
Whither my many crymes and vse of sinn
       May yet forbid the banes and bliss ?   bans

Onely my soule hangs on Thy promises,
Wth face and hands clinging vnto Thy brest;
Clinging and crying, crying wthout cease,   15
    'Thou art my Rock, Thou art my Rest.'
                (Fol. 76.)

VII. THE CONVERT.

If ever tears did flow from eyes,
If ever voice was hoarse with cries,
If ever heart was sore with sighs,—
    Let now my eyes, my voice, my heart
    Strive each to play their part.

My eyes, from whence these tears did spring,
Where treach'rous Syrens us'd to sing,
Shall flow no more, untill they bring
    A deluge on my sensual flame,
    And wash away my shame.

My voice, that oft with foolish lays,
With vows and rants and senseless praise,
Frail Beauty's charms to heav'n did raise,
    Henceforth shall only pierce the skies
    In penitential cryes.

My heart, that gave fond thoughts their food—
Till now averse to all that's good,
The Temple where an idol stood,
    Henceforth in sacred flames shall burn,
    And be that idol's urn.

NOTES AND ILLUSTRATIONS.

1. *The Holy Communion.* Lines 13-18=Whether Thou comest direct to the believer, or comest first into the bread and wine, and thence to the receiver. Lines 25-6=I could believe God becoming bread (impanation), and hold it as of the same value as God becoming man, if &c. Line 38, ' *keeps his grass:*' *i. e.* keeps that natural substance which is in the grass and herbs from which all flesh is immediately or intermediately derived. Line 41, ' *meres :*' generally said to be a boundary; but perhaps more correctly what it certainly is sometimes, a boundary-mark. See Drayton's Polyolb. i.

"₊" I printed '*ff*' originally, but I have since discovered that this was merely a form of capital F.

11. *Love.* Line 20, ' *Upon y^e matter*'=in this matter [of love].

111. *Trinity Sunday.* In this there is a play on 'one' at the beginning and end, and intermediately on 'three.' He that is one (Nature) &c. Two (Nature and Grace) reacheth &c. He that has 'one' of the three, *i.e.* 'Heaven,' has all.

1v. *Euen-song.* Line 3, ' *more paces:*' and therefore advanced with more exertion and expense of energy and flesh.

v1. *Perseverance.* Line 3, ' *moue*'=intend to speak.

v11. *The Convert.* See Note prefixed to this section.

G.

III.

PSALMS.

HITHERTO UNCOLLECTED AND INEDITED.

These Psalms are taken from the following now extremely rare book:

PSALMS AND HYMNS

IN SOLEMN MUSICK

OF FOURE PARTS,

Or the common tunes to the Psalms in Metre:
Used in Parish-Churches.

Also six Hymns for one Voice to the Organ.

For God is King of all the earth; sing ye praises with understanding.
PSALM xlvii. 7.

By JOHN PLAYFORD.

[Picture of K. David playing, surrounded by a square margin containing
'the music of Gloria in excelsis, Deo Cantato, &c.]

London: Printed by W. Godbid for J. Playford at his shop in the
Inner-Temple. 1671. [A folio.]

It is dedicated to William Sancroft, D.D., Dean of St. Paul's.
In the Preface occur these explanations: 'To those which are
Bishop King's, there is H. K.; those of Mr. [Miles] Smith [yet
living], M. S.; those with G. H. are supposed to be Mr. George
Herbert's.' The translation of the 23d Psalm in 'The Temple'
is also given by Playford, who was well acquainted with Her-
bert's sacred poems. In the same volume he sets the Altar to
music, and in his preface quotes Herbert's first Antiphon (Vol.
I. pp. 59-60). Probably, therefore, the 23d Psalm was added from
'The Temple,' and this is the more likely, as the other Psalms
signed G. H. run on continuously from 1 to 7. Edward Farr, in
his 'Select Poetry, chiefly sacred, of the Reign of King James
the First' (Cambridge, 1847), gives 'Psalm V.' (pp. 87-8). On
his uncharacteristically incorrect Note hereon, and other points,
see our Preface (Vol. I.) and Essay (Vol. II.).   G.

PSALM III.

How are my foes increasèd, Lord!
    many are they that rise
Against me, saying, for my soul
    no help in God there is.
But Thou, O Lord, ar't still the shield
    of my deliverance ;
Thou art my glory, Lord, and He
    that doth my head advance.

I cry'd unto the Lord, He heard
    me from His holy hill ;
I laid me down and slept, I wak't ;
    for God sustain'd me still.
Aided by Him, I will not fear
    ten thousand enemies,
Nor all the people round about
    that can against me rise.

Arise, O Lord, and rescue me ;
    save me, my God, from thrall ;
'Tis Thou upon the cheek-bone smit'st
    mine adversaries all.

And Thou hast brok th' ungodly's teeth :
 salvation unto Thee
Belongs, O Lord ; Thy blessing shall
 upon Thy people be. G. H. (p. 12.)

PSALM IV.

Another translation.

Lord, hear me when I call on Thee,
 Lord of my righteousness ;
O Thou that hast enlargèd me
 when I was in distress.

Have mercy on me, Lord, and hear
 the prayer that I frame ;
How long will ye, vain men, convert
 my glory into shame ?

How long will ye seek after lies,
 and vanity approve ?
But know the Lord Himself doth chuse
 the righteous man to love.

The Lord will hearken unto me
 when I His grace implore ;
O learn to stand in awe of Him,
 and sin not any more.

Within your chamber try your hearts ;
 offer to God on high
The sacrifice of righteousness,
 and on His grace rely.

Many there are that say, ' O, who
    will show us good ?'   But, Lord,
Thy countenance's cheering light
    do Thou to us afford.

For that, O Lord, with perfect joy
    shall more replenish me
Then worldlings joy'd with all their store
    of corn and wine can be.

Therefore will I lie down in peace
    and take my restful sleep ;
For Thy protection, Lord, alone
    shall me in safety keep.   G. II. (p. 18.)

PSALM VI.

Rebuke me not in wrath, O Lord,
    nor in Thine anger chasten me ;
O pity me ; for I, O Lord,
    am nothing but infirmitie.

O heal me, for my bones are vex'd,
    my soul is troubled very sore ;
But, Lord, how long so much perplex'd
    shall I in vain Thy grace implore ?

Return, O God, and rescue me,
    my soul for Thy great mercy save ;
For who in death remember Thee ?
    or who shall praise Thee in the grave ?

With groaning I am wearied,
     all night I make my couch to swim,
And water with salt tears my bed ;
     my sight with sorrow waxeth dim.

My beauty wears and doth decay,
     because of all mine enemies ;
But now from me depart away
     all ye that work iniquities.

For God Himself hath heard my cry ;
     the Lord vouchsafes to weigh my tears ;
Yea, He my prayer from on high
     and humble supplication hears.

And now my foes the Lord will blame
     that e'rst só sorely vexèd me,
And put them all to utter shame,
     and to confusion suddainly.

Glory, honour, power, and praise
     to the most glorious Trinity ;
As at the first beginning was,
     is now, and to eternity.   G. H. (p. 26.)

GLORIA TO PSALM XXIII.

To Father, Son, and Holy Ghost,
     one consubstantial Three,
All highest praise, all humblest thanks,
     now and for ever be.   G. H.

PSALM VII.

Save me, my Lord, my God, because
    I put my trust in Thee;
From all that persecute my life,
    O Lord, deliver mee.

Lest like a lion swollen with rage
    he do devour my soul;
And peace-meal rent it, while there's none
    his mallice to controul.

If I have done this thing, O Lord,
    if I so guilty be;
If I have ill rewarded him
    that was at peace with me;

Yea, have not oft deliver'd him
    that was my causeless foe;
Then let mine enemie prevail
    unto mine overthrow.

Let him pursue and take my soul,
    yea, let him to the clay
Tread down my life, and in the dust
    my slaughter'd honour lay.

Arise in wrath, O Lord, advance
    against my foes' disdain;
Wake and confirm that judgment now
    which Thou did'st foreordain.

So shall the people round about
    resort to give Thee praise ;
For their sakes, Lord, return on high,
    and high Thy glory raise.

The Lord shall judge the people all :
    O God, consider me
According to my righteousness
    and mine integritie.

The wicked's malice, Lord, confound,
    but just me ever guide ;
Thou art that righteous God by whom
    the hearts and rains are try'd.

God is my shield, Who doth preserve
    those that in heart are right ;
He judgeth both the good and those
    that do His justice slight.

Unless the wicked turn again,
    the Lord will whet His sword ;
His bow is bent, His quiver is
    with shafts of vengeance stor'd.

The fatal instruments of death
    in that preparèd lie ;
His arrows are ordain'd 'gainst him
    that persecuteth me.

Behold, the wicked travelleth
    with his iniquitie ;

Exploits of mischief he conceives,
　　but shall bring forth a lye.

The wicked diggèd, and a pit
　　for others' ruine wrought ;
But in the pit which he hath made
　　shall he himself be caught.

To his own head his wickedness
　　shall be returnèd home ;
And on his own accursèd pate
　　his cruelty shall come.

But I, for all His righteousness,
　　the Lord will magnifie ;
And ever praise the glorious Name
　　of Him that is on high.　　　G. H. (p. 30.)

PSALM I.

Blest is the man that never would
　　In councels of th' ungodly share,
Nor hath in way of sinners stood,
　　Nor sitten in the scorner's chair.

But in God's Law sets his delight,
　　And makes that Law alone to be
His meditation day and night :
　　He shall be like an happy tree,

Which, planted by the waters, shall
　　With timely fruit still loden stand ;
His leaf shall never fade, and all
　　Shall prosper that he takes in hand.

The wicked are not so ; but they
  Are like the chaff, which from the face
Of earth is driven by winds away,
  And finds no sure abiding place.

Therefore shall not the wicked be
  Able to stand the Judge's doom ;
Nor in the safe society
  Of good men shall the wicked come.

For God Himself vouchsafes to know
  The way that right'ous men have gone ;
And those ways which the wicked go
  Shall utterly be overthrown.   (p. 54.)

PSALM II.

Why are the heathen swell'd with rage,
  The people vain exploits devise ?
The kings and potentates of earth
  Combin'd in one great faction rise ?

And taking councels 'gainst the Lord
  And 'gainst His Christ, presume to say,
' Let us in sunder break their bonds,
  And from us cast their cords away.'

But He that sits in heaven shall laugh,
  The Lord Himself shall them deride ;
Then shall He speak to them in wrath,
  And in sore anger vex their pride.

' But I am God, and seated King
   On Sion, His most holy hill;
I will declare the Lord's decree,
   Nor can I hide His sacred will.

He said to Me, Thou art My Son,
   This day have I begotten Thee;
Make Thy request, and I will grant
   The heathen shall Thy portion be.

Thou shalt possess earth's farthest bounds,
   And there an awful sceptre sway;
Whose pow'r shall dash and break them all,
   Like vessels made of brittle clay.'

Now therefore, O ye kings, be wise;
   Be learnèd, ye that judge the earth;
Serve our great God in fear; rejoice,
   But tremble in your highest mirth.

O kiss the Son, lest He be wroth,
   And straight ye perish from the way:
When once His anger burns, thrice blest
   Are all that make the Son their stay.

                     G. H. (p. 54.)

PSALM V.

Lord, to my words encline Thine ear,
   My meditation weigh;
My King, my God, vouchsafe to hear
   My cry to Thee, I pray.

Thou in the morn shalt hear my mone ;
  For in the morn will I
Direct my prayers to Thy throne,
  And thither lift mine eye.

Thou art a God, Whose puritie
  Cannot in sins delight ;
No evil, Lord, shall dwell with Thee,
  Nor fools stand in Thy sight.

Thou hat'st those that unjustly do,
  Thou slay'st the men that lye ;
The bloody man, the false one too,
  Shall be abhorr'd by Thee.

But in th' abundance of Thy grace
  Will I to Thee draw near,
And toward Thy most holy place
  Will worship Thee in fear.

Lord, lead me in Thy righteousness,
  Because of all my foes ;
And to my dym and sinful eyes
  Thy perfect way disclose.

For wickedness their insides are,
  Their mouths no truth retain,
Their throat an open sepulcher,
  Their flattering tongues do fain.

Destroy them, Lord, and by their own
  Bad councels let them fall
In hight of their transgression ;
  O Lord, reject them all ;

Because against Thy Majesty
  They vainly have rebell'd.
But let all those that trust in Thee
  With perfect joy be fill'd :

Yea, shout for joy for evermore,
  Protected still by Thee ;
Let them that do Thy name adore
  In that still joyfull bee.

For God doth righteous men esteem,
  And them for ever bless ;
His favour shall encompass them,—
  A shield in their distress.

NOTES AND ILLUSTRATIONS.

Psalm viii. p. 35, st. ix. l. 3, misprinted 'Good' for 'God.'

,, i. p. 37. This has no signature, but Psalm ii., which follows immediately, has; and above Psalm i. is 'Two other Psalms to this Tune, of a new translation.'

Psalm ii. p. 38, st. iv. l. 1, is printed 'But I by God.' This might be by=through God . . . I will declare. But it is harsh, and forestalls what becomes a repetition, 'He said to me.' I have ventured to read 'am.' Vulg. 'Rex ab eo.'

Psalm vi. p. 33. With reference to the 'Gloria,' wherever it is added to a psalm or hymn, whether the psalm be King's, G. H.'s, or other, it is in italics if the psalm be in roman, and *vice versa*. The 'Gloria' to Psalm xxiii., which bears Herbert's initials, occurs also after a hymn (p. 85) by the 'unknown author.' That after Psalm vi. is twice repeated, but in a slightly varied form, after Psalm xcv. by H. K. and after an unsigned hymn (p. 74). Hence these were probably added by Playford, according to his own judgment.   G.

IV.

SECULAR POEMS.

WITH ADDITIONS FROM MSS.

I. SONNETS.

SENT BY GEORGE HERBERT TO HIS MOTHER AS A NEW-
YEAR'S GIFT FROM CAMBRIDGE.

My God, where is that ancient heat towards Thee
   Wherewith whole shoals of martyrs once did burn,
Besides their other flames?   Doth poetrie
   Wear Venus' liverie, onely serve her turn?
   Why are not sonnets made of Thee, and layes   5
   Upon Thine altar burnt?   Cannot Thy love
Heighten a spirit to sound out Thy praise
   As well as any she?   Cannot Thy Dove
Outstrip their Cupid easilie in flight?
   Or, since Thy wayes are deep, and still the same, 10
   Will not a verse runne smooth that bears Thy Name?
Why doth that fire, which by Thy power and might
   Each breast does feel, no braver fuel choose
   Then that which one day worms may chance refuse?

Sure, Lord, there is enough in Thee to drie   15
   Oceans of ink; for, as the Deluge did
Cover the earth, so doth Thy Majestie.
   Each cloud distills Thy praise, and doth forbid
Poets to turn it to another use;
   Roses and lilies speak Thee, and to make   20

A pair of cheeks of them is Thy abuse.   =abuse of Thee
   Why should I women's eyes for crystal take?
Such poor invention burns in their low minde,
   Whose fire is wild, and doth not upward go
   To praise, and on Thee, Lord, some ink bestow. 25
Open the bones, and you shall nothing finde
   In the best face but filth; when, Lord, in Thee
   The beauty lies in the discoverie.

II. INSCRIPTION IN THE PARSONAGE, BEMERTON.

TO MY SUCCESSOR.

If thou chance for to find
   A new House to thy mind,
And built without thy Cost;
   Be good to the Poor
   As God gives thee store,
And then my Labour's not lost.

Another Version.

Fuller writes in his character of The Faithful Minister: 'A clergyman who built his house from the ground wrote on it this counsel to his successor:'

If thou dost find
An house built to thy mind,
   Without thy cost;
Serve thou the more
God and the poor;
   My labour is not lost.

III. ON LORD DANVERS.

Sacred marble, safely keepe
His dust who under thee must sleepe
Untill the graves againe restore
Theire dead, and time shal be no more.
Meane while, if Hee which all thinges weares　　　5
Doe ruine thee, or if the tears
Are shed for him dissolve thy frame,
Thou art requited; for his fame,
His vertues, and his worth shal bee
Another monument for thee.　　　G. Herbert.　　　10

IV. ON SIR JOHN DANVERS.

By the same (Geo. Herbert), Orator of [the] University at Cambridge; pinned on the curtaine of the picture of the old Sir John Danvers, who was both a handsome and a good man :

Passe not by ;　　　Sr John Danvers' earthly part,
Search, and you may　　　Here is copied out by art ;
Find a treasure　　　But his heavenly and divine
Worth your stay.　　　In his progenie doth shine.
What makes a Danvers　　　Had he only brought them forth,
Would you find ?　　　Know that much had been his worth.
In a fayre bodie　　　Ther's no monument to a sonne ;
A fayre mind.　　　Read him there, and I have done.

V. A PARADOX.

THAT THE SICK ARE IN A BETTER CASE THEN THE WHOLE.

(From Rawlinson MSS. *in Bodleian, Oxford, p. 78.)*

You who admire yourselves because
    You neither grone nor weepe,
And think it contrary to nature's laws
    To want one ounce of sleepe ;
       Your strong beleife   5
Acquits yourselves, and gives ye sick all greife.

Your state to ours is contrary ;
    That makes you thinke us poore :
So Black-Moores think us foule, and wee
    Are quit wth y^m, and more :   10
      Nothing can see
And judg of things but mediocrity.

The sick are in y^{m}selves a state
    W^{ch} health hath nought to doe ;
How know you that o^r tears p^{r}ceed from woe,   15
    And not frō better fate ?
      Since that Mirth hath
Her waters alsoe and desyrèd bath.

How know you y^t ye sighs wee send
    Frō want of breath p^{r}ceede,   20
Not frō excesse ? and therefore we do spend
    That wch we do not neede :
      So trembling may
As well shew inward warblings as decay.

Cease y^u to judge calamityes   25
   By outward forme and shew,
But view yourselves, and inward turn yor eyes,
   Then you shall fully know
      That your estate
Is, of y^e two, y^e farre more desperate.   30

You allwayes feare to feele those smarts   = continually
   W^ch we but sometimes p^rve ;
Each little comfort much affects o^r hearts,   = our
   None but gross joyes you move ;
      Why, then confesse   35
Your feares in number more, yor joyes are lesse.

Then for yo^rselves not us embrace
   Plaints to bad fortune due ;
For though you visitt us, and plaint o^r case,   = our
   Wee doubt much whether you   40
      Come to our bed
To comfort us, or to be comforted.   G. Herbert.

VI. G. H.

TO Y^E QUEENE OF BOHEMIA.

Bright soule, of whome if any countrey knowne
Worthy had bin, thou hadst not lost thine owne;
No Earth can bee thy Jointure, For the sunne
And starres alone vnto ye pitch doe runne
And pace of thy swift vertues; onely they   5
Are thy dominion.   Those that rule in clay

Stick fast therein, but thy transcendent soule
Doth for two clods of earth ten spheres controule,
And though starres shott from heauen loose their light,
Yet thy braue beames, excluded from there right,   10
Maintaine there Lustre still, & shining cleere   their
Turne watrish Holland to a chrystalline sphere.
Mee thinkes, in that Dutch optick I doe see
Thy curious vertues much more visibly:
There is thy best Throne, for afflictions are   15
A foile to sett of worth & make it rare.
Through y^t black tiffany thy vertues shine
Fairer and richer.   Now wee know what's thine,
And what is fortune's.   Thou hast singled out
Sorrowes & griefs, to fight with them about   20
At there owne weapons, wthout pomp or state
To second thee against there cunning hate.
O what a poore thing 'tis to bee a Queene
When scepters, state, Attendants are ye screene
Betwixt us & the people! when-as glory   25
Lyes round about us to helpe out ye story,
When all things pull & hale, y^t they may bring
A slow behauiour to the style of king;
When sense is made by Comments, But y^t face
Whose natiue beauty needs not dresse or lace   30
To serue it forth, & being stript of all
Is self-sufficient to bee the thrall
Of thousand harts: y^t face doth figure thee
And show thy vndiuided Maiestye

W^{ch} misery cannot vntwist, but rather   35
Addes to the vnion, as lights doe gather
Splendour from darknes.   So close sits ye crowne
About thy temples y^t ye furious frowne
Of opposition cannot place thee where
Thou shalt not be a Queene, & conquer there.   40
Yet hast thou more dominions : God doth giue
Children for kingdomes to thee ; they shall liue
To conquer new ones, & shall share ye frame
Of th' vniuerse, like as ye windes, & name
The world anew : ye sunne shall neuer rise   45
But it shall spy some of there victories.
There hands shall clipp ye Eagles winges, & chase
Those rauening Harpyes wch peck at thy face
At once to Hell, without a baiting while
At Purgatory, there inchanted Ile   50
And Paris garden.   Then let there perfume
And spanish sents, wisely layd vp, presume
To deale wth brimstone, y^t vntamed stench
Whose fier, like there malice, nought can quench.
But ioyes are stord for thee ; thou shalt returne   55
Laden wth comforts thence, where now to morne
Is thy chief gouerment, to manage woe,
To curbe some Rebell teares wch faine would flow,
Making a Head & spring against thy Reason.
This is thy empire yet : till better season   60
Call thee from out of y^t surrounded Land ;
That habitable sea, & brinish strand,

Thy teares not needing.   For y^t hand Divine,
W^{ch} migles water wth thy Rhenish wine,
Will power full ioyes to thee; but dregs to those   65
And meet theire tast who are thy bitter foes.

LENVOY.

Shine on, Maiestick soule, abide
Like Dauid's tree, planted beside
The Flemmish riuers: in the end   70
Thy fruite shall wth there drops contend;
Great God will surely dry those teares,
Which now y^t moist land to thee beares.
Then shall thy Glory, fresh as flowers
In water kept, maugre the powers   75
Of Diuell, Jesuitt, & Spaine,
From Holland saile into the Maine:
Thence wheeling on, it compass shall
This oure great Sublunary Ball,
And with that Ring thy fame shall wedd   80
Eternity into one Bedd.

NOTES AND ILLUSTRATIONS.

I. *Sonnets.* On these Sonnets see our Memorial-Introduction and our Essay, as before. They are taken from Walton's 'Life' of Herbert, where they are called 'a Sonnet'=a double one, like Shakespeare's Sonnets v. and vi., xv. and xvi., xxvii. and xxviii., &c. Lines 10-11. Suggested by a remembrance of the proverb, 'Still waters run deep.'

II. *Inscription.* The original slab, or whatever it was, has disappeared; but it has been modernly carved and placed in back-front of the 'Parsonage,' facing the little church. The

second version is derived from Dr. Thomas Fuller's ' Holy and
Profane State' (1642). The first is from Walton's ' Life' of Herbert (1670). Fuller's readings are surely the better.

III. *On Lord Danvers.* Our text is taken from the monument in the church of Dauntsey. There are corrections of the
hitherto printed texts: *e.g.* l. 3, 'graves' for 'yeares;' l. 6,
' the' for ' thy;' l. 10, ' for' for ' to'—the second very important.
Line 7 is=if the tears [that] are shed [by mourners] for him
[do] dissolve thy frame, &c.

The quaint idea of the name and virtues of the dead being
a monument to the marble beneath which they rest, is not
original. A similar thought is found in an epitaph on Euripides, among the Greek epigrams by uncertain authors (Jacobs,
iv. 231, dxxxvi.). The following translation of it is taken from
No. 551 of the Spectator :

> ' Divine Euripides, this tomb we see,
> So fair, is not a monument for thee,
> So much as thou for it, since all will own
> Thy name and lasting praise adorn the stone.'

In the monument of Drayton (Westminster Abbey) there is
almost a parallel to Herbert's on Danvers altogether :

> ' Do, pious marble, let thy readers know
> What they and what their children owe
> To Drayton's name, whose sacred dust
> We recommend unto thy trust.
> Protect his memory, and preserve his story,
> Remain a lasting monument of his glory.
> And when thy ruins shall disclaim
> To be the treasurer of his name,
> His name, that cannot fade, shall be
> An everlasting monument to thee.'

See also Nugæ Canoræ (1827) for another. (Dodd's Epigrammatists, 1870, pp. 232, 234.)

IV. *On Sir John Danvers.* I take this from Aubrey and
Jackson's ' Wiltshire' (pp. 224-6), where the preceding also appears, and in its text of it is found the source of the after-misprint of ' thy' for ' the.' The following is Jackson's note on the
lines, so far as required here : ' Sir John Danvers *senior* married Elizabeth Nevill, fourth daughter and co-heiress of John,
Lord Latimer. She remarried Sir Edmund Carey. Her fine
monument in the church of Stowe, co. Northampton, is described
in Baker's History of that county, i. 147. George Herbert of
cmerton, having been in the first year of his age in 1594, when

Sir John Danvers *senior* died, could only have known his character by report.'

v. *A Paradox*. Written, as shown by l. 7, in sickness, or rather when ailing. Line 12, 'mediocrity' is here used for one who is in the mean or middle state between the two; neither in perfect health nor under the full sway of sickness; one who was, in fact, in the state in which Herbert then was—failing. Line 14, a curious ellipse of 'with.' Can 'which' be an error for 'where'? There is a distinct misreading of 'or' for ' our' (often in the ms. 'or'). From the Rawlinson ms., corrective of the text, as furnished by Dr. Bliss to Pickering. ' The Synagogue,' by C. Harvey, contains a parallel poem, showing that he knew of this of Herbert's.

vi. *To the Queen of Bohemia*. From Harleian ms. 3910, pp. 121-2 — never before printed. G. H. is placed prominently at the head of this poem in the ms. It has a good deal of the rhythm and breaks of Donne, and this I take as a confirmation of the Herbert authorship, for elsewhere he remembered and copied his friend Dean Donne. So too with L'Envoy, as at end of The Church Militant. Line 13, 'optick'= the crystalline sphere. I do not think the reference is to the magnifying effect of the sphere, but to it as an optic or glass in which we see the proportion and form of lines, which, looked at otherwise, are mere confusion. Such optic is the perspective-glass so noticeably spoken of by Herbert in The Temple (Vol. I. p. 138), and which in other authors are called optics. Thus an undistinguishable picture revealed itself when seen in a cylindrical mirror into a portrait of Charles I. This out-of-the-way illustration, as being common to Herbert in The Temple with this, perhaps additionally confirms his authorship of these Lines. See Glossarial Index under 'perspective.' Miss Benger (1825) has written the life of Elizabeth Stuart, Queen of Bohemia. She died February 13th, 1662. See our Essay for remarks on this Poem, as having been composed while Donne was still strongly influential over Herbert.   G.

V.

PARENTALIA.

PARENTALIA.

SACRED TO A MOTHER'S MEMORY.

I.

Ah Mater, quo te deplorem fonte? Dolores
    Quae guttae poterunt enumerare meos?
Sicca meis lacrymis Thamesis vicina videtur,
    Virtutumque choro siccior ipse tuo.
In flumen moerore nigrum si funderer ardens,
    Laudibus haud fierem sepia justa tuis.
Tantum istaec scribo gratus, ne tu mihi tantum
    Mater : et ista Dolor nunc tibi Metra parit.

Ah, Mother! where is Grief's full-flowing fount?
What drops my sorrows ever can recount?
Dry, to my tears, seems Thames that murmurs by,
Myself for all thy virtues all too dry.
Into the grief-black stream pour burning me;
Fit ink to write thy praise I should not be.
These things I pen in love, that all may know,
Mother means Music when Grief wills it so ![1]

R. WI.

[1] Or to preserve the play on the words, 'Mater' is Metre
when Grief wills it so.

II.

Corneliae sanctae, graves Semproniae,
Et quicquid uspiam est severae foeminae,
Conferte lacrymas; Illa quae vos miscuit
Vestrasque laudes, poscit et mixtas genas.
Namque hanc ruinam salva Gravitas defleat,
Pudorque constet vel solutis crinibus;
Quandoque vultus sola majestas, Dolor.

 Decus mulierum periit; et metuunt viri
Utrumque sexum dote ne mulctaverit.
Non illa soles terere comptu lubricos,
Struices superbas atque turritum caput
Molita, reliquum deinde garriens diem,—
Nam post Babelem linguae adest confusio,—
Quin post modestam, qualis integras decet,
Substructionem capitis et nimbum brevem,
Animam recentem rite curavit sacris
Adorta numen acri et ignea prece.

 Dein familiam lustrat, et res prandii,
Horti colique distributim pensitat.
Suum cuique tempus et locus datur.
Inde exiguntur pensa crudo vespere.
Ratione certa vita constat et domus,
Prudenter inito quot-diebus calculo.
Tota renident aede decus et suavitas
Animo renidentes prius.   Sin rarior
Magnatis appulsu extulit se occasio,
Surrexit una et illa, seseque extulit:

Occasione certat imo et obtinet.
Proh! quantus imber, quanta labri comitas,
Lepos severus, Pallas mixta Gratiis;
Loquitur numellas, compedes, et retia;
Aut si negotio hora sumenda est, rei
Per angiportus et maeandros labitur,
Ipsos Catones provocans oraculis.
Tum quanta tabulis artifex? quae scriptio?
Bellum putamen, nucleus bellissimus
Sententiae cum voce mire convenit.
Volant per orbem literae notissimae:
O blanda dextra, neutiquam istoc pulveris,
Quo nunc recumbis, scriptio merita est tua,
Pactoli arena tibi tumulus est unicus.

    Adde his trientem Musices, quae molliens
Mulcensque dotes caeteras, visa est quasi
Caelestis harmoniae breve praeludium.
Quam mira tandem sublevatrix pauperum?
Languentium baculus, teges jacentium,
Commune cordis palpitantis balsamum:
Benedictiones publicae cingunt caput,
Caelique referunt et praeoccupant modum.
Fatisco, referens tanta quae numerant mei
Solum dolores,—et dolores, stellulae!

    At tu qui inepte haec dicta censes filio,
Nato parentis auferens Encomium,
Abito trunce cum tuis pudoribus.
Ergo ipse solum mutus atque excors ero

Strepente mundo tinnulis pracconiis?
Mihine Matris urna clausa est unico,
Herbae exoletae, ros-marinus aridus?
Matrine linguam refero, solum ut mordeam?
Abito barde!   Quam pie istic sum impudens!
Tu vero Mater perpetim laudabere   ·
Nato dolenti: literae hoc debent tibi
Queis me educasti; sponte chartas illinunt
Fructum laborum consecutae maximum
Laudando Matrem, cum repugnant inscii.

Holy Cornelias, and Sempronias grave,
And all of serious womanhood, I crave
Your tears; for she, who blended what in you
Shines good and beautiful, claims as her due
Your blended sorrows.   For this downfall raise
Loud weepings, Dignity, nor lose thy praise:
Stand, Modesty, with locks loose flowing down;
Sorrow is sometimes Beauty's loftiest crown.
    The glory of women has perish'd; and men dread
Lest of each sex with her the dower has fled.
The fleeting suns she would not wear away
In vanity of dress and self-display,
Piling proud structures in the morning hour
Upon her head, rear'd upwards like a tow'r;
Then spending the long day in talk and laughter—
For tongues' confusion comes tower'd Babel after!—
But after modest braiding of her hair,

Such as becomes a matron wise and fair,
And a brief bath, her freshen'd mind she brought
To pious duties and heart-healing thought,
Addressing to the Almighty Father's throne
Such warm and earnest prayers as He will own.
    Next she goes round her family, assigning
What each may need for garden, distaff, dining.
To everything its time and place are given ;
Then are call'd in the tasks at early even.
By a fix'd plan her life and house go on,
By a wise daily calculation;
Sweetness and grace through all her dwelling shine,
Of both first shining in her mind the sign.
But if at times a great occasion rise—
With visit of some noble—she likewise
Rises, and raises up herself, and vies
With the occasion, and the victory gains.
O, what a shower of courteous speech she rains!
Grave pleasantry, grace mix'd with wit is heard ;
Fetters and chains she weaves with every word.
Or if some business for the hour should ask,
She glides through turns and windings of the task,
With her replies a match for wisest men.
Then what a mistress was she of the pen !
What graceful writing hers !   Mark the fair shell,
Wherein a kernel fairer still may dwell,
The voice and sentiment agreeing well.
Through all the world her well-known letters flit :

Charming right hand, that dust[1] is all unfit,
Where now thou liest, for thy writing fine;
Pactolus' sand sole fitting tomb of thine.

    Add music, smoothing, soothing other gifts,
Which, for a moment, the rapt spirit lifts
As with a prelude of Heaven's harmony.
Then what a helper of the poor you see
In her! A prop of languid folk and slow,
A roof for those who live forlorn and low,
A common balm on throbbing bosoms shed,
While public blessings hover round her head,
Rehearsing now the manner of the sky,
Anticipating her reward on high.
I droop as all her virtues I relate,
Which by my sorrows I enumerate;
Stars are they now, my tearful griefs of late.

    But thou who think'st these things not fitly done,
A mother's praise forbidding to a son,
Away with thy false foolish modesty!
Heartless and silent then shall only I
Be found, when her fine praise rings to the sky?
My mother's urn, is't closed only to me—
Wither'd the herbs, and dry the rosemary?
Owe I to her a tongue only to grieve?
Away, thou foolish one and give me leave
Shame to forget while pious praise I weave.

---

[1] Alluding probably to the dust sprinkled from a small castor, which was formerly used in letter-writing to dry the ink.

Thou shalt be prais'd for ever, mother mine,
By me, thy sorrowing son; for surely thine
This learning is, which I deriv'd from thee,
Which o'er the page now flows spontaneously,
Its highest fruit of labour seen to attain
In praising thee, though Folly may arraign. R. WI.

III.

Cur splendes, o Phoebe? ecquid demittere matrem
    Ad nos cum radio tam rutilante potes?
At superat caput illa tuum, quantum ipsa cadaver
    Mens superat; corpus solum elementa tenent.
Scilicet id splendes: haec est tibi causa micandi
    Et lucro apponis gaudia sancta tuo.
Verum heus si nequeas coelo demittere matrem,
    Sitque omnis motus nescia, tanta quies,
Fac radios saltem ingemines, ut dextera tortos
    Implicet, et matrem, matre manente, petam.

Why shin'st thou, sun? Canst thou send down to me
My mother, with thy beam so bright to see?
Ah, she o'ertops thy head as soul the clay;
The elements but round her body play.
Sure, thus thou shinest, and adorn'st thy face,
And holy joys to thy account dost place.
But if thou canst not send her down from heav'n,
And rest to her, deep and serene, be giv'n,—
Double thy rays, that I, my hand being twin'd
In them, my mother in her bliss may find. R. WI.

IV.

Quid nugor calamo favens?
Mater perpetuis uvida gaudiis,
   Horto pro tenui colit
Edenem Boreae flatibus invium.
   Quin coeli mihi sunt mei
Materni decus, et debita nominis;
   Dumque his invigilo frequens
Stellarum socius, pellibus exuor.
   Quare Sphaeram egomet meam
Connixus, digitis impiger urgeo:
   Te, mater, celebrans diu,
Noctu te celebrans luminis aemulo.
   Per te nascor in hunc globum,
Exemploque tuo nascor in alterum:
   Bis tu mater eras mihi,
Ut currat paribus gloria tibiis.

Why do I trifle, still with my pen playing?
My mother, now in heavenly Eden straying
     'Stead of her little garden bow'rs,
     Tends there ever-blooming flow'rs.
Nor there amid the still-increasing joy
May blast of Boreas blow, or once annoy;
     Nay, my mother dear, in thee
     Heaven comes down to me.
And while I muse, companion of the stars,
I am a spirit, free of my body's bars;

Wherefore in this my lower sphere
I sing, with sweet soft tear;
Still praising thee, mother, throughout the day,
And the hush'd night when light has pass'd away;
Dark night rivalling e'en the morn,
Though I am lone and lorn.
From thee my birth, through thee my second birth—
Twice mother to me—showing heav'n on earth,
That here and there I might thy praise
In song still grateful raise.   G.

V.

Horti, deliciae Dominae, marcescite tandem ;
Ornastis capulum, nec superesse licet.
Ecce decus vestrum spinis horrescit, acuta
Cultricem revocans anxietate manum :
Terram et funus olent flores : Dominaeque cadaver
Contiguas stirpes afflat, eaeque rosas.
In terram violae capite inclinantur opaco,
Quaeque domus Dominae sit, gravitate docent.
Quare haud vos hortos, sed coemeteria dico,
Dum torus absentem quisque reponit heram.
Euge, perite omnes ; nec posthac exeat ulla
Quaesitum Dominam gemma vel herba suam.
Cuncta ad radices redeant, tumulosque paternos,
Nempe sepulcra Satis numen inempta dedit ;
Occidite ; aut sane tantisper vivito, donec
Vespere ros maestis funus honestet aquis.

Gardens, your Lady's joy, now meet your doom;
Ye've deck'd her bier, no longer ye may bloom:
Your beauty, bristling now with briers and thorns,
Her tending hand with a keen sorrow mourns.
Of earth the flowers smell, and where she reposes
Death taints the neighbouring stems, and these the roses.
With dim heads violets to the ground bend low,
And by their grief their Lady's dwelling show.
Not gardens, cemeteries here I find;
Of absent mistress all the beds remind.
Die all! nor in this garden, from this hour,
To seek their Lady spring forth bud or flower!
Back to your roots and fathers' tombs all glide;
Graves without price God does for plants provide.
Die; or live only till sad Eve appears
To deck your obsequies with dewy tears.   R. WI.

VI.

Galene, frustra es, cur miserum premens
Tot quaestionum fluctibus obruis,
   Arterias tractans micantes
      Corporeae fluidaeque molis
Aegroto mentis? quam neque pixides
Nec tarda possunt pharmaca consequi,
   Utrumque si praederis Indum,
      Ultra animus spatiatur exlex.
Impos medendi, occidere si potes,
Nec sic parentem ducar ad optimam:

Ni sancte, uti Mater, recedam,
Morte magis viduabor illa.
Quin cerne ut erres inscie, brachium
Tentando sanum : si calet, aestuans,
Ardore scribendi calescit,
Mater inest saliente vena.
Si totus infler, si tumeam crepax,
Ne membra culpes, causa animo latet
Qui parturit laudes parentis :
Nec gravidis medicina tuta est.
Irregularis nunc habitus mihi est :
Non exigatur crasis ad alterum.
Quod tu febrem censes, salubre est,
Atque animo medicatur unum.

O Galen, altogether vain art thou,
Still questioning me with moody brow ;
Thy fingers on my wrist inclin'd,
So searching me,—me, sick in mind :
In mind, not body ; which nor thy pills many
Nor aught slow med'cines yield, nor any
Spoil o' the Indies, e'er can cure :
Mind soaring free, like spirit pure.
Pow'rless to heal, O if thou couldst but kill !
Nay, not e'en so should I obtain my will :
Save by a holy death reliev'd,
I should but be the more bereav'd.
How ignorantly, Galen, thou dost err,

Feeling my pulse !   If it be fever'd, there
   Burns the desire to write of Mother ;
   She's in the throbbing veins, none other.
Or if I flat'lent swell, blame not my members ;
The cause hides in my mind, as fire in embers—
   Trav'ling with her praise, my Mother styl'd ;
   Med'cine's unsafe to those with child.
My frame's disorder'd, yet don't mixtures weigh
For an unreal state ; what thou dost say
   Is fever brings alone my cure,
   For troubl'd mind a medicine sure.   G.

VII.

Pallida materni Genii atque exsanguis imago,
In nebulas similesque tui res gaudia numquid
Mutata? et pro Matre mihi phantasma dolosum
Uberaque aëria hiscentem fallentia natum ?
Vae nubi pluvia gravidae, non lucte, measque
Ridenti lacrymas quibus unis concolor unda est.
Quin fugias? mea non fuerat tam nubila Juno,
Tam segnis facies aurorae nescia vernae,
Tam languens genitrix cineri supposta fugaci ;
Verum augusta parens, sanctum os caeloque locandum,
Quale paludosos jamjam lictura recessus
Praetulit Astraea, aut solio Themis alma vetusto
Pensilis, atque acri dirimens Examine lites.
Hunc vultum ostendas, et tecum nobile spectrum
Quod superest vitae, insumam ; Solisque jugales

Ipse tuae solum adnectam, sine murmure, thensae.
Nec querar ingratos, studiis dum tabidus insto,
Effluxisse dies, suffocatamve Minervam,
Aut spes productas, barbataque somnia vertam
In vicium mundo sterili, cui cedo cometas
Ipse suos, tanquam digno, pallentiaque astra.

    Est mihi bis quinis laqueata domuncula tignis
Rure; brevisque hortus, cujus cum vellere florum
Luctatur spatium, qualem tamen eligit aequi
Judicii dominus, flores ut junctius halent
Stipati, rudibusque volis impervius hortus
Sit quasi fasciculus crescens, et nidus odorum.
Hic ego tuque erimus, variae suffitibus herbae
Quotidie pasti: tantum verum indue vultum
Affectusque mei similem; nec languida misce
Ora meae memori menti: ne dispare cultu
Pugnaces, teneros florum turbemus odores,
Atque inter reliquos horti crescentia foetus
Nostra etiam paribus marcescant gaudia fatis.

Pale bloodless image of maternity,
Into such misty likenesses of thee
Are my joys changed?   For mother do I see
A treacherous phantasm, and aerial breast
Mocking a son who fain would there find rest?
Woe for a cloud fill'd not with milk but rain,
And laughing at my tears as I complain,—
Tears which reflect the watery tint again!

Nay, wouldst thou fly?   Not such a cloudy face
My Juno show'd ; where you could see no trace
Of vernal dawn.   She was no mother pale,
Conceal'd behind a fleeting ashy veil.
Parent august was she, whose holy face,
Star-like, in yonder sky deserv'd a place ;
Such as Astræa wore, about to leave
Her haunt amid the reeds some cloudless eve ;
Or Themis, o'er her old throne hovering seen,
Settling contentions with discernment keen.
Show such a face, and with thee, image fair,
My life's remainder I will gladly share ;
Myself the horses of the sun will tie
Unto thy car alone, unmurmuringly ;
Nor while on such pursuits, wasting, I pore,
Will mourn my days unpleasingly past o'er ;
Nor sigh for learning quench'd or thrown away,
And hopes deferr'd to some far-distant day.
And for my uncouth fancies I shall blame
An empty world, which well deserves to claim
Its comets, spreading consternation far,
And many a pale and pallor-striking star.
    I have a rural cottage, ceil'd with beams
Scanty and bare, where a small garden gleams,
Whose fleecy growth of flowers with radiant bloom
Struggles for light in the too narrow room :
But 'tis a garden which a master's mind
Well balanced to its wish exact would find,

That crowded flowers more closely might exhale
Their odours, and rude hands might ne'er prevail
To burst its bounds ; a growing bouquet fair,
A nest of sweets, enriching all the air.
Here thou and I, my Mother dear, will stray,
Inhaling flowery incense day by day ;
Only do thou assume feelings and face
Where I an image of myself may trace ;
Nor a dim drooping countenance let me find
Oppos'd to my too-well-remembering mind ;
Lest, differing in discordant look and act,
The tender fragrant flower-beds we distract,
And mid the garden's other offspring fair,
Our growing joys should wither in despair.   R. WI.

VIII.

Parvam piamque dum lubetner semitam
    Grandi reaeque praefero,
Carpsit malignum sidus hanc modestiam
    Vinumque felle miscuit.
Hinc fremere totus et minari gestio
    Ipsis severus orbibus,
Tandem prehensa comiter lacernula
    Susurrat aure quispiam,
Haec fuerat olim potio Domini tui.
    Gusto proboque dolium.

Whilst I a humble holy path prefer
To grand and guilty wherein others err,

An envious star my modest choice arraigns,
And mingles gall i' my wine, nor ill restrains.
Alas, on this I fling me down, repining,
And the orbs of heaven menace in their shining ;
Till Some One grasps my cloak, and whispers kindly
Into my ear, the while I murmur blindly :
' *This is the cup thy Lord drank.*'   Then I ask,
Adoring, taste it, and approve the cask.   G.

IX.

Hoc, Genitrix, scriptum proles tibi sedula mittit.
    Siste parum cantus, dum legis ista, tuos.
Nosse sui quid agant, quaedam est quoque musica sanctis,
    Quaeque olim fuerat cura, manere potest.
Nos misero flemus, solesque obducimus almos
    Occiduis, tanquam duplice nube, genis.
Interea classem magnis Rex instruit ausis :
    Nos autem flemus : res ea sola tuis.
Ecce solutura est, ventos causata morantes :
    Sin pluviam : fletus suppeditasset aquas.
Tillius incumbit Dano, Gallusque marinis :
    Nos flendo : haec nostrum tessera sola ducum.
Sic aevum exigitur tardum, dum praepetis anni
    Mille rotae nimiis impediuntur aquis.
Plura tibi missurus eram ; nam quae mihi laurus,
    Quod nectar, nisi cum te celebrare diem ?
Sed partem in scriptis etiam dum lacryma poscit,
    Diluit oppositas candidus humor aquas.

Mother, thy child this letter sends to thee;
To read it, stay awhile thy melody :
'Tis music to the saints, news of their own:
The cares abide which they of old have known.
Sadly we weep, and the fair suns we shroud
With darkening cheeks, as with a double cloud.
Our king prepares a fleet with grand design ;
We weep; sole interest is this to thine.
About to sail, they blame the winds that blow;
If rain, our tears the hindering cause might show.
The Dane claims Tilly;[1] sea-affairs the Gaul;
But weeping occupies our leaders all.
So Time rolls slowly, while full many a tear
Retards the thousand wheels of the swift year.
Fain would I write thee more ; for what know I
Of crown or joy, save thought of thee is nigh?
But while of this my page tears ask a share,
The ink they meet is blurr'd with moisture fair.   R. WI.

X.

Nempe hujusque notos tenebricosos,
Et maestum nimio madore coelum,
Tellurisque Britannicae salivam
Injuste satis arguit viator.
At te commoriente, magna Mater,
Recte, quem trahit, aërem repellit
Cum probro madidum, reumque difflat.

---

[1] John Tzerclaes, Count de Tilly; born 1559; died 1632. G.

Nam te nunc ager, urbs, et aula plorant :
Te nunc Anglia Scotiaeque binae
Quin te Cambria pervetusta deflet,
Deducens lacrymas prioris aevi
Ne serae meritis tuis venirent.
Non est angulus uspiam serenus,
Nec cingit mare, nunc inundat omnes.

Surely the trav'ller censures wrongly
Our cloudy south-winds blowing strongly,
Our gray skies with rain o'ercharg'd,
Still spitting, and yet ne'er discharg'd,
      In this our British land.
But thou dying, great Mother, now
Rightly he speaks; for I do vow
This over-moisture well he may
As guilty name, and drive away
      With breath and tongue and hand.
For thee, now country, city, hall,
For thee, Anglia, two Scotias call,   Ireland and Scotland
And ancient Cambria; tears down-pour,
Such as were wept in classic lore,
      Fearing too late they come.
Not anywhere is there quiet spot
That tears of sorrow do not blot ;
Nor doth grief's sea merely surround ;
It all o'erflows without a bound,
      And leaves me stricken dumb.   G.

XI.

Dum librata suis haeret radicibus ilex
    Nescia Vulturnis cedere firma manet;
Post ubi crudelem sentit divisa securem,
    Quo placet oblato, mortua fertur, hero:
Arbor et ipse inversa vocor: dumque insitus almae
    Assideo Matri, robore vinco cedros.
Nunc sorti pateo, expositus sine matre procellis,
    Lubricus, et superans mobilitate salum.
Tu radix, tu petra mihi firmissima, Mater,
    Ceu polypus, chelis saxa prehendo tenax:
Non tibi nunc soli filum abrupere sorores
    Dissutus videor funere et ipse tuo.
Unde vagans passim recte vocer alter Ulysses,
    Alteraque haec tua mors, Ilias esto mihi.

While balanc'd by its roots the oak holds fast,
Firm it remains, nor fears or flood or blast;
But when its trunk the cruel hatchet hews,
Dead it is borne where'er its chance lord choose.
I am a tree o'erthrown; while planted by
My Mother's side, with cedars strong I vie.
Now, motherless, to Fate and storms I bow,
Tottering and wavering like a billow now.
Thou art my root, a rock most firm to me;
Like limpet to the crags I cling to thee.
Not thy thread only have the Fates unspun,
I also by thy death appear undone;

Wandering, a new Ulysses may I be,
And a new Iliad be thy death to me.   R. WI.

XII.

Facesse Stoica plebs, obambulans cautes.
Exuta strato carnis, ossibus constans,
Iisque siccis, adeo ut os Molossorum
Haud glubat inde tres teruncios escae.
Dolere prohibes? aut dolere me gentis
Adeo inficetae, plumbeae, Meduseae,
Ad saxa speciem retrahentis humanam,
Tantoque nequioris optima Pyrrha.
At forte Matrem perdere haud soles demens :
Quin nec potes; cui praebuit tigris partum.
Proinde parco belluis, nec irascor.

Begone, O Stoic race !—a walking rock
Stript of all softer flesh as e'er was block;
Made up of bones alone, and these so dry
That e'en Molossians, were they to try,
Should not peel from them three grains of bare food.
And do ye bid me grieve not? or as rude
And leaden Medusean tribes do grieve,
Who call men back to stones, naught human leave,
More harsh than exc'llent Pyrrha?   Insensate crew !
Ye nor e'er mother lost, nor mother knew.
A tiger bore ye—is not this your boast?
I spare my ire; on your hard hearts 'twere lost.   G.

XIII.

Epitaphium.

Hic sita foeminei laus et victoria sexus :
    Virgo pudens, uxor fida, severa parens :
Magnatumque inopumque aequum certamen et ardor :
    Nobilitate illos, hos pietate rapit.
Sic excelsa humilisque simul loca dissita junxit,
    Quicquid habet tellus, quicquid et astra fruens.

Here lies her sex's triumph and its praise :
As maid shamefast, as wife faithful always,
      As mother gently grave ;
Alike of great and poor, strife and desire :
These to her nobleness ravish'd aspire ;
      Those her sweet goodness crave.
High, lowly—she unites opposing things,
Enjoying all that earth, all heaven brings.
      Whoe'er may her deprave
      Of grace or glory brave ?   G.

XIV.

Ψυχῆς ἀσθενὲς ἕρκος, ἀμαυρὸν πνεύματος ἄγγος
    Τῷδε παρὰ τύμβῳ δίζεο, φίλε, μόνον.
Νοῦ δ' αὐτοῦ τάφος ἐστ' ἀστήρ. φέγγος γὰρ ἐκείνου
    Φεγγώδη μόνον, ὡς εἰκὸς, ἔπαυλιν ἔχει.
Νῦν ὁράας ὅτι κάλλος ἀπείριτον ὠπὸς ἀπαυγοῦς
    Οὐ σαθρὸν, οὐδὲ μελῶν ἔπλετο, ἀλλὰ νοός.

"Ὃς διὰ σωματίου πρότερον καὶ νῦν δι' Ὀλύμπου
  Ἀστράπτων, θυρίδων ὡς δία, νεῖμε σέλας.

The spirit's dim vessel and soul's barrier weak
Within this sepulchre, friend, only seek:
The mind's tomb is a star; for its fair light
A lightsome home has only, as 'tis right.
The boundless beauty of bright face you find
Decays not, nor belong'd to form, but mind;
Which through the body once, as now o'erhead
Lightening, as through a window, radiance shed.   R. WI.

XV.

Μῆτερ, γυναικῶν ἄγλη, ἀνθρώπων ἔρις,
 Ὀδύρμα δαιμόνων, Θεοῦ γεώργιον,
Πῶς νῦν ἀφίπτασαι, γόου καὶ κινδύνου
 Ἡμᾶς λιποῦσα κυκλόθεν μεταιχμίους.
Μενοῦνγε σοφίην, εἰ δ' ἀπηλλάχθαι χρεών,
Ζωῆς ξυνεργὸν σήνδε διαθεῖναι τέκνοις
 Ἔχρην φυγοῦσα, τήν τ' ἐπιστήμην βίου.
Μενοῦν τὸ γλαφυρὸν, καὶ μελίῤῥοον τρόπων.
Λόγων τε φίλτρον, ὥστ' ὑπεξελθεῖν λεών.
Νῦν δ' ὤχου ἔνθενδ' ὡς στρατὸς νικηφόρος
Φέρων τὸ πᾶν, κἄγων ἢ ὡς Ἀπαρκτίας
Κήπου συνωθῶν ἀνθινὴν εὐωδίαν,
Μίαν τ' ἄταρπον συμπορεύεσθαι δράσας.
 Ἐγὼ δὲ ῥινὶ ξυμβαλὼν ἰχνηλατῶ
Εἴπου τύχοιμι τῆςδ' ἀρίστης ἀτραποῦ,
Θανεῖν συνειδὼς κρεῖττον, ἢ ἄλλως βιοῦν.

O Mother! of thy sex the glory,
Contest of men—as in old story,—
The dread of devils, ' God's husbandry ;'
How then from us dost thou now fly?
And leavest us all standing round,
'Twixt tears and threatening danger found.
Surely if thou must needs depart,
It yet behov'd thee to impart
To thy children,—in their weeping
That thou i' the cold grave art sleeping ;
Of thy wisdom, guide of life,
With all rich experience rife ;
Of thy manners, sweet and smooth ;
And thy words, which charm and soothe :
So that thou from earth wouldst go,
And the world would scarcely know.

But now, like banner'd army, hence
Thou bear'st away all excellence ;
Or like a north-wind flowers beguiling,
All a garden's fragrance spoiling ;
I seek to trace thy sweet ascending
By the perfumes interblending,
Which bewray how thou hast gone,
And stir up aspiration,
That I might light on that best path
Which thy dainty footprints hath :
For to die thus were better bliss
Than to live and thee to miss.   G.

XVI.

Χαλεπὸν δοκεῖ δακρῦσαι,
Χαλεπὸν μὲν οὐ δακρῦσαι·
Χαλεπώτερον δὲ πάντων
Δακρύοντας ἀμπαύεσθαι.
Γενέτειραν οὔ τις ἀνδρῶν
Διδύμαις κόραις τοιαύτην
Ἐποδύρεται πρεπόντως.
Τάλας, εἴθε γ' Ἄργος εἴην
Πολυόμματος, πολύτλας,
Ἵνα μητρὸς εὐθενούσης
Ἀρετὰς διακριθείσας
Ἰδίαις κόραισι κλαύσω.

To weep a grievous thing appears;
Grievous it is not to shed tears;
But 'tis more grievous still than all,
Weeping, to cease to let tears fall.
But such a Mother what man could,
With two eyes, grieve for as he should?
O wretched me! would that e'en I
Own'd Argus-like full many an eye,
And power to bear enduringly;
That all the gifts of my rich Mother,
And virtues sunder'd one from other,
Each with its own peculiar eyes,
I might bewail to the dark skies!

R. WI.

XVII.

Αἰάζω γενέτειραν, ἐπαιάζουσι καὶ ἄλλοι,
Οὐκ ἔτ' ἐμὴν ἰδίας φυλῆς γράψαντες ἀρωγὸν,
Προυνομίῳ δ' ἀρετῆς κοινὴν γενέτειραν ἑλόντες.
Οὐκ ἔνι θαῦμα τόσον σφετερίζειν· οὐδὲ γὰρ ὕδωρ,
Οὐ φέγγος, κοινὸν τ' ἀγαθὸν, μίαν εἰς θύραν εἴργειν
Η θέμις, ἢ δυνατόν. σεμνώματος ἔπλετο στάθμη,
Δημόσιον τ' ἴνδαλμα καλοῦ, θεῖόν τε κάτοπτρον.

　　Αἰάζω γενέτειραν, ἐπαιάζουσι γυναῖκες,
Οὐκ ἔτι βαλλομένης χάρισιν βεβολημέναι ἦτορ,
Αὐταρ ἄχει μεγάλῳ κεντούμεναι· εὗτε γὰρ αὗται
Τῆς περὶ συλλαλέουσιν, ἑοῦ ποικίλματος ἄρδην
Λήσμονες, ἡ βελόνη σφαλερῷ κῆρ τραύματι νύττει
Εργου ἁμαρτηκυῖα, νέον πέπλον αἵματι στικτὸν
Μητέρι τικταίνουσα, γόῳ καὶ πένθεσι σύγχρουν.

　　Αἰάζω γενέτειραν, ἐπαιάζουσιν ὀπῶραι,
Οὐκ ἔτι δεσποίνης γλυκερᾷ μελεδῶνι τραφεῖσαι·
Ης βίος ἠελίοιο δίκην, ἀκτῖνας ἱέντος
Πραεῖς εἰαρινούς τε χαραῖς ἐπικίδνατι κῆπον·
Αὐταρ ὅδ' αὖ θάνατος κυρίης ὡς ἥλιος αὖος
Σειρίου ἡττηθεὶς βουλήμασι, πάντα μαραίνει.
Ζῶ δ' αὐτὸς βραχύ τι πνείων, ὥς ἔμπαλιν αὐτῆς
Αἶνον ὁμοῦ ζώειν καὶ πνεύματος ἄλλο γενέσθαι
Πνεῦμα, βίου πάροδον μούνοις ἐπέεσσι μετρῆσαν.

I bewail a Mother, and other men bewail her too;
Yet not as she is my Mother do they their sorrow show,

But, as having taken her into their loftiest strain
For a common mother of Virtue, they weep amain.
Nor marvel is it at all they should my Mother claim,
For idle 'twere to limit her to those who bear her name ;
Vain as within one door to shut the water or fire,
Or any common bounty from our heavenly Sire :
She was a measure of majesty, image of beauty rare,
A mirror to reflect what of divine still lingers here.
　　I bewail a Mother; and women her bewail,
No longer struck by Envy's shafts, that still the good
　　　　　assail,
But pierc'd by a mighty grief for her by Death struck low,
Mourning that they no more shall see her on earth below:
For when they speak of her, their embroidery they let
　　　　　fall,
The needle pricking their hearts, and blood spotting the
　　　　　garment all ;
And so a new robe for my Mother, a mourning robe,
　　　　　they make,
While their hands and hearts together in grief and an-
　　　　　guish shake.
　　I bewail a Mother; the orchard fruit-trees also weep,
No longer tended by her, who doth in the cold ground
　　　　　sleep;
Whose life, like the sun, emitting gentle and vernal
　　　　　beams,
Dispers'd itself o'er the garden in gracious as lovely
　　　　　streams ;

But now this death of their mistress, like arid-parching
    sun
O'erpower'd by burning Sirius, blights all he looks upon;
And now I myself shall live faintly but a little while,
So using my breath that I may in her my grief beguile:
Another spirit is born of her spirit within me,
Measuring its course with words only, weak, empty, as
    you may see.   G.

XVIII.

Κύματ' ἐπαφριοῶντα Θαμήσεος, αἶκε σελήνης
   Φωτὸς ἀπαυρομένης, ὄγκου ἐφεῖσθε πλέον.
Νῦν θέμις ὀρφναίῃ μεγάλης ἐπὶ γείτονος αἴσῃ,
   Οὐλυμπόνδε βιβᾶν ὔμμιν ἀνισταμένοις.
'Αλλὰ μενεῖτ', οὐ γὰρ τάραχος ποτὶ μητέρα βαίνῃ,
   Καὶ πρέπον ὦδε παρὰ δακρυόεσσι ῥέειν.

If when, ye froaric waves of Thames,
The Moon's fair face a cloud defames,
Filching from her the pallid light
That gleams upon the brow of Night,
Ye rise in wrathful majesty,—
How much more may ye mount on high,
Since she, fairer than moon, is gone,
Her life's light in extinction,
Who lately dwelt your banks upon!
Now 'twere but right o'er such a fate,
'Gainst the heavens to strike elate:

Yet rest ye, hush ye, where ye are,
My Mother's ear no noise may jar;
More fitting 'tis ye murm'ring flow,
Beside us weeping here below.   G.

XIX.

Excussos manibus calamos falcemque resumptam
    Rure, sibi dixit Musa fuisse probro.
Aggreditur Matrem, conductis carmine Parcis,
    Funereque hoc cultum vindicat aegra suum.
Non potui non ire acri stimulante flagello:
    Quin Matris superans carmina poscit honos.
Eia, agedum, scribo: vicisti, Musa; sed audi,
    Stulta semel scribo, perpetuo ut sileam.

My pen laid by, and pruning-hook retaken,
The Muse's indignation soon awaken:
She seeks my Mother, the Fates by song being won,
And, sad, demands the worship of her son
For this dark death : and what she asks is done.
I needs must go, urg'd on by scourge so strong;
My Mother's honour claims it, passing song.
Ah, well, I write : thou hast conquer'd, Muse; but see
These follies once for all I write for thee,
That ever after I may silent be.   R. WI.

VI.

ANTI-TAMI-CAMI-CATEGORIA

ET

GEORGII HERBERTI, ANGLI MUSAE RESPONSORIAE,
AD ANDREAE MELVINI, SCOTI,
ANTI-TAMI-CAMI-CATEGORIAM.

VERSES OF GEORGE HERBERT, ENGLISHMAN,
IN REPLY TO THE 'ANTI-TAMI-CAMI-CATEGORIA' OF
ANDREW MELVILLE, SCOTCHMAN;

OR

ACCUSATION AGAINST THE THAMES AND CAM
= THE UNIVERSITIES OF OXFORD AND CAMBRIDGE.   G.

In our Memoir (Vol. I.) and Essay (Vol. II.) we have stated
and examined critically the historic grounds on which the ' An-
ti-Tami-Cami-Categoria' rests, as well as the controversy in re-
lation to Melville and Herbert. Thither the reader is referred.
This memorable satire was originally published in 1604. My
text is taken from the following excessively rare edition, with
which David Laing, Esq., LL.D. Edinburgh, favoured me:

PARASYNAGMA PERTHENSE

ET

IVRAMENTUM ECCLESIAE

SCOTICANAE

ET

A. M. ANTITAMICA-
MICATEGORIA.

Anno M.DC.XX.

Quarto—Title and pp. 3-47. ' Anti-Tami-Cami-Categoria' oc-
cupies pp. 41-47. Stanza 43 in this edition differs from the
usual text, which is as follows :

> ' Quisquis hanc, surda negat aure, qua se
> Fundit ubertim liquidas sub auras,
> Ille ter prudens, sapiens que, et omni ex
>   Parte beatus.'

that is :

> Who turns a deaf ear to all these,
> Nor sinfully will himself please,
> As from the air and sea and earth
> Pleasure her tempting snares pours forth,
> He is thrice prudent and wise of heart,
> Perfectly happy in every part.

and furnishes variations and an additional stanza thereafter, as inserted in its place. Mr. W. Aldis Wright, as before, informs me that in the copy of above edition of 'Anti-Tami,' &c. in the University Library, Cambridge, there are inserted after 'Porr'gerre Regi' (l. 12), in a contemporary hand, the following—the end of the lines being, unfortunately, cut off by the binder:

> Rege quo maius, meliusne
> Fata donavere nihil, dab
> Gratius, quamuis rodean
> Tempora pris
>
> Cuius in scripto Themis, i
> Suda, sub fibris Sophie ex
> Suauis in vultu Charis in
> Entheus ardo.

Another edition is given in 'Ecclesiastes Solomonis. Auctore Joan. Viviano. Canticum Solomonis: Nec non Epigrammata Sacra, Per Ja. Duportum. Accedunt Georgii Herberti, Musae Responsoriae, ad Andreae Melvini, Anti-Tami-Cami-Categoriam. Cant. 1662. 12°.' There is a separate title-page, as follows: 'Georgii Herberti, Angli Musae Responsoriae, ad Andreae Melvini, Scoti, Anti-Tami-Cami-Categoriam. Cantabrigiae: Ex Officina Joannis Field, celeberrimae Academiae Typographi. Anno Dom. 1662.' pp. 1-30 (separate pagination). This seems to have been the first edition of the 'Musae Responsoriae.' Our text of Herbert's 'Response' is from it.   G.

PRO SUPPLICI

*Evangelicorvm Ministrorvm in Anglia, ad Serenissimum Regem
contra Larvatam geminae Academiae Gorgonem Apologia ;*

SIVE

ANTI-TAMI-CAMI-CATEGORIA,

Authore A [NDREA] M [ELVINO].

Responsum, non dictum.

INSOLENS, audax, facinus nefandum,
Scilicet, poscit ratio ut decori,
Poscit ex omni officio ut sibi mens
    Conscia recti

Anxiam Christi, vigilemque curam,   5
Quae pias terris animas relictis
Sublevans deducit in astra, nigroque
    Invidet Orco,

De sacri casta ratione cultus,
De Sacro-sancti Officii decoro,   10
Supplicem ritu veteri libellum
    Porr'gere Regi,

Simplici mente atque animo integello,
Spiritu recto, et studiis modestis,
Numinis sancti veniam, et benigni   15
    Regis honorem

Rite praefantem: Scelus expiandum
Scilicet tauro[rum], et ovium, suumque
Millibus centum, voluisse nudo
　　　　　Tangere verbo　　　　　　　20

Praesulum fastus; monuisse Ritus
Impios, deridiculos, ineptos,
Lege, ceu labes maculasque lecta ex
　　　　　Gente fugandos.

Jusque-jurandum ingemuisse jura　　　25
Exigi contra omnia; tum misellis
Mentibus tristem laqueum injici per
　　　　　Fasque nefasque.

Turbida illimi crucis in lavacro
Signa consignem? magico rotatu　　　30
Verba devolvam? sacra vox sacrata im-
　　　　　murmuret unda

Strigis in morem? Rationis usu ad
Fabor Infantem vacuum? canoras
Ingeram nugas minus audienti　　　35
　　　　　Dicta puello?

Parvulo impostis manibus sacrabo
Gratiae foedus? digitone Sponsae
Annulus sponsi impositus sacrabit
　　　　　Connubiale　　　　　　　40

Foedus aeternae bonitatis? Unda
Num salutari mulier sacerdos

Tinget in vitam, Sephoramque reddet
    Lustrica mater?

Pilei quadrum capiti rotundo   45
Rite quadrabit? Pharium Camillo
Supparum Christi, et decus Antichristi
    Pontificale?

Pastor examen gregis exigendum
Curet invitus, celebrare coenam   50
Promptus arcanam, memorando Jesu
    Vulnera dira?

Cantibus certent Berecinthia aera
Musicum fractis? reboentve rauco
Templa mugitu? Illecebris supremi ah   55
    Rector Olympi

Captus humanis? libitumque nobis,
Scilicet, Regi id Superum allubescet?
Somniumque aegri cerebri profanum est
    Dictio sacra?   60

Haud secus lustri Lupa Vaticani
Romuli faccem bibit, et bibendum
Porrigit poc'lo, populisque et ipsis
    Regibus aureo.

Non ita aeterni Wittakerus acer   65
Luminis vindex patriaeque lumen
Dixit aut sensit; neque celsa summi
    Penna Renoldi.

Certa sublimes aperire calles,
Sueta coelestes iterare cursus,   70
Laeta misceri niveis beatae
          Civibus aulae;

Nec Tami aut Cami accola saniore
Mente, qui coelum sapit in frequenti
Hermathenaeo et celebri Lycaeo   75
          Culta juventus,

Cujus affulget genio Jovae lux:
Cui nitens Sol justitiae renidet:
Quem jubar Christi radiantis alto
          Spectat Olympo.   80

Buccrum laudem? memoremque magnum
Martyrem? Gemmas geminas renati
Aurei saec'li, duo dura sacri
          Fulmina belli?

Alterum Camus liquido recursu,   85
Alterum Tamus trepidante lympha
Audiit, multum stupuitque magno
          Ore sonantem.

Anne mulcentem Rhodanum et Lemanum
Praedicem Bezam viridi in senecta?   90
Octies cujus trepidavit aetas
          Claudere denos

Solis anfractus, reditusque, et ultra
Quinque percurrens spatiosa in annos

Longius florem viridantis aevi
        Prorogat et ver.   95

Oris erumpit scatebra perenni
Amnis exundans, gravidique rores
Gratia fecunda animos apertis
        Auribus implent.   100

Major hic omni invidia, et superstes
Millibus mille, et Sadeele, et omnium
Maximo CALVINO, aliisque veri
        Testibus aequis;

Voce olorina liquidas ad undas   105
Nunc canit laudes Genitoris almi,
Carmen et nato canit eliquante
        Numinis aura,

Sensa de castu sacra puriore,
Dicta de cultu potiore sancta,   110
Arma quae in castris jugulent severi
        Tramitis hostes.

Cana cantanti juga ninguidarum
Alpium applaudunt, resonantque valles;
Jura concentu nemorum sonoro,   115
        Et pater Ister.

Consonant longe; pater et bicornis
Rhenus ascensum ingeminat: Garumna,
Sequana, atque Arar, Liger: insularum et
        Undipotentum   120

Magna pars intenta Britannicarum
Voce conspirat liquida: solumque
Et salum coeli aemula praecinentis
        More modoque

Concinunt Bezae numeris modisque   125
Et polo plaudunt ; referuntque leges
Lege quas sanxit pius ardor, et Rex
        Scoto-britannus.

Sicut edictum in tabulis ahenis
Servat aeternum pia cura Regis,   130
Qui mare et terras variisque mundum
        Temperat horis :

Cujus aequalis Soboles Parenti
Gentis electae Pater atque Custos ;
Par et ambobus, veniens utrinque   135
        Spiritus almus ;

Quippe Tres-unus Deus ; unus actus,
Una natura est tribus ; una virtus,
Una Majestas, Deitas et una,
        Gloria et una.   140

Una vis immensa, perennis una
Vita, lux una, et sapientia una,
Una mens, una et ratio, una vox, et
        Una voluntas.

Lenis, indulgens, facilis, benigna ;   145
Dura et inclemens, rigida et severa ;

Semper aeterna, omnipotens, et aequa,
    Semper et alma:

Lucidum cujus speculum est, reflectens
Aureum vultus jubar, et verendum,   150
Virginis proles, sata coelo, et alti In-
    terpres Olympi:

Qui Patris mentemque animumque sancti
Filius pandit face noctiluca,
Sive doctrinae documenta, seu com-   155
    pendia vitae,

Publicae, privae, sacra scita Regni
Regis ad nutum referens, domusque
Ad voluntatem Domini instituta
    Singula librans,   160

Luce quam Phoebus melior refundit,
Lege quam legum- tulit ipse -lator,
Cujus exacti officii suprema est
    Norma voluntas.

Caeca mens humana, hominum voluntas   165
Prava, et affectus rabidi: indigetque
Luce mens, norma officii voluntas,
    Lege libido:

Quisquis hanc surda negat aure et orba
Mente dat ferri rapidis procellis,   170
Ter quater caudex, stolidusque et omni ex
    Parte misellus[1]

[1] This additional stanza from the original edition.

Quisquis hanc prava bibit aure, qua se
Fundit ubertim liquidas sub auras,
Ille ter prudens sapiensque et omni   175
       Ex parte beatus.

Ergo vos Cami proceres, Tamique,
Quos via flexit malesuadus error,
Denuo rectum, duce Rege Regum, in-
       sistite callem.   180

Vos metus tangit si hominum nec ullus,
At Deum fandi memorem et nefandi
Vindicem sperate, et amoena solis
       Tartara Diris;

Quae manent sontes animas trucesque   185
Praesulum fastus, male quos perurit
Pervigil zelus vigilum, et gregis cus-
       todia pernox.

Veste bis tincta Tyrio superbos
Murice, et pastos dape pinguiore   190
Regia quondam aut Saliari inuncta ab-
       domine coena.

Qualis Ursini, Damasique fastus   Ammianus Marcell. lib. 27
Turgidus, luxuque ferox, feroque
Ambitu pugnax, sacram et aedem et urbem   195
       Caede nefanda

Civium incestavit, et ominosum
Traxit exemplum veniens in aevum

Praesulum quod nobilium indecorus
    Provocat ordo. 200

Quid fames auri sacra? quid cupido
Ambitus diri fera non propagat
Posteris culpae? mala damna quanta
    Plurima fundit?

NOTES.

The text of 1662 furnishes these slight variations:
St. v. l. 18, 'taurorum, ovium.'
  ,, xvi. l. 62, 'bibendam.'
  ,, xxxi. l. 123, 'coeli.'
  ,, xliii. xliv. of 1622 were displaced in Duport's edition
(1662) by that given in the Note before this section.   G.

A Defence in behalf of the Petition of the Evangelical Ministers
    in England [=the Puritans] to the most serene King,
    against the masked Gorgon of the twin Universities; or Anti-
    Tami-Cami-Categoria,—Andrew Melville being author.

Answered, not spoken.

' Insolent, impudent, impious crime
As e'er was written in annals of Time :'
So I am jeer'd and flouted forsooth,
Although what I contend for is—TRUTH ;
Right, becoming, conscience-rul'd, as I
Would faithful speak for Him on high ;

As I vigilant under-shepherd would be,
Anxious and watchful as was He,
To lead souls upward and upward still,
Seeking to do the Master's will ;

Drawing from Earth and all its jars,
Rising exultant to the stars;
Rescuing souls from Shades infernal,
Gaining them for the light eternal.

Of SACRED WORSHIP, as simple and pure,
Of the HOLY OFFICE, what shall allure,
I now am to write; and petition bring
Humbly, in olden wise, to my King:

With a 'single mind' and purpose upright,
In spirit meek and motive right,
I venture to hope for Almighty ruth
And my Sovran's face as I stand for THE TRUTH;
Thus in due form favour bespeaking,
I unconscious am of aught self-seeking.

But, lo, 'tis a crime, that I expiate may
By holocausts only, in ancient way:
A hundred thousand bulls, sheep, swine,
A victim, and more, for my every line.

That I by so much as one word should dare
To brand Prelates' pride, and Rites lay bare—
Impious and foolish and absurd,
Such as are found not in The Word;
That I should seek such Rites to expel
As blots on God's chosen; and rebel,

Yea, groan, that an oath exacted should be
Against all law; and that I should see

A sorrowful trap or net spread along,
To catch wretched souls by right or by wrong!

O, how could I sign dark signs of the Cross
Over the Laver, withouten loss?
How dare I roll out set words of prayer
In magic rotation through the air?

How, with solemn voice, o'er the water-fill'd bowl
Murmur, as screeches the hooting owl?
Shall I speak to a babe unknowing
Harmonious trifles, it no heed showing?

Or solemn hands on young heads place,
Confirming thus the promis'd GRACE?
Or shall I to the bridegroom elate

On bride's finger a ring consecrate?
As though, forsooth, 'twere in my mind
The ETERNAL GOODNESS thus to bind!

With healing water shall the priest
In long attire like woman drest,
Sprinkle the babe, and make it live,
As if a man could sins forgive?
And shall the 'churching' mother bring
Her 'customary offering,'
And, like another Zipporah, fling   Exodus iv. 25
Before his feet the odious thing?

Shall he, the Minister of Christ,
Don cap four-squar'd? or o'er him twist

Egyptian robes or pomp externe,
Such as in papal glory worn?
Shall he, Christ's simpleness denying,
Be found old Antichrist out-vying?
Or should Pastor perforce drive out
His flock, as he The Supper's about;
Seeking in secret that confounds
To celebrate Christ's awful wounds?
Or voice-music's sweet melody
By clash of Phrygian cymbals die?
Or House of God with bellowings roar
Hoarse as sea-waves on a lee shore?
Ah, is the Ruler, God Most High,
Pleas'd with such heathen minstrelsy?

And what to human ears is sweet,
Shall it Divine approval meet?
And shall the dreams of sickly brain
The name of Sacred Worship gain?

Just so the Roman she-wolf slakes
Her thirst; to Vat'can puddle takes
A golden cup, and filling it there
Holds it still forth, alluring, fair,
For peoples and for kings to share.

Not so did WHITAKER[1] speak or feel,
When he Rome's darkness did reveal:
Champion of the Eternal Light,
Forth-bearing to defend the RIGHT,

Himself light of his native land;
Nor he that did beside him stand,
The great RAINOLDS,[2] pen in hand.

Ah, that lofty pen was sure
To open ways sublime and pure,
Tracing the paths celestial still,
Joyous all minds and hearts to fill
With visions of the City of Gold,
And hosts in snow-white vesture stol'd.

Nor of sounder mind by Cam or Thames
Dwells any whom Athenæum names;
Or throng'd Lyceum as learn'd, and given
Such joys as mixes man with heav'n :

Whose light effulgent God did give,
And by Sun of Righteousness did live ;
Fetching still from Christ on high
Radiance to th' upward-gazing eye.

Shall I laud BUCER ?[3] or proclaim
The great PETER MARTYR'S[4] lustrous name ?
Twin gems of our Golden Age they are,
Twin thunderbolts of the Holy War.

Cam, listening backward, heard the one ;
Thames, tremulous, look'd the other upon ;
Both wond'ring as 'fore flashing swords
How each grand mouth spoke burning words.

Or should I celebrate BEZA hoar,
Soothing the Rhone and Leman's shore

In his green old age? who, white-hair'd, saw

His fourscore years; and still doth draw
For five years more his line of life,
Fruitful as Spring with young flow'rs rife;

His mouth—like stream o'erflowing, rushing—
Still his prime eloquence forth-gushing,
Filling men's minds as they list attent
With grace as rich as dews heaven-sent;

Above all envy, thousands outliving,
And holy SADEEL[5] and CALVIN[6] surviving—
Greatest of names that Europe boasts,
Grandest e'er led the Lord's own hosts:

With swan-like voice to the flowing waves,
He sings the praise of Him Who saves:
Now of God the Father kind,
Now of the Son, now of the Wind
Divine, e'en God the Spirit holy,
Sanctifier of the meek and lowly:

He sings what he feels of Truth more pure,
Of simpler Worship that shall endure;
The pure an added pureness taking,
The already worthy worthier making;
Furnishing arms to smite the foes
Of Him Whose Cross on Calv'ry rose.

To him singing, Alpine summits hoar,
Which up to the heavens serenely soar,

Shout forth his praise; the valleys beneath
Take up the echo, and their breath
Far Jura rolls back in his thund'ring woods,
And Father Ister with his floods—

They ring together from afar;
And two-horn'd Rhine doubles the war;
Garonne, Seine, Saône, and Loire,

And our British Isles, that rule the sea,
In great part join the melody,
Lifting a liquid voice on high;
And earth and sea and the wide sky,
In emulation to prolong
His form and mode who leads the song,

Together sing, and seek to move
In measures which BEZA will approve,
And renew those laws, by zeal inspir'd,
Which our Scoti-British[7] king requir'd;
Laws which he order'd to stand fast,
That the FAITH REFORM'D for aye may last.

Thus His eternal, fix'd decree
On brazen tablets keepeth He,—
The King Who rules the earth and sea,
And governs all things wondrously.

Whose Offspring takes coequal place
With's Father—Guard of the Elect Race,
And nurt'ring Spirit, equal to Both,
Proceeding from them as BREATH doth—

In fine, the Tri-une God, yet One
In nature, virtue, action ;
One Glory and one Majesty,
One self-containèd Deity ;

One boundless Power, One Endless Life,
One Light, one Wisdom superlative ;
One Mind, one Reason, and One Voice,
One Will, according in all choice ;

Gentle, indulgent, easy, kind—
Yet other attributes are join'd ;
Stern, rig'rous, unyielding, and severe—
O, weak our words how deep soe'er !—
Omnipotent, eternal, just,
Yet ever mild to all Him trust.

Clear Mirror of Whose Face of Wonder—
Golden and awful in its splendour—
Is He the Virgin-born from above,
And Mediator there of Love ;

The Son Who doth the Father show
All that He feels, all He doth know,
With such a keen and piercing light
As drives away the blackest night ;
Whether He holy doctrine preacheth,
Or Way of Christian life He teacheth ;

Public or private ordinances—
Whate'er His Kingdom great advances ;

Referring all unto the King,
'Neath Whose will he all doth bring;

By light which better Sun bestows
Than our dim sky or earth e'er knows;
By a law which The Lawgiver made,
Whose Will may never be gainsaid;
Of perfect duty the supreme rule—
He who denies it is a fool!

Blind, alas, is mind of man;
His will deprav'd and under ban;
Passions outrageous, soul benighted;
His choice from duty disunited;
Lust at the call of Appetite,
That doth all obedience slight.

Whoe'er to Duty turns deaf ear,
And yields to Passion without fear,
While like a storm it bears along
His foolish heart with impulse strong,—
Fool—blockhead—thrice, four times, we say,
And wholly wretched every way.

Whoe'er drinks-in with ready ear
The voice of Duty stern yet clear,
As freely it makes known abroad,
Throughout the world, the will of God;
He is thrice prudent and wise of heart,
Perfectly wise in every part.

Therefore, ye foremost men of Cam,
And ye whom famous Thames doth claim,
Whom ill-advising Error hath
Turnèd aside from the right path,
O, return now, and once again
Guidance of King of Kings obtain.

And if no fear of man will awe,
Think—God will yet avenge His Law ;
The right, the wrong, is 'neath His eye,
Nor may you hope Him to defy ;
Bethink ye too o' the realms below,
Which only fiends as pleasant know ;
And of the doom that there awaits

All guilty souls whom Pride elates.
Ah, pomp-full Prelates, ye shall feel
Strange fiery overseers' zeal,
And through Hell's night shall ye their flock
Be held—who the Almighty mock !

Prelates ! in twice-dipt Tyrian dyes,
As proud ye court admiring eyes ;
Gorging your paunches in banquets high,
Outvying all regal revelry ;

Such pride as did Ursinus show—
Such pride as Damasis did blow,
Swelling in luxury, insolent,
Pugnacious, to fierce ambition bent ;

Polluting God's House and the City
With vilest slaughter—without pity ;

Drawing precedent for our age,
Kindling e'en now to utmost rage
Against the prelate-order, who
All the old wrong-doings full renew ;

What will not this dire thirst of gold
Lead men to do? Crimes manifold.
What guilt will not Ambition
From age to age bring mortals on ?
Alas, how many woes, and great,
Doth it not pour, unconsecrate!   G.

NOTES.

[1] Whitaker (William), the illustrious Master of St. John's,
Cambridge : b. 1547, d. 1595.

[2] Rainolds (John), a famous Puritan divine and controver-
sialist : b. 1549, d. 1607. See our Life of him prefixed to re-
print of his Commentaries on Obadiah and Haggai, in Nichol's
Puritan Commentaries.

[3] Bucer (Martin), the reformer : b. 1491, d. 1551.

[4] Martyr (Peter), another venerable reformer and scholar :
b. 1500, d. 1562.

[5] Sadeel (Anthony), a celebrated French Huguenot divine :
b. 1534, d. 1591. Hitherto misprinted Sadecle, to the ruin of
the verse and of the memory of a great and good man.

[6] Calvin. Nothing more is needed but the name. The small
stone at Geneva, with ' J. C.' on it, seemed to me magnificent by
its very simplicity, as I looked on neighbouring stone-tawdry
monuments. For a noble tribute to Calvin as a commentator,
see Perowne's recent most masterly Exposition of the Psalms
(2 vols.).

[7] James VI. of Scotland and I. of England. See the histo-
rical fact in Life of Herbert by Walton (in Vol. III.).   G.

PRO DISCIPLINA ECCLESIAE NOSTRAE
EPIGRAMMATA APOLOGETICA.

I.

Augustissimo Potentissimoque Monarchae Jacobo, D. G. Magnae
Britanniae, Franciae, et Hiberniae Regi, Fidei Defensori,
&c. Geo. Herbertus.

Ecce recedentis foecundo in littore Nili
    Sol generat populum luce fovente novum.
Ante tui, Caesar, quam fulserat aura favoris,
    Nostrae etiam Musae vile fuere lutum ;
Nunc adeo per te vivunt, ut repere possint,
    Sintque ausae thalamum solis adire tui.

EPIGRAMS IN DEFENCE OF THE DISCIPLINE OF
OUR CHURCH.

To the Most August and Mighty Monarch, James, by the Grace
of God of Great Britain, France, and Ireland King, Defender
of the Faith, &c. George Herbert.

Lo, on the fruitful banks of ebbing Nile
The sun begets new tribes with nurturing smile.
So, Cæsar, ere thy favouring ray had gleam'd,
Nothing but common mud our Muses seem'd.
Now these, through thee, so live that they can creep,
And into thy sun's bedchamber dare peep.   n. wi.

II.

Illustris. celsissimoque Carolo, Walliae et Juventutis Principi.

Quam chartam tibi porrigo recentem,
Humanae decus atque apex juventae,
Obtutu placido benignus affles,
Namque aspectibus e tuis vel unus
Mordaces tineas, nigrasque blattas,
Quas livor mihi parturit, retundet,
Ceu, quas culta timet seges, pruinas
Nascentes radii fugant, vel acres
Tantum dulcia leniunt catarrhos.
Sic, o te, juvenem senemve, credat
Mors semper juvenem, senem Britanni.

*To the most illustrious and exalted Charles, Prince of Wales
and of our Youth.*

On this new page which in thy hand I place,
O crown and glory of the youthful race,
Breathe thou with tranquil countenance benign.
Surely before a single glance of thine
Devouring worms and dusky moths will flee—
The carping race which Envy bears to me;
E'en as the rising sunbeams put to flight
Hoar-frosts, which cultivated crops affright;
Or as sweet syrups soothe a wearing cold;
So—shall I call thee young, O prince, or old?—
May Death believe thee always young in years,
While to our eyes thy wisdom old appears.　　R. WI.

III.

Reverendissimo in Christo Patri ac Domino Episcopo
Vintoniensi, &c.

Sancte Pater, cœli custos, quo doctius uno
    Terra nihil, nec quo sanctius astra vident ;
Cum mea futilibus numeris se verba viderent
    Claudi, pene tuas præteriere fores.
Sed propere dextreque reduxit cuntia sensus,
    Ista docens soli scripta quadrare tibi.

To the Right Reverend Father in Christ and Lord Bishop of
Winchester, &c. ⌊*Launcelot Andrewes.*⌉

Blest sire, Heaven's guard, than whom more learnèd
           seems
Nought upon Earth, on High nought holier gleams ;
When in weak numbers were imprison'd fast
My words, thy friendly doors they well-nigh past :
But quickly, cleverly there issu'd thence,
And stay'd them as they went along, GOOD SENSE—
Teaching my poetry henceforth to find
Its fair proportion only from thy mind.   R. WI.

IV.

Ad Regem Epigrammata duo.
Instituti Epigrammatici Ratio.

Cum millena tuam pulsare negotia mentem
    Constet, et ex illa pendeat orbis ope ;
Ne te productis videar lassare camœnis,
    Pro solido, CAESAR, carmine frusta dabo.

Cum tu contundens, Catharos, vultuque librisque,
Grata mihi mensae sunt analecta tuae.

To the King : Two Epigrams.

1. The reason of the epigrammatic form.

Since thousand matters knock at thy mind's gates,
Upon whose aid a world dependent waits ;
Lest with long poems I should tedious be,
For solid verse, fragments I offer thee.

2. Second Epigram of the two.

With looks and books the Puritans crush thou ;
Thy table's pickings be for me enow.   R. WI.

V.

Ad Melvinum.

Non mea fert aetas, ut te, veterane, lacessam ;
    Non ut te superem: res tamen ipsa feret.
Aetatis numerum supplebit causa minorem ;
    Sic tu nunc juvenis factus, egoque senex.
Aspice, dum perstas, ut te tua deserat aetas ;
    Et mea sint canis scripta referta tuis.
Ecce tamen quam suavis ero ! cum, fine duelli,
    Clauserit extremas pugna peracta vices,
Tum tibi, si placeat, fugientia tempora reddam ;
    Sufficiet votis ista juventa meis.

To Melville.

Nor to attack, vet'ran, my age befits,
Nor conquer thee; but yet the theme permits.

Let my good cause my want of years supply;
So thou a youth art found, an old man I.
As thou contendest, shorten'd see thine age,
While with thy hoary hairs I deck my page.
But how obliging am I ! when our blows
Have brought the changing conflict to a close,
Then thy fleet years, an't please thee, I'll resign,
And rest contented with this youth of mine. R. WI.

VI.

In Monstrum vocabuli Anti-Tami-Cami-Categoria.
Ad eundem.

O quam bellus homo es ! lepido quam nomine fingis
 Istas Anti-Tami-Cami-Categorias !
Sic Catharis nova sola placent; res, verba novantur :
 Quae sapiunt aevum, ceu cariosa jacent.
Quin liceat nobis aliquas procudere voces :
 Non tibi fingendi sola taberna patet.
Cum sacra perturbet vester furor omnia, scriptum
 Hoc erit, Anti-furi-Puri-Categoria.
Pollubra vel cum olim damnaris Regia in ara,
 Est Anti-pelvi-Melvi-Categoria.

On the Monster of a Word, ' Anti-Tami-Cami-Categoria.'
To the same [=Melville].

What a fine man thou art ! a pretty word to say,
This 'Anti-Tami-Cami-Categoria' !
Thus Puritans in words and things love novelties ;
What smacks of age or hoary time neglected lies.

To hammer-out some words now also grant to me ;
The shop for forging them is not confin'd to thee.
Accept, since Puritanic fury rules the day,
My ' Anti-furi-Puri-Categoria ;'
Or since you blam'd the bowls which on James'altar lay,
Take ' Anti-pelvi-Melvi-categoria.'[1]   R. WI.

VII.
Partitio Anti-Tami-Cami-Categoriae.

Tres video partes, quo re distinctius utar,
    Anti categoriae, Scoto-Britanne, tuae :
Ritibus^e una sacris opponitur ;[3] altera sanctos
    Praedicat autores ;[4] tertia plena Deo est.
Postremis ambabus idem sentimus uterque ;
    Ipse pios laudo ; numen et ipse colo.
Non nisi prima suas patiuntur praelia lites.
    O bene quod dubium possideamus agrum !

The division of Anti-Tami-Cami-Categoria.

Three parts, O Scot, to make the thing more clear,
Of ' Anti-categoria' appear.
One Sacred Rites attacks : Two, lifts on high
Holy Divines : Three, treats of Deity.
Concerning the two last we think the same :
I praise the Good, and I adore God's Name.
About the first alone debate is found :
O, well that we possess some fighting-ground !   R. WI.

[1] See our Essay for the historical reference here.   G.
[2] Ab initio ad vers. 65.   [3] Inde ad vers. 128.   [4] Inde 170.

VIII.

In Metri Genus.

Cur, ubi tot ludat numeris antiqua poësis,
    Sola tibi Sappho feminaque una placet?
Cur tibi tam facile non arrisere poëtae
    Heroum grandi carmina fulta pede?
Cur non lugentes elegi? non acer Iambus?
    Commotos animos rectius ista decent.
Scilicet hoc vobis proprium, qui purius itis,
    Et populi spurcas creditis esse vias;
Vos ducibus missis, missis doctoribus, omnes
    Femineum blanda fallitis arte genus:
Nunc etiam teneras quo versus gratior aures
    Mulceat, imbelles complacuere modi.

On the kind of Metre of Anti-Tami-Cami-Categoria (Sapphics).

Why, when the Classics deal in many a measure,
Does female Sappho only give thee pleasure?
How came thy poet-fancy to decline
So readily the grand Heroic line,
Iambics quick, and mournful Elegies?
Hearts agitated best find words in these.
This style suits you, who wear so demure face,
And deem the people's ways defil'd and base.
Leaders and learnèd men ye bid depart,
And 'silly women' guile with cozening art.
And now to suit your verse to tender ears,
The unwarlike Sapphic on your page appears.   R. WI.

IX.

De Larvata Gorgone.[1]

Gorgona cur diram larvasque obtrudis inanes ?
    Cum prope sit nobis Musa, Medusa procul !
Si, quia felices olim dixere poëtae
    Pallada gorgoneam, sic tua verba placent.
Vel potius liceat distinguere.   Tuque tuique
    Sumite gorgoneam, nostraque Pallas erit.

Concerning the Masked Gorgon.

Why thrustest thou on us a Gorgon dire
And senseless masks, our patience thus to tire ?
Near is the Muse—Medusa, far be thou ! ·
Or if, as happy poets, we allow
Once on a time Pallas Gorgonean nam'd,
Then thy words please me, nor must thou be blam'd ;
Or if between us we must draw a line,
Gorgonean shall belong to thee and thine,
While Pallas shall be left to me and mine.   G.

X.

De Praesulum Fastu.

Praesulibus nostris fastus, Melvine, tumentes
    Saepius aspergis.   Siste, pudore vacas.
An quod semotum populo laquearibus altis
    Eminet, id tumidum protinus esse feres ?
Ergo etiam solem dicas, ignave, superbum,
    Qui tam sublimi conspicit orbe viam :
                In titulo.

Ille tamen, quamvis altus, tua crimina ridens
   Assiduo vilem lumine cingit humum.
Sic laudandus erit nactus sublimia Praesul,
   Qui dulci miseros irradiabit ope.

Concerning the Pride of Prelates.

Our Prelates, Melville, oft dost thou asperse
As swoll'n with pride. Stay, list my answering verse.
Whate'er above ' the people' towering high
Is elevated to the ceilèd sky
As puff'd-up, straightway wilt thou that decry?
Then thou must designate as proud the Sun
Holding its lofty course, O foolish one!
Disdaining thee, he speeds his heavenly round,
Yet ceaselessly illumes the lowest ground.
So Prelates, who, when to high places rais'd,
Lighten with help the wretched, should be prais'd.   α.

XI.

De Gemina Academia.

Quis hic superbit, oro? tunc, an Praesules?
   Quos dente nigro corripis?
Tu duplicem solus Camaenarum thronum
   Virtute percellis tua;
Et unus impar aestimatur viribus,
   Utrumque sternis calcitro;
Omnesque stulti audimus, aut hypocritae,
   Te perspicaci atque integro.

An rectius nos, si vices vertas, probi,
    Te contumaci et livido ?
Quisquis tuetur perspicillis Belgicis
    Qua parte tractari solent,
Res ampliantur, sin per adversam videt,
    Minora fiunt omnia ;
Tu qui superbos caeteros existimas,
    Superbius cum te nihil,
Vertas specillum ; nam, prout se res habent,
    Vitro minus recte uteris.

Concerning the Twin Universities.

Who here is proud ?　Prelates, or thou, forsooth ?
Prelates, whom thou dost seize with thy black tooth ?
Thou dost strike through the Muses' double throne
By thine own merit, mighty though alone.
Powerless is one the conflict to maintain ;
A valiant kicker, thou dost floor them twain.
All fools, or hypocrites, we are esteem'd ;
Clever and upright thou alone art deem'd.
Are we not rather, changing places, good ?
Thou full of obstinate and envious blood ?
If through perspective you make inspection,　See Glos. s.v.
Holding it in the usual direction,
Objects are magnified ; but turn it round
The other way, all things are lessen'd found.
Thou who dost deem all others proud to be,
Although naught prouder do we know than thee,

Just turn the perspective ; for now, I wis,
You use the magnifying glass amiss !   R. WI.

XII.

De S. Baptismi Ritu.

Cum tener ad sacros infans sistatur aquales,
    Quod puer ignorat, verba profana putas?
Annon sic mercamur agros? quibus ecce Redemptor
    Comparat aeterni regna beata Dei.
Scilicet emptorem si res aut parcior aetas
    Impediant, apices legis amicus obit.
Forsitan et prohibes infans portetur ad undas,
    Et per se templi limen adire velis:
Sin, Melvine, pedes alienos postulet infans,
    Cur sic displiceat vox aliena tibi?
Rectius innocuis lactentibus omnia praestes,
    Quae ratio per se, si sit adulta, facit.
Quid vetat ut pueri vagitus suppleat alter,
    Cum nequeat claras ipse litare preces?
Saevus es eripiens parvis vadimonia coeli :
    Et tibi sit nemo praes, ubi poscis opem.

Concerning the Rite of holy Baptism.

When to the Font a tender babe is brought,
Must the accustom'd words profane be thought,
Because the child knows not? Thus buy we fields
For whom Christ's blood a heavenly kingdom yields?
If circumstance or nonage buyer prevent,
A friend to go through points of law is sent.

Would you the carrying of the babe escheat,
Bidding it cross the church on its own feet?
But if another's feet a babe demands,
How is't another's voice displeasing stands?
Rightly may innocent sucklings claim from you
All things which Sense mature itself would do.
Why should not one make good an infant's cries,
Powerless itself to supplicate the skies?
Cruel, dost snatch from babes the pledge of heaven?
No surety be to thee in thy need given.   G.

XIII.

De Signaculo Crucis.

Cur tanta sufflas probra in innocuam crucem?
Non plus maligni daemones Christi cruce
Unquam fugari, quam tui socii solent.
Apostolorum culpa non levis fuit
Vitasse Christi spiritum efflantis crucem.
Et Christianus quisque piscis dicitur
Tertulliano, propter undae pollubrum,
Quo tingimur parvi.   Ecquis autem brachiis
Natare sine clarissima potest cruce?
Sed non moramur: namque vestra crux erit,
Vobis faventibusve vel negantibus.

Concerning the Sign of the Cross.

Why 'gainst the harmless Cross do you thus puff
Reproaches keen and fierce and ne'er enough?

Not more precip'tate flee demons malign
Than you and yours before the sacred Sign !
It was of the Apostles no light blame
To eschew Christ's Sp'rit, breathing Cross's shame :
Each Christian, Tertullian styles a fish
From Baptism's waters in the sacred dish
Wherein when we are children we are dipp'd,
And thereby for life's warfare are equipp'd.
Who looks upon the arms of one who swims,
Nor sees the Cross in his outstretchèd limbs?
I will not waste more time : your Cross will come,
Whether you welcome it, or meet it dumb.   G.

XIV.

De Juramento Ecclesiae.

Articulis sacris quidam subscribere jussus,
    Ah, Cheiragra vetat, quo minus, inquit, agam.
O vere dictum et belle ! cum torqueat omnes
    Ordinis osores articulare malum.

Concerning the Church's Oath.

To sign the Articles when one was told,
' Ah, gout forbids my hand a pen to hold !'
O finely said ! when all who order hate
Find rack'd articulations is their fate !   R. WI.

XV.

De Purificatione post Puerperium.

Enixas pueros matres se sistere templis
    Displicet, et laudis tura litare Deo.

Forte quidem, cum per vestras Ecclesia turbas
   Fluctibus internis exagitata natet,
Vos sine maternis hymnis infantia vidit,
   Vitaque neglectas est satis ulta preces.
Sed nos, cum nequeat parvorum lingua parentem
   Non laudare Deum, credimus esse nefas.
Quotidiana suas poscant si fercula grates,
   Nostra caro sanctae nescia laudis erit?
Adde piis animis quaevis occasio lucro est,
   Qua[1] possint humili fundere corde preces.
Sic ubi jam mulier decerpti conscia pomi
   Ingemat ob partus, ceu maledicta, suos,
Apposite quum[2] commotum subfugerat olim,
   Nunc redit ad mitem, ceu benedicta, Deum.

On Purification (= Churching) after Childbirth.
Childbearing mothers you object to find
In God's House, praising Him with grateful mind.
Perchance, since with such waves of mutual strife
The harass'd Kirk of Scotland still was rife,   [years,
No mother's prayers and hymns bless'd your young
And the neglect in your marr'd life appears.
But we, when children's tongue to God is still,
That parent should not praise Him, think it ill:
If for our daily food our thanks we raise,
For our own flesh shall we ascribe no praise?
Nay, pious souls for gain the occasion count   [mount.
When from meek hearts their prayers to heaven may

----

[1] Printed 'Quae.'   [2] Printed 'quem.'

So when a woman, conscious of the gloom
Of the pluck'd apple and the sorrowing womb,
Groans bitterly beneath the Curse's doom,
Rightly does she, escap'd from storm to rest,
Go to her kind Preserver, as one blest.   R. WI.

XVI.

De Antichristi decore Pontificali.

Non quia Pontificum sunt olim afflata veneno,
   Omnia sunt temere projicienda foras.
Tollantur si cuncta malus quae polluit usus,
   Non remanent nobis corpora, non animae.

Concerning the Pontifical Beauty (=decency) of Antichrist.

Not 'cause of old poison'd with Papal breath,
   Are all things to be flung straight out o' door;
If all misusèd things are due to death,
   'Tis time our souls and bodies were no more.   G.

XVII.

De Superpelliceo.

Quid sacrae tandem meruere vestes?
Quas malus livor jaculis lacessit,
Polluens castam chlamydis colorem
          Dentibus atris?

Quicquid ex urna meliore ductum
Luce praelustri, vel honore pollet,
Mens sub insigni specie coloris
          Concipit albi.

Scilicet talem liquet esse solem ;
Angeli vultu radiante candent ;
Incolae coeli melioris alba
                    Veste triumphant.

E creaturis sine mentis usu
Conditis binas homini sequendas
Spiritus proponit, et est utrique
                    Candor amicus.[1]

Ergo ringantur pietatis hostes,
Filii noctis, populus malignus,
Dum suum nomen tenet et triumphat
                    Albion albo.

Concerning the Surplice.

What have the sacred vestments done, I pray,
Which Envy thus assails as beast of prey,
Staining the Surplice's chaste hue, forsooth,
                    With venomous black tooth?

Whate'er's drawn from the heav'nly urn of Brightness,
Or Honour, men conceive of it as whiteness ;
The sun around his glorious circuit turning,
                    Angels in splendour burning.

So the redeemèd throng from Earth below,
Cloth'd in the blood-bought raiments white as snow ;
Yea look on Sheep and Dove, by whom Christ teacheth,
                    The favour'd White still preacheth.

[1] Ovis et columba.   Columel. l. 7. c. 2, and l. 8. c. 8.

Then let Religion's foes, the sons of Night,
Gnash their malignant teeth in jealous spite,
So long as Albion by ' white' is named,
　　　　Nor of ' white' Surplice is ashamèd.　α.

XVIII.

De Pileo Quadrato.

Quae dicteria fuderat Britannus
Superpellicei tremendus hostis,
Isthaec pileus audiit propinquus,
Et partem capitis petit supremam ;
Non sic effugit angulus vel unus
Quo dictis minus acribus notetur.
Verum heus ! si reputes, tibi tuisque
Longe pileus anteit galerum,
Ut fervor cerebri refrigeretur,
Qui vestras edit intime medullas.
Sed qui tam male pileos habetis,
Quos Ecclesia comprobat, verendum
Ne tandem caput ejus impetatis.

Concerning the Square College-cap.

The words of the North-Briton—witty,
Foe of the Surplice, without pity—
The neighb'ring College-cap has heard,
And flies incont'nent, terror-stirr'd,
Right to the upmost part o' the head ;
But even there astonièd

It too must list—for naught escapes—
Sharp twittings from this Jack-o'-napes.
    But, ah, if but ye will attend,
You and each North-Briton friend,
You will see our College-cap
Would better suit you far, mayhap,
Even than that close-fitting hood:
Why ? To cool your hot brains' blood ;
Which consumes—I say't with sorrow—
Even your very inmost marrow.
But ye who treat our cap so badly,
Prating 'gainst it thus so madly,
Which our Church of old approves,
As she decent vestment loves ;
Ah, we have reason much to dread,
Lest next ye should assail her HEAD!   G.

XIX.

In Catharum.

Cur Latiam linguam reris nimis esse profanam ?
   Quam praemissa probant secula, nostra probant ?
Cur teretem Graecam damnas, atque Hellada totam,
   Qua tamen occisi foedera scripta Dei ?
Scilicet Hebraeam cantas, et perstrepis unam :
   Haec facit ad nasum sola loquela tuum.

To a Puritan.

The Latin tongue why common dost thou deem,
Which former ages and our own esteem ?

Why the smooth Greek, and Hellas all disdain,
Which holds the Covenants of the Godhead slain?
Hebrew, forsooth, you sing and sound alone,
Because that language suits your nasal tone!   n. wl.

XX.

De Episcopis.

Quos charos habuit Christus Apostolos
Testatosque suo tradiderat gregi ;
Ut cum mors rabidis unguibus imminens
Doctrinae fluvios clauderet aureae,
Mites acciperent Lampada Praesules,
Servarentque sacrum clavibus ordinem ;
Hos nunc barbaries impia vellicat
Indulgens propriis ambitionibus,
Et quos ipsa nequit scandere vertices
Hos ad se trahere, et mergere gestiens.
O coecum populum ! si bona res siet
Praesul, cur renuis? sin mala, pauculos
Quam cunctos fieri praestat Episcopos.

Concerning Bishops.

Holy Apostles, whom the Saviour lov'd,
And to His flock commended as approv'd,
That, when impending Death fierce-talon'd rose
His golden Doctrine's living streams to close,
Such Rulers mild the sinking torch might seize,
And the blest Order keep with power of keys ;

An impious rudeness now plucks at these heights,
Indulging its ambitions and its spites;
And since it cannot reach, itself, this crown,
Eager to drag it to the earth, or drown.
O blinded people! if a Bishop be
A good thing, why refuse it wantonly?
If bad, 'tis well to have them very few,
And not have all men bishops over you!　　R. WI.

XXI.

De iisdem: ad Melvinum.

Praesulibus dirum te Musa coarguit hostem:
An quia textores artificesque probas?

Concerning the same : to Melville.

To prelates the Muse proves thee a dire foe;
Weavers and workmen is't thou lovest so?　　R. WI.

XXII.

De Textore Catharo.

Cum piscatores Textor legit esse vocatos,
　　Ut sanctum Domini persequerentur opus;
Ille quoque invadit Divinam Flaminis artem,
　　Subtegmen reti dignius esse putans,
Et nunc perlongas Scripturae stamine telas
　　Torquet, et in textu doctor utroque cluet.

Concerning a Puritan Weaver.

That fishermen were call'd, a Weaver heard,
To do the work of Christ, and preach His Word;

So at the priestly office straight he caught;
'A shirt more noble than a net,' he thought.
Long yarns he twists a Scripture thread around,
For text and texture equally renown'd !   R. WI.

XXIII.
De Magicis Rotatibus.

Quos tu rotatus, quale murmur auscultas
In ritibus nostris? Ego audio nullum.
Age, provocemus usque ad angelos ipsos
Auresque superas: arbitri ipsi sint litis,
Utrum tenore sacra nostra sint, nec ne
Aequabili facta.   Ecquid ergo te tanta
Calumniandi concitavit urtica,
Ut quae Papicolis propria, assuas nobis,
Falsumque potius, quam crepes versu ?·
Tu perstrepis tamen; utque tingeat carmen
Tuum tibi, poëta belle non mystes
Magicos rotatus, et perhorridas striges,   vers. 33
Dicteriis mordacibus notans, clausus
Non convenire precibus ista Divinis.
O saevus hostis ! quam ferociter pugnas !
Nihilne respondebimus tibi?   Fatemur.

Concerning Magical Circles.

What circlings and what murmur hearest thou
In our Church-rites?   I hear none, I avow.
Come, let us give a challenge, ev'n above,
To angels and all ears in realms of Love ;

Let them the umpires of our strife now be,
Whether our sacred rites they do not see
To have been form'd with equal-flowing course,
Neither too slack, nor with immoderate force.
What fresh itch stings you to calumniate,
And patch on us things popish that we hate?
Chatt'ring all falsely, and thy lines to swell,
Like ill-instructed bard, in sarcasms tell
Of magic circlings, and screech-owls malign,
Crying, 'O how unfit for prayers divine!'
Harsh enemy, how savagely you fight!
Shall we reply naught to thee?   We own all: good-
       night!   G.

XXIV.

Ad Fratres.

O sacclum lepidum! circumstant undique Fratres,
    Papicolisque sui sunt Catharisque sui.
Sic nunc plena boni sunt omnia Fratris, amore
    Cum nil fraterno rarius esse queat.

On the Brethren.

Fine age! on all sides brethren stand—no less.
Papists and Puritans each theirs possess.
So now 'Good brother' you may hear all round;
Though nought more rare than brotherly love is found.
                             '   R. WI.

XXV.

De labe maculisque.

Labeculas maculasque, nobis objicis:
Quid? hoccine est mirum? Viatores sumus.
Quo sanguis est Christi, nisi ut maculas lavet,
Quas spargit animae corporis propius lutum?
Vos ergo puri! O nomen appositissimum
Quo vulgus ornat vos! At audias parum;
Astronomus olim, ut fama, dum maculas diu,
Quas luna habet, tuetur, in foveam cadit,
Totusque caenum Cynthiae ignoscit notis.
Ecclesia est mihi luna; perge in fabula.

On Spots and Blemishes.

Small spots and blemishes in us appear;
Why, is this wonderful? we're travellers here.
Is not Christ's blood to wash the stains away
Which the soul takes from contact with base clay?
Ye're Puritans indeed!   Appropriate style
Which the crowd decks you with!   But list awhile.
Once an astronomer, as he eyes long
The spots which to the silvery moon belong,
Falls in a ditch; with mire all cover'd o'er,
Of spots upon the moon he thinks no more.
The Church of England is to me the moon:
Follow the fable—and fulfil it soon!   R. WI.

XXVI.

De Musica Sacra.

Cur efficaci, Deucalion, manu,
Post restitutos fluctibus obices,
    Mutas in humanam figuram
        Saxa supervacuasque cautes?

Quin redde formas, O bone, pristinas,
Et nos reducas ad lapides avos:
    Nam saxa mirantur canentes,
        Saxa lyras citharasque callent.

Rupes tenaces et silices ferunt
Potentiori carmine percitas
    Saltus per incultos lacusque
        Orphea mellifluum secutas.

Et saxa diris hispida montibus
    Amphionis testitudine nobili
        Percussa dum currunt ad urbem,
            Moenia contribuere Thebis.

Tantum repertum est trux hominum genus,
Qui templa sacris expoliant choris,
    Non erubescentes vel ipsas
        Duritia superare cautes.

O plena centum musica gratiis,
Praeclariorum spirituum cibus,
    Quo me vocas tandem, tuumque
        Ut celebrem decus insusurras?

Tu Diva miro pollice spiritum
Caeno profani corporis exuens
    Ter millies caelo reponis :
        Astra rogant, Novus hic quis hospes ?
Ardore Moses concitus entheo,
Mersis revertens laetus ab hostibus
    Exsuscitat plebem sacratos
        Ad Dominum properare cantus.
Quid hocce ? Psalmos audion' ? O dapes !
O succulenti balsama spiritus !
    Ramenta caeli, guttulaeque
        Deciduae melioris orbis !
Quos David, ipsae deliciae Dei,
Ingens piorum gloria Principum,
    Sionis excelsas ad arces
        Cum citharis lituisque miscet.
Miratur aequor finitimum sonos,
Et ipse Jordan sistit aquas stupens;
    Prae quo Tibris vultum recondit,
        Eridanusque pudore fusus.
Tun' obdis aures, grex nove, barbaras,
Et nullus audis ? cantibus obstrepens,
    Ut, quo fatiges verberesque
        Pulpita, plus spatii lucreris ?
At cui videri prodigium potest
Mentes, quietis tympana publicae,
    Discordiis plenas sonoris
        Harmoniam tolerare nullam

Concerning Sacred Music.

Deucalion, why, with wondrous hand,
When their old banks the waves withstand,
    The rocks and useless stones dost take,
    And thence the human figure make ?

Nay, kindly our old forms restore,
Leave us the stones we were of yore ;
    For rocks the voice of song admire,
    Rocks answer to the lute and lyre.

The stedfast cliffs and flints, they say,
Stirr'd by some mighty moving lay,
    Through lake and wilderness and wood
    The sweet-voic'd Orpheus once pursu'd.

And shaggy rocks from mountains dire,
Smit by Amphion's noble lyre,
    While ancient Thebes they gather'd round,
    A strong protecting wall were found.

To cruel mankind it remains
God's House to rob of hallow'd strains ;
    Yea, and they blush not when, alas,
    E'en rocks in hardness they surpass.

O Music, of all graces blent,
Of noble souls blest aliment,
    Whither dost whisper me away
    To celebrate thy praise to-day?

Thou, goddess, dost the soul divorce
From contact with the body coarse,

And oft in heaven dost bid it rest ;
The stars ask : ' Who is this new guest ?'

Exultant o'er his whelmèd foes,
Moses, with zeal inspir'd, arose,
   And summon'd Israel's sacred throng
   To lift on high their timbrell'd song.

What's this ?   Psalms do I hear ?   O feast !
O balsam of the drooping breast !
   Sweet bits of heaven and dewdrops clear
   Down-sliding from a happier sphere ;

Which David, the Lord's own delight—
Of pious kings the pride and might—
   Seated on Zion's turrets high,
   Mix'd with his harp melodiously.

The sound amazes Ocean near,
And Jordan stays his stream to hear ;
   Tiber to Jordan veils his face,
   And Po is cover'd with disgrace.

Your barbarous ears, strange race, d'ye close,
And not one hears ?   Hymns ye oppose,
   That ye the time may lengthen out,
   To beat the pulpit and to shout.

To wonder, surely, men may cease,
That minds, the drums of public peace,
   Fill'd full of all discordant hate,
   No harmony can tolerate !   R. WI.

XXVII.

De eadem.

Cantus sacros, profane, mugitus vocas?
Mugire multo mavelim quam rudere.

Concerning the same.

Our sacred songs are bellowings, dost thou say?
To bellow I think better far than bray.   R. WI.

XXVIII.

De Rituum Usu.

Cum primum ratibus suis
Nostram Caesar ad insulam
Olim appelleret, intuens
Omnes indigenas loci
Viventes sine vestibus,
O victoria, clamitat,
Certa ac perfacilis mihi !
   Non alio Cathari modo
Dum sponsam Domini piis
Orbam ritibus expetunt,
Atque ad barbariem patrum
Vellent omnia regredi,
Illam tegminis insciam
Prorsus daemoni, et hostibus
Exponunt superabilem.
   Atqui vos secus, o boni,
Sentire sapere addecet,

Si vestros animos regant
Scripturae canones sacrae :
Namque haec, jure, cuipiam
Vestem non adimi suam,
Sed nudis et egentibus
Non suam tribui jubet.

Concerning the Use of Ceremonies.

When Cæsar steer'd to Britain's shore,
With his great fleet in days of yore,
Seeing the natives of the place
To have of clothing not a trace,
He cried out as they caught his eye,
' O certain and easy victory !'
    Just so, the Puritans austere,
While they the Lord's Spouse would strip bare
Of all ceremonies holy,—
Howe'er reverent and lowly ;
Seeking with perverse earnestness,
Such as nor God nor man may bless
Forefathers' rudeness primitive
To go back on, and revive.
    Thus would they straightway her expose,
Destitute of seemly clothes,
To the Devil and enemies,
Conqu'ring easily as so she lies.
    But, good friends, false is your zeal,
Far otherwise ought ye to feel,

If Holy Scripture rule your minds,
And to its precepts conscience binds;
For Scripture precepts plainly say,
Clothing from no one take away;
Nay, that to naked and to needy
We succour give and clothing speedy.   G.

XXIX.

De Annulo Conjugali.

Sed nec conjugii signum, Melvine, probabis?
    Nec vel tantillum pignus habebit amor?
Nulla tibi si signa placent, e nubibus arcum
    Eripe caelesti qui moderatur aquae.
Illa quidem a nostro non multum abludit imago,
    Annulus et plenus tempore forsan erit.
Sin nebulis parcas, et nostro parcito signo,
    Cui non absimilis sensus inesse solet.
Scilicet, ut quos ante suas cum conjuge tedas
    Merserat in lustris perniciosa Venus,
Annulus hos revocet, sistatque libidinis undas
    Legitimi signum connubiale tori.

Concerning the Wedding-Ring.

Of wedlock's symbol dost thou not approve?
So small a pledge wilt thou deny to love?
If no signs please thee, bid the braided bow
Which stays the rain of heaven to hide its glow.
A ring and rainbow well may go together,
Both may be tokens of the coming weather.

So, if you spare the bow, our symbol spare,
Which may a meaning not unlike it bear;
Since those whom hurtful love in mire had drown'd
Before the comfort of a wife was found,
The ring may rescue, and lust's waves arrest,
Of lawful marriage joy the symbol blest.   n. wi.

XXX.

De Mundis et Mundanis.

Ex praelio undae ignisque, si physicis fides,
        Tranquillus aër nascitur:
Sic ex profano Cosmico et Catharo potest
        Christianus extundi bonus.

Concerning Puritans and Worldlings.

To strife of fire and water, naturalists say,
        Calm atmosphere is due;
So from a Worldling and a Puritan may
        Be found a Christian true.   R. WI.

XXXI.

De Oratione Dominica.

Quam Christus immortalis innocuo gregi
        Voce sua dederat,
                Quis crederet mortalibus
Orationem rejici septemplicem,
                Quae miseris clypeo
                        Ajacis est praestantior?

Haec verba, superos advolaturus thronos
      Christus, ut auxilii
         Nos haud inanes linqueret,
Cum dignius nil posset aut melius dare,
      Pignora cara sui
         Fruenda nobis tradidit.
Quis sic amicum excipiet, ut Cathari Deum,
      Qui renovare sacri
         Audent amoris symbolum?
Tu vero quisquis es, cave, ne dum neges,
      Improbe, verba Dei,
         Te deneget VERBUM Deus.

Concerning the Lord's Prayer.

The Pray'r of the Lord Jesus sevenfold
More excellent than shield of Ajax old
For wretched ones; Pray'r which with His own voice
He gave to cause His innocent Flock rejoice,—
Who would believe mortals should it neglect,
Nay, as 'twere e'en an evil thing, reject?
    Those holy words He, Ever-living One,
Ere He left earth, ascending to His throne,
Bestow'd—nought sweeter had He to bestow—
That we might none of us unsuccour'd go:
Pledges of Heaven, giving joy below.
As Puritans their God, who would treat friend,
Daring Love's sacred symbol thus to rend?
Beware, lest while God's words thou dost deny,
The Word of God deny thee from on high !   c.

XXXII.

In Catharum quendam.

Cum templis effare, madent sudaria, mappae,
    Trux caper alarum, suppara, laena, sagum.
Quin populo, clemens, aliquid largire caloris:
    Nunc sudas solus; caetera turba riget.

To a certain Puritan.

When thou dost preach in church, the sweat runs down
Thy handkerchief and bands and coat and gown.
A little heat be to the rest allow'd;
Thou only dost perspire—stark sits the crowd.   R. WI.

XXXIII.

De Lupa lustri Vaticani.

Calumniarum nec pudor quis nec modus,
Nec Vaticanae desines unquam lupae?
Metus inanes! Nos pari praetervehi
Illam Charybdim cautione novimus
Vestramque Scyllam, aequis parati spiculis
Britannicam in vulpem inque Romanam lupam.
Dicti fidem firmabimus anagrammate.

Concerning the She-Wolf of the Vatican Puddle.

Is there no bound or blush to calumny?
Shall ' Roman she-wolf' be your ceaseless cry?
Vain are your fears !   We know with equal care
To sail by that Charybdis, and beware

Your Scylla; with our darts prepar'd alike
The British fox and Roman wolf to strike;
And our sincerity to carry home,
Here is a stinging anagram on Rome.　　　　r. wi.

XXXIV.

De Impositione Manuum.

Nec dextra te fugit almi amoris emblema?
Atqui manus imponere integras praestat
Quam, more vestro, imponere inscio vulgo.
Quanto impositio melior est impostura!

Concerning Imposition of Hands.

And so this emblem meet of fostering love
Thou thinkest needful also to reprove?
But to impose pure hands, 'twill be allow'd,
Excels your way,—to impose on the dull crowd.
Such imposition, surely all will say,
Is better than imposture, any day.　　　　r. wi.

XXXV.

Supplicum Ministrorum Raptus κωμῳδούμενος.

Ambitio Cathari quinque constat actibus.
 1. Primo, unus aut alter parum ritus placet.
　　Jam repit impietas volatura illico.
 11. Mox displicent omnes.　Ubi hoc permanscrit
 111. Paulo, secretis mussitans in angulis
　　Quaerit recessus.　Incalescit fabula,

iv. Erumpit inde, et continere nescius
  v. Sylvas pererrat. Fibulis dein omnibus
     Prae spiritu ruptis, quo eas resarciat
     Amstellodamum corripit se. Plaudite.

The Petitioning Ministers' Taking-off : treated as a Comedy.
    The progress of a Puritan, his round,
    In these five acts is regularly found.
  i. First, he is scarcely pleas'd with some one rite,
    And then and there he meditates a flight.
 ii. Soon all displease. When this awhile has grown,
iii. Muttering in secret corners with his own,
    He seeks withdrawal. Hotter grows the play,
 iv. He bursts forth now, unable there to stay,
  v. And roams the woods. Then every clasp being rent
    Before the Spirit, see him straightway bent
    To Amsterdam to mend them. Meanwhile hark
    What ' Plaudits' follow his departing bark ! R. WI.

XXXVI.
De Auctorum Enumeratione.

Quo magis invidiam nobis, et crimina confles,
    Pertrahis in partes nomina magna tuas ;
Martyra, Calvinum, Bezam, doctumque Bucerum,
    Qui tamen in nostros fortiter ire negant.
Whitaker, erranti quem praefers carmine, miles
    Assiduus nostrae papilionis erat.
Nos quoque possemus longas conscribere turmas,
    Si numero starent praelia, non animis.

Primus adest nobis, Pharisaeis omnibus hostis,
    Christus Apostolici cinctus amore gregis.
Tu geminas belli portas, o Petre, repandis,
    Dum gladium stringens Paulus ad arma vocat.
Inde Patres pergunt quadrati, et tota Vetustas.
    Nempe novatores quis veteranus amat?
Jam Constantinus multo se milite miscet;
    Invisamque tuis erigit hasta Crucem.
Hipponensis adest properans, et torquet in hostes
    Lampada, qua studiis invigilare solet.
Teque Deum alternis cantans Ambrosius iram,
    Immemor antiqui mellis, eundo coquit.
Haec etiam ad pugnam praesens, qua vivimus, aetas
    Innumeram nostris partibus addit opem.
Quos inter plenusque Deo genioque Jacobus
    Defendit veram mente manuque fidem.
Interea ad sacrum stimulat sacra Musica bellum,
    Qua sine vos miseri lentius itis ope.
Militat et nobis, quem vos contemnitis, Ordo,
    Ordine discerni maxima bella solent.
O vos invalidos! audi quem talibus armis
    Eventum Naso vidit et admonuit;
Una dies Catharos ad bellum miserat omnes:
    Ad bellum missos perdidit una dies.

On the Enumeration of Authors.

The more to give thy envious charges way,
Great names upon thy side thou dost display;

World-famous Calvin, Bucer erudite,
Martyr and Beza, thy own chief delight,
Who yet 'gainst us stoutly refuse to fight.
Whitaker, nam'd with a false quantity,
Rank'd with our party you may always see.
We too might muster-up a long array,
If numbers, and not spirit, won the day.
Foe to all Pharisees first see Christ stand,
Girt with His loving Apostolic band;
While Peter opens the twin gates of war,
Paul with drawn sword to battle calls from far;
Next go the Fathers in a mighty square,
And all Antiquity, in arms, is there;
What ancient can raw innovators bear?
Now Constantine with his vast host draws nigh,
The Cross thou hatest on a spear rais'd high;
Augustine, hastening, hurls against the foe
The torch which o'er his midnight task would glow;
In strains alternate, praising God, Ambrose,
Mindless of dew from classic hives which flows,
Nurses his wrath against you as he goes;
And for the fight, this present living age
Succour untold on our side can engage;
James, in whose soul Godhead and genius blend,
With mind and hand the true faith will defend.
To sacred war hear sacred Music call;
Without whose aid your poor ranks falter all.
Order, which you despise, fights on our side;

Order is wont great battles to decide.
O ye poor strengthless ones! the issue know,
Which Ovid sang to such arms long ago :
Behold, to battle one day sent them all,
And, sent to battle, one day saw them fall !   R. WI.

XXXVII.

De Auri sacra Fame.

Claudis avaritia satyram, statuisque sacrorum
    Esse recidendas, Aeace noster, opes.
Caetera condonabo tibi, scombrisque remittam :
    Sacrilegum carmen, censeo, flamma voret.

Concerning the accursed Hunger for Gold.

Your satire ends with avarice, and you say
That our endowments must be cut away,
The Æacus of this our modern day.
To thee and thine the rest I will condone ;
But for such sacrilegious verse, I own,
Devouring fire must be reserv'd alone.   R. WI.

XXXVIII.

Ad Scotiam Protrepticon ad Pacem.

Scotia, quae frigente jaces porrecta sub Arcto,
    Cur adeo immodica relligione cales ?
Anne tuas flammas ipsa Antiperistasis auget,
    Ut nive torpentes incaluere manus ?
Aut ut pruna gelu summo mordacius urit,
    Sic acuunt zelum frigora tanta tuum ?

Quin nocuas extingue faces, precor: unda propinqua est,
    Et tibi vicinas porrigit aequor aquas;
Aut potius Christi sanguis demissus ab alto,
    Vicinusque magis nobiliorque fluit:
Ne, si flamma novis adolescat mota flabellis,
    Ante diem vestro mundus ab igne ruat.

To Scotland: an Exhortation to Peace.

Scotland, outstretcht beneath the freezing North,
Why such immoderate Church-heat dost put forth?
By force of contraries do thy flames glow,
As hands benumb'd have gather'd warmth from snow?
Or as in frosts more heat from coal we feel,
Does thy chill climate sharpen-up thy zeal?
Nay, quench thy hurtful flames, water is nigh,
On either hand contiguous oceans lie.
Or, better still, Christ's blood pour'd down from heaven,
A nearer and a nobler stream is given;
Lest if thy flames, stirr'd by new fans, should grow,
Earth from your fire to untimely ruin go.   R. WI.

XXXIX.

Ad seductos Innocentes.

Innocuae mentes, quibus inter flumina mundi
    Ducitur illimi candida vita fide,
Absit ut ingenuum pungant mea verba pudorem;
    Perstringunt vestros carmina sola duces.
O utinam aut illorum oculi, quod comprecor unum,
    Vobis, aut illis pectora vestra forent!

To Innocent ones led astray.

O innocent minds, who this earth's tumults thread
With fair white life by faith unspotted led,
Far be it my words should hurt your modesty,
Or even smite your leaders angrily.
O would their eyes—'tis my one prayer to Heav'n—
Were given to you,—your breasts to them were given!

C.

XL.
Ad Melvinum.

Atqui te precor unice per ipsam,
Quae scripsit numeros, manum; per omnes
Musarum calices, per et beatos
Sarcasmos quibus artifex triumphas;
Quin per Presbyteros tuos; per urbem
Quam curto nequeo referre versu;
Per caras tibi nobilesque dextras,
Quas subscriptio neutiquam inquinavit;
Per quicquid tibi suaviter probatur;
Ne me carminibus nimis dicacem,
Aut saevum reputes.   Amica nostra est
Atque edentula Musa, nec veneno
Splenis perlita contumeliosi.

Nam si te cuperem secare versu,
Totamque evomerem potenter iram
Quam aut Ecclesia despicata vobis,
Aut laesae mihi suggerunt Athenae,
Et quem non stimularet haec simultas,

Jam te funditus igneis Camoenis,
Et Musa crepitante subruissem :
Omnis linea sepiam recusans
Plumbo ducta fuisset aestuanti,
Centum stigmatibus tuos inurens
Profanos fremitus bonasque sannas :
Plus charta haec mea delibuta dictis
Haesisset tibi, quam suprema vestis
Olim accreverit Herculi furenti :
Quin hoc carmine lexicon probrorum
Extruxissem, ubi, cum moneret usus,
Haurirent tibi tota plaustra Musae.

　　Nunc haec omnia sustuli, tonantes
Affectus sociis tuis remittens.
Non deridiculumve sive ineptum,
Non striges magiamve vel rotatus,
Non fastus tibi turgidos repono ;
Errores, maculas superbiamque,
Labes somniaque ambitusque diros,
Tinnitus Berecynthios omittens
Nil horum regero tibi merenti.

　　Quin te laudibus orno : quippe dico,
Caesar sobrius ad rei Latinae
Unus dicitur advenire cladem :
Et tu solus ad Angliae procellas,
Cum plerumque tua sodalitate
Nil sit crassius impolitiusve,
Accedis bene doctus, et poëta.

To Melville.

Now your ear, I pray thee, lend.
By the hand thy poem penn'd;
By the sacred founts which flow
Where the Muses' footsteps go ;
By thy artist-powers sarcastic,
Keen, triumphant, trenchant, drastic ;
Nay, by thine own Presbyters, and
By the chief city of thy land,   Edinburgh
Which in short verse I'd fail to name ;
By the right-hands thou wilt not blame,
Noble, venerable, holy,
Lov'd of highest and of lowly ;
Right-hands on which e'en thou canst smile,
Which ne'er SUBSCRIPTION did defile ;
By all that doth itself approve
As sweet to thee, and wins thy love,—
Do not count me harsh, severe ;
My Muse is toothless and sincere,
Nor would with Spleen's abuse besmear.
For if I wish'd in cutting verse
Thy many failings to rehearse,
Or if indeed I should desire
To pour forth all the mighty ire
Which THE CHURCH, by thee despisèd,
And LEARNING, wroth, as she's advisèd,
Of thy scholarship misus'd
And of thy genius abus'd,

Might suggest—I should thee scorn,
And in passionate anger burn;
And whom would not this jealousy
Spur to indignation high?
Then I should thee have overwhelm'd,
Rushing on thee like warrior helm'd;
While along my fiery page
The Muse should thunder forth its rage
In ev'ry line—refusing ink
Fast as I could my vengeance think;
I should with furious leaded pen
Have torn thy verse 'gain and again;
Branding thy mutterings profane,
Thy pretty grimaces o'er thy strain;
And thus my page of pois'nous ire
Have clung to thee like shirt of fire
That clave to Hercules loud-raging,
Naught his agony assuaging;
Nay, in this very poem now
I should have pilèd-up aglow
A lexicon of reproachful words,
Whence the Muses, as sharp swords,
Might have chosen a wagon-load
O' weapons thee to smite and goad.

    Now all these things I have borne,
Nor thund'ring passions have me torn;
These to thy coarse friends resigning,
Still envious and still maligning.

I have not call'd thee in my verse
' Fierce,' ' ridic'lous,' ' absurd,' or worse ;
I do not give thee back in taunt
' Screech-owls,' ' magic-circles,' ' avaunt,'
Nor 'swollen-pride,' nor terms accusing,
All charity and ruth refusing ;
Passing o'er ' errors,' ' spots,' ' blots,' ' state,'
' Ambitions dire' and ' dreams' elate,
Yea ' Berecynthian tinkling,' and all ;
I don't retaliate or mis-call
Thee,—the heaviest deserving,
Full-giv'n, and with hand unswerving ;
Nay, with my praise I thee adorn,
Nor to place thee with Cæsar scorn ;
Cæsar sober found alone
In the Commonwealth o'erthrown.
And now thee alone I see,
Midst thy brutal company
That seeks to wreck our Church august,
And hurl it prone unto the dust,
Thoroughly learn'd and poet, such
As words are weak to praise too much.   o.

XLI.

Ad eundem.

Incipis irridens ; stomachans in carmine pergis ;
Desinis exclamans : tota figura vale.

To the same.

First mocking, storming next, thy verses swell ;
Shouting thou endest : every style farewell.   n. wi.

XLII.

Ad seren. Regem.

Ecce pererratas, regum doctissime, nugas,
Quas gens inconsulta, suis vexata procellis
Libandas nobis absorbendasque propinat ;
O caecos animi fratres ! quis vestra fatigat
Corda furor, spissaque afflat caligine sensus ?
Cernite quam formosa suas Ecclesia pennas
Explicat, et radiis ipsum pertingit Olympum ;
Vicini populi passim mirantur, et aequos
Mentibus attonitis cupiunt addiscere ritus ;
Angelicae turmae nostris se coetibus addunt ;
Ipse etiam Christus coelo speculatus ab alto
Intuituque uno stringens habitacula mundi,
Sola mihi plenos, ait, exhibet Anglia cultus.
Scilicet has olim divisas aequore terras
Seposuit Divina sibi, cum conderet orbem,
Progenies gemmamque sua quasi pyxide clausit.

    O qui Defensor Fidei meritissimus audis,
Responde aeternum titulo ; quoque ordine felix
Coepisti, pergas simili res texere filo.
Obrue ferventes, ruptis conatibus, hostes ;
Quasque habet aut patulas aut caeco tramite, moles
Haeresis, evertas.   Quid enim te fallere possit ?

Tu venas laticesque omnes quos sacra recludit
Pagina gustasti, multoque interprete gaudes ;
Tu Synodosque Patresque et quod dedit alta vetustas
Haud per te moritura, Scholamque introspicis omnem.
Nec transire licet quo mentis acumine findis
Viscera naturae, commistusque omnibus astris
Ante tuum tempus coelum gratissimus ambis.
Hac ope munitus securior excipis undas,
Quas Latii Catharique movent, atque inter utrasque
Pastor agis proprios, medio tutissimus, agnos.

    Perge, decus Regum ; sic, Augustissime, plures
Sint tibi vel stellis laudes et laudibus anni ;
Sic pulsare tuas, exclusis luctibus, ausint
Gaudia sola fores ; sic quicquid somnia mentis
Intus agunt, habeat certum meditatio finem ;
Sic positis nugis, quibus irretita libido
Innumeros mergit vitiata mente poëtas,
Sola Jacobaeum decantent carmina nomen.

To his most Serene Majesty [James I.].

Behold, at last, most erudite of kings,
We have discuss'd in full the trifling things
Which an unwise race, hither, thither blown,
Offers to us to taste and make our own.
O brethren blind, what madness wraps your souls,
And with pitch-darkness round your senses rolls ?
Behold our beauteous Church its plumes unfold,
And brush the very sky with wings of gold.

All neighbouring peoples wonder, and desire,
With minds amaz'd, our just rites to acquire.
Angelic bands with our assemblies join,
And Christ Himself, from heavenly heights divine
Down-looking, and with one glance of His eye
Surveying all earth's dwellings easily,
Says: England only My full service yields.
Forsooth, of old these ocean-sunder'd fields
Christ for Himself claim'd when the world He made,
And in a box as 'twere His jewel laid,
' Defender of the Faith !' O most just style,
Fulfil thy title always, as erewhile.
Nobly thou hast begun—to all 'tis clear ;
In the same line of action persevere.
Break their attempts, confound the fervid foe ;
All the designs of Heresy o'erthrow,
Open or secret, howsoe'er She go.
What can deceive thee? Thou hast tasted all
The secret springs and waters, great or small,
Which Holy Writ unfolds ; and dost rejoice
In them, and in the exegetic voice
Of many a scholar.   Thou dost look within
Synods and Fathers, and whate'er we win
From the far depths of hoar Antiquity,
Never to perish now, by means of thee ;
Through every School thy footsteps wander free.
Nor is it possible the bounds to find
Of that acute discernment of the mind

With which great Nature's secrets thou dost probe ;
And quitting ere thy time this earthly globe,
To mingle with the stars to thee is given,
And walk, a welcome guest, the floor of Heaven.
Arm'd with these aids thou dost securely scan
The agitating waves of Puritan
And Papist, and between them, as they rock,
Dost lead, as a good shepherd, thine own flock
The middle way, safest from danger's shock.

Glory of kings, go on ! thus mayst thou see,
O most august, more praises given to thee
Than stars are counted in the evening sky ;
And may thy years thy praises still outvie.
So, knocking at thy door may only joys
Dare to appear, while far away the noise
Of grief is banish'd.   So, what dreams soe'er
Dwell in my mind, be it my only care
That all my thoughts a certain issue bear.
So, trifles laid aside with which lust binds
Innumerable Poets, whose base minds
Are plung'd in folly ; be it my sole aim
That all my verses chant great James's name.   R. WI.

XLIII.

Ad Deum.

Quem tu, summe Deus, semel
Scribentem placido rore beaveris,
   Illum non labor irritus

Exercet miserum ; non dolor unguium
  Morsus increpat anxios ;
Non macret calamus ; non queritur caput :
  Sed fecunda poëseως
Vis, et vena sacris regnat in artubus ;
  Qualis nescius aggerum
Exundat fluvio Nilus amabili.
  O dulcissime spiritus
Sanctos, qui gemitus mentibus inseris
  A te turture defluos,
Quod scribo, et placeo, si placeo, tuum est.

To God.

On whom Thy blessing, Lord, descendeth,
When soft as dew his strains he blendeth,
Him no more vain toil perplexeth,
Nor nail-biting trouble vexeth ;
His pen mourns not, his head aches not ;
But Nile-like from its fountain shot
Bounds along its far-drawn course
With an unrestrainèd force,
The fecund strength of Poesy,
And the vein that in it doth lie,
Reign in scarce-measurable wealth,
Giving to mind and body health.
 O most sweet celestial Spirit,
From Whom these breathings we inherit,
Murmurings of quiet love
Flowing down from Thee, the Dove,—
That I write and that each line
Pleases, if it please, is Thine.   G.

VII.

ALIA POEMATA LATINA.

OTHER LATIN POEMS.

I.

Ad Auctorem Instaurationis Magnae [Franciscum Bacon].

Per strages licet auctorum veterumque ruinam
    Ad famae properes vera tropaea tuae,
Tam nitide tamen occidis, tam suaviter hostes,
    Se quasi donatum funere quisque putat.
Scilicet apponit pretium tua dextera fato,
    Vulnereque emanat sanguis, ut intret honos.
O quam felices sunt, qui tua castra sequuntur,
    Cum per te sit res ambitiosa mori !

To the Author of the Instauratio Magna, Francis Bacon.

Although the Ancients thou o'erthrowest,
And their many errors showest,
Building up trophies of thy fame,
Placing 'mong greatest thy proud name ;
So tenderly thou dost them kill,
Not even death can they take ill;
In sooth, beneath thy hand to fall,
Destruction seems a prize to all.
When from the wound the blood flows forth
Honour flows in t' exalt their worth.

O, then, how favour'd must they be
Who to the battle follow thee,
When even at thy hands to die
Puts fire into Ambition's eye!   *a.*

II.

In honorem illustrissimi Domini Francisci de Verulamio, Vice-Comitis Sti Albani.

Post editam ab eo Instaur. Magnam.

Quis iste tandem? non enim vultu ambulat
Quotidiano.   Nescis, ignare? audies.
Dux Notionum; Veritatis Pontifex;
Inductionis Dominus et Verulamii;
Rerum Magister Unicus, at non Artium;   5
Profunditatis Pinus atque Elegantiae;
Naturae Aruspex intimus; Philosophiae
Acrarium; Sequester Experientiae
Speculationisque; Acquitatis Signifer;
Scientiarum sub pupillari statu   10
Degentium olim Emancipator; Luminis
Promus; Fugator Idolum atque Nubium;
Collega Solis; Quadra Certitudinis;
Sophismatum Mastix; Brutus Literarius,
Authoritatis exuens Tyrannidem;   15
Rationis et Sensus Stupendus Arbiter;
Repumicator mentis; Atlas Physicus,
Alcide succumbente Stagiritico;
Columba Noae, quae in vetustate Artibus

Nullum locum requiemque cernens, praestitit   20
Ad se suamque matris, arcam regredi ;
Subtilitatis terebra ; Temporis nepos
Ex Veritate matre ; mellis alveus ;
Mundique et animarum Sacerdos unicus ;
Securisque errorum ; inque natalibus   25
Granum sinapis, acre aliis, crescens sibi ;
    O me prope lassum ! Juvate Posteri.

GEOR. HERBERT,
Orat. Pub. in Academ. Cantab.[1]

*To the honour of the most illustrious Francis, Baron Verulam,
Viscount St. Albans, on the publication of the Instauratio
Magna.*

Who is this approaching, pray ?
'Tis not a face seen ev'ry day :
Knowest thou not, ignorant one,
Gazing astonied as he pass'd on ?
Listen to me, and thou shalt hear,
As eager to me thou drawest near :
'Tis the Prince of Ideas great,
High-Priest of Truth consecrate,
Lord of Induction and VERULAM ;
Master of all things thou couldst name,
Though ' Master of Arts' give him not fame ;

[1] In a MS. contemporary copy in possession of the Duke
of Devonshire (erroneously signed ' Gulielmus Herbert') there
are these slight variations : l. 14, ' matrix ;' l. 19, ' vetustatis ;'
l. 20, ' perstitit ;' l. 21, ' suamqne ;' l. 25, ' Naturalibus.' It is
headed ' D. D. Verulamij . . . Al. magni sigilli Custodis . . . In-
staurationem magnam.' G.

Like a pine that towers on high,
Strong-rooted, yet tapering gracefully ;
Inmost diviner Nature hath,
Tracking her every secret path ;
Umpire of Experience golden,
And all Speculation olden ;
Of Equity the standard-bearer ;
Of Science the deliverance-sharer,—
For ere he came Science was bound,
In statu pupillari found ;
Steward of Light, as is the sun ;
Driver away of ' idola,' dun
As clouds that drift the sky athwart;
Four-squar'd foundation of all Art ;
Of Sophisms the mighty scourge,
Let them howe'er wise-seeming urge ;
A Brutus of Lit'rature, off-shaking
Authority,—the tyrant quaking ;
The Brightness of the mental eye ;
Atlas of Natural Philosophy,
When the Hercules-Stagyrite
He with deadly wounds doth smite ;
A Noah's dove, with unresting wing
Flitting o'er all the ancients bring,
Finding nor foot-hold there, nor rest,
And so within itself is blest ;
Fetching from his own mighty brain
What ne'er Antiquity did attain ;

Piercer of nicest subtlety
That in all darkest problems lie ;
Heir of Time, by Truth for mother,
Can the World show such another?
The river-bed of honey flowing,
All richest eloquence still showing ;
Of Earth and Souls the only Priest ;
The Axe of errors, greatest or least ;
At birth a grain of mustard-seed,
To others pungent, found indeed
To itself gathering fame with speed.
O, I am worn his might to tell;
Help me, Posterity, and—farewell!　　　　G.

III.

Comparatio inter Munus Summi Cancellariatus et Librum.

Munere dum nobis prodes, libroque futuris,
　　In laudes abeunt saecula quaeque tuas ;
Munere dum nobis prodes, libroque remotis,
　　In laudes abeunt jam loca quaequo tuas :
Hac tibi sunt alae laudum.　Cui contigit unquam
　　Longius aeterno, latius orbe decus ?

*Comparison between the Office of the Lord High Chancellorship
and (Lord Bacon's) Book (presented to the University).*

Thou with thine Office this our time dost bless,
And with thy Book all future times no less ;
And thus all ages join thy praise to express.

Thou with thine Office blessest this our day,

And with thy Volume countries far away;
All regions to thy praise their tribute pay.

These are the wings of thy illustrious Name:
Who such eternal glory e'er could claim,
Or the high meed of such a world-wide fame?   R. WI.

NOTE.

In Fry's 'Bibliographical Memoranda,' Bristol, 1816 (4to), pp. 188-9, is a poem which is thus described: 'Extracted from a small quarto volume of MS. Latin poetry, containing 40 pages, to which the above name [A. Melvin] is prefixed as that of the author. Its date is nearly ascertained from two poems addressed to James I., and his son Charles as Prince of Wales, consequently after the death of Prince Henry.' The poem is as follows:

'TO THE RIGHT HON. THE LO. CHANCELLOR.
My Lord, a Diamond to mee you sent,
And I to you a Blackamoore present.
Gifts speake the givers, for as those refractions,
Shining and sharpe, poynt out your rare perfections;
So by the other you may read in mee,
Whome Scholler's habite and obscurity
Hath soyl'd with black, the color of my state
Till your bright gift my darknes did abate:
Onely, my noble Lord, shutt not the doore
Agaynst this meane and humble blackamoore;
Perhaps some other subject I had tryed,
But that my inke was factious for that side.'

Fry continues: 'This was addressed to *The Chancellor*, accompanied by a Latin poem, which is subjoined to the MS., *Aethiopissa ambit Cestum diversi coloris virum*. Perhaps it may have been sent to Lord Bacon in return for a copy of his Essays, the volume of which is indeed a Diamond, shining and sharpe, and pointing out his rare perfections. Of the authour, Melvin, I do not trace, in our literary collections, any notice or mention of his name.' It seems abundantly clear that these lines were by George Herbert, not Melville, whose Latinised name, 'Melvin,' misled Fry. The 'Aethiopissa' &c. is one of Herbert's recognised Latin poems. See it in its place next to this. Dr. M'Crie, in his Life of Melville, pointed out Fry's error, or rather the error of his MS.   C.

IV.

Aethiopissa ambit Cestum diversi coloris Virum.

Quid mihi si facies nigra est? hoc, Ceste, colore
    Sunt etiam tenebrae, quas tamen optat amor.
Cernis ut exusta semper sit fronte viator;
    Ah longum, quae te deperit, errat iter.
Si nigro sit terra solo, quis despicit arvum?
    Claude oculos, et erunt omnia nigra tibi :
Aut aperi, et cernes corpus quas projicit umbras ;
    Hoc saltem officio fungar amore tui.
Cum mihi sit facies fumus, quas pectore flammas
    Jamdudum tacite delituisse putes?
Dure, negas?   O fata mihi praesaga doloris,
    Quae mihi lugubres contribuere genas !

A Negress courts Cestus, a Man of a different colour.

What if my face be black?   O Cestus, hear !
Such colour Night brings, which yet Love holds dear.
You see a Trav'ller has a sunburnt face ;
And I, who pine for thee, a long road trace.
If earth be black, who shall despise the ground?
Shut now your eyes, and, lo, all black is found ;
Or ope, a shadow-casting form you see ;
This be my loving post to fill for thee.
Seeing my face is smoke, what fire has burn'd
Within my silent bosom, by thee spurn'd !
Hard-hearted man, dost still my love refuse?
Lo, Grief's prophetic hue my cheek imbues !   G.

V.

In Obitum incomparabilis Vice-Comitis Sancti Albani,
Baronis Verulamii.

Dum longi lentique gemis sub pondere morbi,
    Atque haeret dubio tabida vita pede,
Quid voluit prudens fatum, jam sentio tandem:
    Constat, Aprile uno te potuisse mori:
Ut flos hinc lacrymis, illinc Philomela querelis,
    Deducant linguae funera sola tuae.

On the Death of the incomparable Francis, Viscount St. Albans,
Baron Verulam.

While thou dost groan 'neath weight of sickness slow,
And wasting Life with doubtful step doth go,
What wise Fates sought I see at last fulfill'd;
Thou needs must die in April—so they will'd;
That here the Flowers their tears might weep forlorn,
And there the Nightingale melodious mourn,
Such dirges only fitting for thy tongue,
Wherein all eloquence most surely hung.   G.

VI.

In Natales et Pascha concurrentes.

Cum tù, Christe, cadis, nascor; mentemque ligavit
    Una meam membris horula, teque cruci.
O me disparibus natum cum numine fatis!
    Cur mihi das vitam, quam tibi, Christe, negas?
Quin moriar tecum: vitam, quam negligis ipse,
    Accipe; ni talem des, tibi qualis erat.

Hoc mihi legatum tristi si funere praestes,
  Christe, duplex fiet mors tua vita mihi :
Atque ibi per te sanctificer natalibus ipsis,
  In vitam, et nervos Pascha coaeva fluet.

On (my) Birthday and Good-Friday coinciding.

While Thou, O Christ, dost droop, lo, I am born ;
One little hour Thee to the Cross forlorn
Binds, and my soul to flesh.   How strange that I
Should then be born when Thou, alas, must die !
Why give to me the life Thou dost deny
Unto Thyself?   Nay, I will die with Thee :
The life Thou dost neglect accept from me,
Unless Thou give to me such life as Thine—
That were a legacy indeed divine,
And thus Thy death a double life would bring
To me, in soul and body—O my King.
Thus were I from my birthday sanctified :
Into my life and limbs with holy tide
Thy Passover that very day should flow,
And all my life with its blest influence glow.   G.

VII.

Ad Johannem Donne, D.D.

De uno Sigillorum ejus, Anchora et Christo.

Quod crux nequibat fixa, clavique additi—
Tenere Christum scilicet, ne ascenderet—
Tuive Christum devocans facundia
Ultra loquendi tempus ; addit Anchora :

Nec hoc abunde est tibi, nisi certae anchorae
Addas Sigillum; nempe symbolum suae
Tibi debet unda et terra certitudinis.
    Quondam fessus Amor, loquens amato,
    Tot et tanta loquens amica, scripsit :
    Tandem et fessa manus dedit Sigillum.

Suavis erat, qui scripta, dolens, lacerando recludi,
Sanctius in regno magni credebat Amoris,
In quo fas nihil est rumpi, donare Sigillum!
    Munde, fluas fugiasque licet, nos nostraque fixi :
    Deridet motus sancta catena tuos.

The same in English.

Although the Cross could not Christ here detain,
Though nail'd unto 't, but He ascends again,
Nor yet thy eloquence here keep Him still,
But only while thou speakst, this Anchor will.
Nor canst thou be content, unless thou to
This certain Anchor add a Seal ; and so
The water and the earth both unto thee
Do owe the symbole of their certainty.

When Love, being weary, made an end
Of kind expressions to his friend,
He writ ; when 's hand could write no more,
He gave the Seal, and so left o're.
How sweet a friend was he, who, being griev'd
His letters were broke rudely up, believ'd

'Twas more secure in great Love's commonweal,
Where nothing should be broke, to add a Seal !
Let the world reel, we and all ours stand sure ;
This holy cable's of all storms secure.   G. H.

On the Anchor-Seal.

When my dear friend could write no more,
He gave this Seal, and so gave o'er.
When winds and waves rose highest, I am sure,
This Anchor keeps my faith ; that, me secure.[1]

VIII.

Cum petit Infantem Princeps, Grantamque Jacobus,
    Quisnam horum major sit, dubitatur, amor.
Vincit more suo Noster : nam millibus, Infans
    Non tot abest, quot nos Regis ab ingenio.

When Charles the Infanta seeks, and James the Cam,
Which love is greater, at a loss I am.
James wins ; with him no man is on a par,
For not in miles the Infanta is so far
From Charles, as we from James in genius are.   R. WI.

IX.

Vero verius ergo quid sit audi :
Verum, Gallice, non libenter audis.[2]

---

[1] From Walton's Life of Herbert.   G.

[2] This is from Martial, Epigr. viii. 76, as pointed out by Professor Mayor in Notes and Queries (first series, vol. ix. p. 301). Because found in Herbert's handwriting, it has hitherto been given to him.   It is printed here simply to correct the error.   G.

What, then, is truer than the truth, give ear:
Frenchman, the truth unwilling thou dost hear.

X.

In Obitum serenissimae Reginae Annae.
(e Lacrymis Cantabrigiensibus.)

Quo te, felix Anna, modo deflere licebit ?
     Cui magnum imperium, gloria major erat :
Ecce meus torpens animus succumbit utrique,
     Cui tenuis fama est, ingeniumque minus.
Quis, nisi qui manibus Briareus, oculisque sit Argus,
     Scribere te dignum vel lacrymare queat ?
Frustra igitur sudo ; superest mihi sola voluptas,
     Quod calamum excusent Pontus et Astra meum :
Namque Annae laudes coelo scribuntur aperto,
     Sed luctus noster scribitur Oceano.

On the Death of her most serene Majesty Queen Anne(of Denmark.)
(From Lacrymae Cantabrigienses.)

How shall I duly mourn blest Anna's name,
Whose power was great, but greater was her fame?
To neither can my mind full justice render,
Whose fame is small, and genius still more slender.
Fitly to weep or write of thee demands
The eyes of Argus and Briareus' hands.
Vain toil ! This joy alone to me remains,
That Sea and Sky excuse my pen's poor pains :
For Anna's praises in the Heavens we trace,
Our grief is written in the Ocean's face.   R. WI

XI.

In Obitum Henrici Principis Walliae.

(Ex Epicedivm Cantabrigiense, In Obitum immaturum, semperq.
deflendum Henrici, &c. 1612.)

Ite, leues, inquam, Parnassia numina, Musae ;
Non ego vos posthac, hederae velatus amictu,
Somnis nescio queis nocturna ad vota vocabo :
Sed nec Cyrrhaei saltus Libethriaue arua
In mea dicta ruaut ; non tam mihi pendula mens est,
Sic quasi diis certem, magnos accerscre montes ;
Nec vaga de summo deducam flumina monte,
Qualia parturiente colunt sub rupe sorores :
Si quas mens agitet moles, dum pectora sacuo
Tota stupent luctu, lacrymisque exaestuet aequis
Spiritus, hi mihi jam montes, haec flumina sunto :
Musa, vale ; et tu, Phoebe, dolor mea carmina dictet ;
Hinc mihi principium : vos, o labentia mentis
Lumina, nutantes paulatim acquirite vires,
Viuite, dum mortem ostendam : sic tempora vestram
Non comedant famam, sic nulla obliuia potent.
Quare age, mens ; effare, precor, quo numine laeso ?
Quae suberant causae ? quid nos committere tantum,
Quod non lanigerae pecudes, non agmina lustrent ?
Annon longa fames miseraeque injuria pestis
Poena minor fuerat, quam fatum Principis aegrum ?
Iam felix Philomela et menti conscia Dido ;
Felices quos bella premunt et plurimus ensis ;
Non metuunt ultra ; nostra infortunia tantum

Fataque fortunasque et spem laescre futuram.
Quod si fata illi longam invidere salutem,
Et patrio regno, sub quo jam Principe nobis
Quid sperare, immo quid non sperare licebat?
Debuit ista pati prima et non nobilis aetas:
Aut cita mors est danda bonis aut longa senectus.
Sic lactare animos et sic ostendere gemmam
Excitat optatus auidos, et ventilat ignem.
Quare etiam nuper Pyrii de pulveris ictu
Principis innocuam servastis numina vitam,
Ut morbi perimant, alioque in pulvere prostet.
Phoebe, tui puduit, quum summo mane redires,
Sol sine sole tuo! quum te tum nubibus atris
Totum offuscari peteres, ut nocte silenti
Humana aeternos agerent praecordia questus,
Tantum etenim vestras, Parcae, non flectit habenas.
Tempus edax rerum, tuque, o mors, improba sola es,
Cui caecas tribuit vires annosa vetustas.
Quid non mutatum est? requierunt flumina cursus;
Plus etiam veteres coelum videre remotum:
Cur ideo verbis tristes effundere curas
Expeto, tanquam haec sic nostri medicina doloris?
Immodicus luctus tacito vorat igne medullas,
Ut fluuio currente, vadum sonat, alta quiescunt.

On the Death of Henry Prince of Wales.

Begone, O trifling Muses! yes, begone,
Ye deities that fork'd Parnassus own!

Not ye, with ivy-fillet round my brow,
Call I in dreams to hear my nightly vow ;
Nor let Crissean nor Libethrian mountains   5
Invade my verse, or pour for me their fountains :
My mind's not so with vanity elate
As that I wish with gods myself to mate ;
To summon mountain-chain or wandering stream,
E'en such as for the sister Muses gleam :   10
If needs I must turn o'er my mighty grief,
While all my heart is dumb, without relief ;
If from my spirit fitting tears do swell,
As labouring I fain my woes would tell,—
Be these my mountains, these my rivers be !   15
Adieu, O Muses, and thou, Phoebus, see
From grief shall flow my songs—not thee, not thee.
Henceforth be ye my Muses, swimming eyes,
Up-gathering such strength as in ye lies,
While I my Prince's mournful death show forth ;   20
So rolling years shall ne'er consume your worth,
Nor dark Oblivion ever drink your fame,
Or stain or raze out his illustrious name.
Come, therefore, come, my Mind ; speak out, I pray,
What god thus wrathful is ; and whence, come, say,   25
Flow woes like ours ? O, ye wool-bearing flocks
Know no such sufferings, no such cruel shocks ;
For, lo, our shepherd-prince, by angry Heaven,
Sudden and swift, alas, from us is riven.
Methinks a wasteful plague had been less curse,   30

Nor had a famine long-drawn-out been worse,
Than mortal sickness of our Prince belov'd,
Toward whom in sweet fealty all hearts mov'd.
Now Philomel, compar'd with us, glad is,
And Dido 'reavèd of her erewhile bliss.   35
Happy are they crush'd by War's frequent sword,—
They have no more to fear of Fates abhorr'd ;
Our dread misfortune, as in gloom we grope,
Is, that woes present quench all future hope.
How lawful 'twas to hope with him for King !   40
Nay, what might we not hope his reign would bring ?
But if the Powers begrudg'd him to us long,
Nor for the Kingdom would his life prolong,
Surely as babe, not in fresh bloom of youth,
We should have borne his loss with smaller ruth ;   45
Or early death, or long-protracted years,
Ought for the good to draw the mourner's tears ;
Thus to delight hearts with a touch of gladness—
Thus just to show a jewel, and then sadness,
Stirs keener longings, fans desire to madness.   50
Why from the damnèd Plot, ye Powers divine,
Sav'd ye his life, by sharp disease to untwine ?
Why cruelly and basely him destroy,
And hide in the dark grave a nation's joy ?
Phœbus, asham'd wast thou, as in clouds dun   55
Thou didst return, a sun without thy sun !
For we did see thee robe thyself in gloom,
That we might wail and plain beside his tomb.

Time, that devours all things, ne'er alters Fate,
And Death has powers which know nor stint nor date.
What changes not? Rivers their courses change ;   61
E'en stars by age forsake their wonted range :
But Fate and Death remain changeless for ever ;
To alter them we hope never, no, never.

    But why with bootless words pour I my grief,   65
As if such medicine e'er could bring relief?
My burning sorrow wastes my inmost strength,—
Sorrow which knows no bounds of depth or length.
Hush, hush, my soul; as in a river's course
The shallow places roar with murmurs hoarse,   70
But the deep current flows with silent force.   G.

XII.

Innupta Pallas, nata Diespatre,
Aeterna summae gloria regiae ;
    Cui dulcis arrident Camoenae
        Pieridis Latiaeque Musae.

Cur tela mortis, vel tibi vel tuis
Quacunque gutta temporis imminent ?
    Tantaque propendet statera
        Regula sanguinolenta fati ?

Numne Hydra talis tantaque bellua est
Mors tot virorum sordida sanguine,
    Ut mucro rumpatur Minervae,
        Utque minax superetur Ægis ?

Tu flectis amnes, tu mare caerulum
Ussisse prono fulmine diceris,
    Ajacis exesas triremes
        Praecipitans graviore casu.

Tu discidisti Gorgoneas manus
Nexas, capillos anguibus oblitos,
    Furvosque vicisti Gigantes
        Enceladum, pharetramque Rhaeci.

Ceu victa, Musis porrigit herbulas
Pennata caeci dextra Cupidinis,
    Non ulla Bellonae furentis
        Arma tui metuunt alumni.

Pallas retortis caesia vocibus
Respondit : Eia ! ne metuas, precor,
    Nam fata non justis repugnant
        Principibus, sed amica fiunt.

Ut si recisis arboribus meis
Nudetur illic lucus amabilis,
    Fructusque post mortem recusent
        Perpetuos mihi ferre rami.

Dulcem rependent tum mihi tibiam
Pulchre renatam ex arbore mortua,
    Dignamque coelesti corona
        Harmoniam dabit inter astra.
                    G. Herbert, *Coll. Trin.*

On the Death of Prince Henry.

O virgin Pallas, goddess bright,
The glory of Heaven's Courts of light,
    To whom in hours of blissful leisure
    The Roman Muse and Greek give pleasure;

Why do Death's darts tow'rds thee or thine
With threat'ning motion e'er incline?
    Why is the balance of stern Fate
    Pull'd down for thee with such dead weight?

Has Death, with blood of thousands stain'd,
A Hydra's monstrous form attain'd,
    That e'en Minerva's sword is broken,
    And crush'd her mighty Ægis-token?

Rivers thou turnest; Ocean blue
Was flush'd by thee with fiery hue,
    When lightning, with a direr blow,
    'Whelmed Ajax' shatter'd ships below.

The Gorgon's knots thou didst divide,
With twisted snakes for locks supplied;
    Didst slay grim giants fam'd of old,
    Enceladus and Rhæcus bold.

The feather'd hand of blind Love brings,
Vanquish'd, to thee green offerings;
    Thy foster-children feel no fear,
    Though fierce Bellona thunder near.

With quick stern answer Pallas cries,
' Let no vain fear, I pray thee, rise ;
    Fates with just princes ne'er contend,
    But always bless them in the end.

What though my trees were all cut down,
This pleasant grove stript of its crown,
    And the dead boughs should bear no more
    The fruits they render'd me before ;

A sweet-ton'd lute they'll yield to me,
Fram'd beauteous from the fallen tree,
    Whose dulcet strains shall float on high,
    And win a garland in the sky.'   R. WI.

NOTE TO

In Natales et Pascha concurrentes, p. 166.

This reminds us of Dr. Donne's very striking poem ' Vppon the Annunciacon and Passiown fallinge vpon one day, 1608' (our edition of his complete Poems, vol. ii. pp. 296-8). By the way, for Winchester, read in the Note, Westminster. Probably both were written on the same occasion. Sir John Beaumont has an equally noticeable poem ' Vpon the two Great Feasts of the Annunciation and Resurrection falling on the same day, March 25th, 1627' (our edition of his Poems, pp. 67-8).. Crashaw and William Cartwright also turn the stable of Bethlehem into quaint symbolisms ; *e.g.* the latter, as less known :

' Blest Babe, Thy birth makes Heaven in the stall,
And we the manger may Thy altar call :
Thine and Thy mother's eyes as stars appear ;
The bull no beast, but constellation here.
Thus both were born—the Gospel and the Law :
Moses in flags did lye, Thou in the straw.'
        (On the Nativity, pp. 317-18.)

Solem ex Oceano Veteres exurgere fingunt
Postquam se gelidis nocte refecit aquis:
Venius hoc olim factum est, ubi Christi lavarit
Illos, qui mundus circumiere, pedes.

In D. Lucam

Cur Deus eligit Medicus, qui numini plenus
Divinâ Christi scriberet acta manu.
Ut discat sibi quisque, quid utile: nempe nocebat
Crudus olim pomum, tristis Adami. sibi.

Papæ titulus
Nec Deus Nec Homo.

Quisnam Antichristus cessantes quaerit; Papa
Nec Deus est nec Homo: Christus utrique fuit.

In iusti solutio

Piscis tributum solvit; Et tu Caesari:
Utrumque mirum est: hoc tamen mirum magis
Quod omnibus tute impendis, nemo tibi.

Tempestas Christo dormitante

Cum dormis, sus sit pelagus: cur Christe resurgis
Dormitat pelagus: Quam bene fraena tenes!

Bonus Civis

Sagax Humilitas Eligens, vires bonos
Atque evehens, bonum facit foecundius,
Etiam si ipse solus omnia interverterit,
Suamque in aliis posuit prudentiam.

In Umbram Petri

Produxit Umbram corpus, umbra corpori
Vitam reduxit: ecce gratitudinem.

Geor. Herbert.

VIII.

PASSIO DISCERPTA. LUCUS.

Printed and translated for the first time.

G. = The Editor.

R. Wi. = Rev. Richard Wilton, M.A. (as before.)

NOTE.

The whole of ' Passio Discerpta' and ' Lucus' are derived from the Williams ms., as before. For details on these and others, see Preface in Vol. I., and Essay in present volume.   G.

PASSIO DISCERPTA.

I.

Ad Dominum morientem.

Cum lacrymas oculosque duos tot vulnera vincant,
    Impar, et in fletum vel resolutus, ero;
Sepia concurrat, peccatis aptior humor,
    Et mea jam lacrymet culpa colore suo.

To the dying Lord.

Since my two eyes and utmost tears
    Thy many wounds exceed;
Weeping will never match their worth,—
    I must dissolve indeed:
O let my ink together run,
    Moisture of fitting hue;
And thus black tears for my black sins
    These guilty cheeks imbue.   G.

II.

In Sudorem sanguineum.

Quo fugies, sudor? quamvis pars altera Christi
    Nescia sit metae, venula cella tua est.

Si tibi non illud placeat mirabile corpus,
   Caetera displiceat turba, necesse, tibi :
Ni me forte petas ; nam quanto indignior ipse,
   Tu mihi subveniens dignior esse potes.

On the bloody Sweat.

Whither wilt thou, O bloody sweat, now flee?
Though other parts of Christ unbounded be,
A vein is surely the fit home for thee.

And if His marvellous body please thee not,
I know no other more alluring spot
Amid the crowd of men stain'd with sin's blot.

Unless thou seekest me, unworthy me !
For succouring me most worthy thou shalt be.   G.

III.

In eundem.

Sic tuus effundi gestit pro crimine sanguis,
   Ut nequeat paulo se cohibere domi.

On the same.

Impatient for man's sin to be pour'd out, Thy blood
   E'en for a little while may not restrain its flood. G.

More freely.

So does Thy blood for sin exult to pour,
It can't itself restrain for one short hour,
     But rains its awful shower.   G.

IV.

In Latus perfossum.

Christe, ubi tam duro patet in te semita ferro,
    Spero meo cordi posse patere viam.

On the pierced Side.

O Christ, where now a path I see
    Made by the cruel spear,
For my poor heart a way to Thee
    I trust will be kept clear.   G.

V.

In Sputum et Convicia.

O barbaros! sic os rependitis sanctum,
Visum quod uni praebet, omnibus vitam,
Sputando, praedicando? sic Aquas Vitae
Contaminatis alveosque caelestes
Sputando, blasphemando? nempe ne hoc fiat
In posterum, maledicta Ficus, arescens
Gens tota fiet, atque utrinque plectetur.
Parate situlas, Ethnici, lagenasque
Graves lagenas, vester est Aquae-ductus.

On the Spittle and Revilings.

O barbarous! e'en thus do ye requite
That holy mouth, which unto one gives sight,
And life to all, by spittle or His word?
Thus foully is the sacred fountain stirr'd?

Dare ye the living waters thus defile,
And wantonly celestial stream-beds soil,
By your base spitting and wild blasphemy,
Commingl'd with that fierce rejecting cry?

Ah, lest such wickedness repeated be,
The Nation shall become a curs'd Fig-tree,
Withering away in wrath, on every side
Punish'd by Him Who as their Victim died.
Gentiles, bring vessels, bring great flagons; lo,
For you, and through you, shall the Water flow.　　G.

VI.

In Coronam spineam.

Christe, dolor tibi supplicio, mihi blanda voluptas;
　　Tu spina misere pungeris, ipse rosa.
Spicula mutemus: capias Tu serta rosarum,
　　Qui Caput es, spinas et tua membra tuas.

On the thorny Crown.

Grief is the source of suffering, Lord, to Thee;
Soft pleasure is its source to guilty me.
Thou, Lord, art piercèd grievously with thorn;
I with a rose: Lord, look on me forlorn!
Exchange the points that pierce; take Thou, the Head,
All roses; and Thy members thorns instead.　　G.

VII.

In Arund., Spin., Genufl., Purpur.

Quam nihil illudis, Gens improba! quam male cedunt
　　Scommata! Pastorem semper Arundo decet.

Quam nihil illudis ! cum quo magis angar acuto
    Munere, Rex tanto verior inde prober.
Quam nihil illudis flectens! namque integra posthac
    Posteritas flectet corque genuque mihi.
Quam nihil illudis ! Si, quae tua purpura fingit,
    Purpureo melius sanguine regna probem:
At non lusus erit, si quem tu laeta necasti
    Vivat, et in mortem vita sit illa tuam.

On the Reed, Crown of Thorns, Bending the Knee, and
Purple Robe.

Vainly ye mock ; your scoffs fly wide, vile race ;
A Reed in Shepherd's hand finds fitting place:
Vainly ye mock ; your pointed thorns may sting,
So much the more they prove Me a true King :
Vainly ye mock, bending ; for unto ME
All times to come shall bend both heart and knee :
Vainly ye mock ; if not with purple vest,
Yet purple blood, I claim My kingdom blest.
But if He lives Whom once in sport ye slew—
His life your death—'twill be no play to you !   R. WI.

VIII.

In Alapas.

Ah, quam caederis hinc et inde palmis !
Sic unguenta solent manu fricari;
Sic toti medicaris ipse mundo.

On the Buffetings.

They smite Thee, Lord, on all sides with their palms;
Thus men are wont to bruise Earth's precious balms :

Thus all the world Thou healest with Thy woes,
And from Thy stripes the Balm of Gilead flows.   R. WI.

IX.

In Flagellum.

Christe, flagellati spes et victoria mundi,
     Crimina cum turgent, et mea poena prope est:
Suaviter admoveas notum tibi carne flagellum,
     Sufficiat virgae saepius umbra tuae.
Mitis agas: tenerae duplicant sibi verbera mentes,
     Ipsaque sunt ferulae mollia corda suae.

On the Scourge.

O Christ, sole Hope of a world scourg'd with woe,
When swelling crimes invite the imminent blow,
Softly apply the scourge once felt by Thee,
Let Thy rod's shadow oft suffice for me:
Deal gently; tender minds their strokes redouble,
And gracious hearts are their own sharpest trouble.

             R. WI.

X.

In Vestes divisas.

Si, Christe, dum suffigeris, tuae vestes
     Sunt hostium legata, non amicorum,
Ut postulat mos; quid tuis dabis?   Teipsum.

On the parted Garments.

If, Lord, while Thou art fasten'd on the Tree,
Thy garments, the accustom'd legacy

Of friends, e'en to Thy foes assign'd we see ;
What to Thy faithful followers wilt Thou give ?
Thyself, Thy dying self, that they may live.   R. WI.

XI.

In pium Latronem.

O nimium Latro ! reliquis furatus abunde,
  Nunc etiam Christum callidus aggrederis.

On the Penitent Thief.

And does he now, this robber overbold,
Who largely on his fellows prey'd of old,
Dare craftily assail the very Christ,
To gain possession of the Pearl unpric'd ?   R. WI.

XII.

In Christum Crucem ascensurum.

Zacchaeus, ut te cernat, arborem scandet ;
Nunc ipse scandis, ut, labore mutato,
Nobis facilitas cedat, et tibi sudor.
Sic omnibus videris ad modum visus :
Fides gigantem sola vel facit nanum.

On Christ about to ascend the Cross.

Zaccheus, to behold Thee, climb'd a tree ;
Now Thou Thyself dost climb that I may see :
The labour chang'd, the toil and sweat are Thine ;
While easiness of vision now is mine.

Thus to Sight's measure Thou art seen by all;
Faith only makes or dwarf or giant tall. R. WI.

XIII.
Christus in Cruce.

Hic, ubi sanati stillant opobalsama mundi,
 Advolvor madidae laetus hiansque Cruci :
Pro lapsu stillarum abeunt peccata ; nec acres
 Sanguinis insultus exanimata ferunt.
Christe, fluas semper; ne, si tua flumina cessent,
 Culpa redux jugem te neget esse Deum.

Christ on the Cross.

Here, where the heal'd World's balm distilleth free,
With yearning joy I cling to the drench'd tree :
E'en as drops fall, sins vanish ; nor are they
Half dead,—by Blood's strong gushing borne away.
O Christ, flow always ; lest if cease Thy streams,
Returning guilt no living God Thee deems. R. WI.

XIV.
In Clavos.

Qualis eras, qui, ne melior natura minorem
 Eriperet nobis, in Cruce fixus eras,
Jam meus es : nunc Te teneo : Pastorque prehensus
 Hoc ligno, his clavis est, quasi falce sua.

On the Nails.

Whate'er Thou wert, Who, lest Thy higher birth
Should take away Thy lower from the earth,
Wast fasten'd on the Cross, while men made mirth,

Now Thou art mine; I grasp Thee now,—this wood,
These nails, hold fast the Shepherd for my good,
As by His pruning-hook bedew'd with blood.   R. WI.

XV.

Inclinato capite.   John xix. 30.

Vulpibus antra feris, nidique volucribus adsunt,
   Quodque suum novit stroma, cubile suum.
Qui tamen excipiat, Christus caret hospite; tantum
   In cruce suspendens, unde reclinet, habet.

On the bowed Head.

Foxes have holes, each bird of air its nest,
All creatures know where they may roost or rest :
Christ has no host to welcome Him ; but now
The Cross permits Him His tir'd head to bow.   R. WI.

XVI.

Ad Solem deficientem.

Quid hoc ? et ipse deficis, coeli gigas,
   Almi choragus luminis ?
Tu promis orbem mane, condis vesperi,
   Mundi fidelis claviger.
At nunc fatiscis, nempe Dominus aedium
   Prodegit integrum penu.
Quamque ipse lucis tesseram sibi negat,
   Negat familiae [jam] suae.
Carere discat verna, quo summus caret
   Paterfamilias lumine.

Tu vero mentem neutiquam despondeas,
 Resurget occumbens Herus:
Tunc instruetur lautius radiis penu,
 Tibi supererunt et mihi.

To the failing Sun. **Matt. xxvii. 45.**

O thou huge giant of the sky,
Wherefore this dimness in thine eye?
Say, what is this? Dost thou fail now,
Darkness enfolding thy great brow?
O fountain of all-nurturing light,
Whence around thee this mid-day night?
Erewhile at morn the earth revealing,
At shut of eve the earth concealing,
Faithful key-bearer of the world,
Art thou from thy grand office hurl'd,
Since thou droopest ominous,
Nor sheddest light on Him or us?
The Master of the House on high
Thy beams methinks spent lavishly;
And what He to Himself denies,
Shines not in our unworthy eyes:
Nor let the servant dare complain,
If from Day's light his Lord abstain:
If the Head Himself deny,
Shall not the Family comply?—
But lose not heart, nor droop amain,
Thy sinking Lord will rise again;

New rays in infinite supply
Shall then relume thy fading eye ;
More than sufficient there will be
For all the world, and thee, and me.　　　　G.

XVII.

Monumenta aperta.

Dum moreris, mea Vita, ipsi vixere sepulti,
　　Proque uno vincto turba soluta fuit.
Tu tamen, haud tibi tam moreris, quam vivis in illis,
　　Asserit et vitam Mors animata tuam.
Scilicet in tumulis Crucifixum quaerite, vivit :
　　Convincunt unam multa sepulcra crucem.
Sic pro majestate Deum non perdere vitam
　　Quam tribuit, verum multiplicare decet.

The open Graves.

Thy death, my Life, the buried saints awoke,
And for One bound, a crowd to freedom broke.
Thou diest not, but in these drawest breath ;
Thy life is prov'd by animated Death.
Seek Him amid the tombs,—He is not dead ;
One Cross by many graves is answerèd :
For it becomes not the Lord's majesty
To waste the life He gave, but multiply.　　　R. WI.

XVIII.

Terrae-motus.

Te fixo, vel Terra movet ; nam cum Cruce totam
　　Circumferre potes, Samson ut ante fores.

Heu, stolidi ! primum fugientem figite Terram,
    Tunc Dominus clavis aggrediendus erit.

The Earthquake.

Though Thou art fasten'd to the fatal Tree,
    Lo, the huge earth is moving ;
For Thou dost bear it all about with Thee,
    The Cross and all ; so proving
That as, of old, the gates strong Samson bore,
His utmost strength, Thy weakness bows before.
Fools ! first the flying earth fix in its place,
Then, with your nails fast-fix the Lord of grace !   G.

XIX.

Velum scissum.

Frustra, Verpe, tumes, propola cultus,
Et Templi parasite ; namque velum
Diffissum reserat Deum latentem,
Et pomaeria terminosque sanctos
Non urbem facit unicam, sed orbem.
Et pro pectoribus recenset aras,
Dum cor omne suum sibi requirat
Structorem et Solomon ubique regnet.
Nunc Arcana patent, nec involutam
·Phylacteria complicant latriam.
Excessit tener Orbis ex ephebis,
Maturusque suos coquens amores
Praeflorat sibi nuptias futuras.
Ubique est Deus, Agnus, Ara, Flamen.

The rent Vail.

Thou circumcisèd ! vain thy swelling,
Parasite of the sacred dwelling !
Huckster of vestments, for gold selling.
For, lo, the vail is rent in twain,
Nor mayst thou seek God to retain :
Surcease thee now thy venal gain.
Ah, the old vail is now up-furl'd,
And not one city, but the world,
Is holy : all place-worship hurl'd.
And now, as He new hearts doth count,
He each a Sol'mon doth account ;
And living altars the old surmount.
One Sol'mon only was of old ;
Now, as believers' names are told,
In each a Sol'mon is enroll'd.
Now the mystery is laid ope,
Nor do phylacteries veil our hope,
Nor legal rites mar Gospel scope.
The world, from tender childhood pass'd,
Attains its manhood, and at last
Rejoices as a spouse to haste.
Look where we may, our God is found;
Lamb! altar! priest! lo, all abound,
And EVERYWHERE is sacred ground.   G.

XX.

Petrae scissae.

Sanus homo factus, vitiorum purus uterque ;
    At sibi collisit fictile Daemon opus.

Post ubi Mosaicae repararent fragmina Legis,
　　Infectas tabulas facta juvenca scidit.
Haud aliter cum Christus obit, prae funere tanto
　　Constat inaccessas dissiluisse petras.
Omnia praeter corda scelus confregit et error,
　　Quae contrita tamen caetera damna levant.

The rent Rocks.

Man was made sound and pure in heart, life, lip,
But Satan shatter'd God's fair workmanship.
When Moses' Law the fragments would refit,
The new-made calf the unmade tablets split.
So when Christ dies, at such a Tragedy
Rocks inaccessible asunder fly :
All things but hearts are broken by Sin's might ;
Yet broken hearts make other losses light.　　R. WI.

XXI.

In Mundi Sympathiam cum Christo.

Non moreris solus ; Mundus simul interit in te,
　　Agnoscitque tuam Machina tota crucem.
Hunc ponas animam mundi, Plato ; vel tua mundum
　　Ne nimium vexet quaestio, pone meam.

On the Earth's Sympathy with Christ.

Alone Thou diest not ; in Thee the World dies ;
The whole Machine Thy Cross must recognise.
Make Him Earth's soul, Plato ; nor pains of thine
Disturb Earth more, after these pains of Mine.　　R. WI.

LUCUS.

I.
Homo Statua.

Sum, quis nescit, Imago Dei, sed saxea certe :
    Hanc mihi duritiem contulit improbitas.
Durescunt propriis evulsa corallia fundis,
    Haud secus ingenitis dotibus orbus Adam.
Tu qui cuncta creans docuisti marmora flere,
    Haud mihi cor saxo durius esse sinas.

Man an Image.

Doubtless I am God's image, but in stone :
This hardness which I feel from sin has grown.
As corals harden from their own beds torn,
Just so does man, of native virtues shorn.
Marbles to weep, Almighty, Thou hast taught :
Let not my heart more hard than stone be thought.

R. WI.

II.
Patria.

Ut tenuis flammae species caelum usque minatur,
    Igniculos legans, manserit ipsa, licet.

Sic mucronatam reddunt suspiria mentem,
 Votaque scintillae sunt animosa meae.
Assiduo stimulo carnem mens ulta lacessit,
 Sedula si fuerit, perterebrare potest.

The Fatherland.

As a small flame threatens to pierce heaven's face,
Sending up sparks, though keeping its own place;
E'en thus sighs make my soul sharp-pointed grow;
Prayers, hearty prayers, the sparks with which I glow.
The keen soul plies the flesh with ceaseless fire;
'Twill penetrate it, if it does not tire.   R. WI.

III.

In Stephanum lapidatum.

Qui silicem tundit—mirum tamen—elicit ignem :
 At Caelum e saxis elicuit Stephanus.

On Stephen stoned.

Who strikes a flint draws fire—wondrous to say ;
But out of stones Stephen drew Heaven one day!
                                              R. WI.

IV.

In Simonem Magum.

Ecquid emes Christum? pro nobis scilicet olim
 Venditus est Agnus, non tamen emptus erit.
Quin nos Ipse emit, precioso fenora solvens
 Sanguine, nec pretium merx emit ulla suum.

Ecquid emes Caelum? quin stellam rectius unam
    Quo pretio venit, fac, liceare prius.
Nempe gravi fertur scelerata pecunia motu,
    Si sursum jacias, in caput ipse ruit.
Unicus est nummus caelo Christoque petitus,
    Nempe in quo clare lucet Imago Dei.

On Simon Magus.

Wilt thou buy Christ? Once, for us, we are taught,
The Lamb was sold, yet will He not be bought.
Himself bought us; with blood our debts He paid:
For such a price no money can be weigh'd.
Wilt thou buy Heaven? Nay, thou hadst better try
What price one star will fetch in yonder sky.
With its own weight curst money downward tends;
Thrown upwards, on your head itself descends.
One only coin to Heaven and Christ is dear;
'Tis that where God's own image shines forth clear.

R. WI.

V.

In S. Scripturas.

Heu, quis spiritus igneusque turbo
Regnat visceribus, measque versat
Imo pectore cogitationes?
Nunquid pro foribus sedendo nuper
Stellam vespere suxerim volantem,   5
Haec autem hospitio latere turpi
Prorsus nescia, cogitat recessum?

Nunquid mel comedens, apem comedi
Ipsa cum domina domum vorando ?
Imo, me nec apes nec astra pungunt ;   10
Sacratissima charta, tu fuisti
Quae cordis latebras sinusque caecos
Atque omnes peragrata es angiportus
Et flexus fugientis appetitus.
Ah, quam docta perambulare calles   15
Maeandrosque plicasque quam perita es ?
Quae vis condidit, ipsa novit aedes.

On the Holy Scriptures.

Ah, what wind, like blast of fire,
Thus sways my inmost soul in ire,
Turning my thoughts e'en upside down
I' th' centre of a heart of stone?
Is it that, seated by my door
At the evening's stilly hour,
I suck'd in a flying star
That thither travell'd from afar,
Ign'rant it hid in my base breast,
And now would out with wild unrest?
Or is't that, eating of my honey,
Golden as e'er is golden money,
While I devour'd the comb rich-dropping,
Queen-bee and all, there interloping,
I too devour'd?

      Nor stars nor bees
Have ever stung, or broke my ease.

O blessèd Book, most holy chart,
Hast thou aye been within my heart;
Thou all its lurking-places showest,
And all its dark recesses knowest,
And all the mazes intricate
Where'er Desire retreating sate :
Ah, how rarely skill'd art thou
Bye-ways to track and turnings show,
And all Sin's foldings hid below !
The Heavenly Power which built my heart
To know it has alone the art.   G.

VI.

In Pacem Britannicam.

Anglia cur solum fuso sine sanguine sicca est,
    Cum natet in tantis caetera terra malis ?
Sit licet in pelago semper, sine fluctibus illa est,
    Cum qui plus terrae, plus habuere maris.
Naufragii causa est aliis mare, roboris Anglo,
    Et quae corrumpit moenia, murus aqua est.
Nempe hic Religio floret, regina quietis,
    Tuque super nostras, Christe, moveris aquas.

On the Peace enjoyed by Britain.

From outpour'd blood why still is England free,
When all the world wades through such misery ?
No waves she feels, though always in the deep,
While seas of woe o'er inland countries sweep.

Their shipwreck, but our strength, the sea we call ;
And rampart-sapping water is our wall.
Forsooth, here reigns Religion, queen of rest,
And Thou, Lord, walkest o'er our waters blest.　　R. WI.

VII.

Avaritia.

Aurum nocte videns, vidisse insomnia dicit ;
　　Aurum luce videns, nulla videre putat.
O falsos homines ! vigilat, qui somniat aurum,
　　Plusque habet hic laetus, quam vel Avarus habet.

Avarice.

He says he saw a dream, beholding gold by night ;
He thinks he sees no dream, seeing gold in the light.
Mistaken men ! he keeps awake who dreams of gold,
And joyful clutches more than ever miser told.　　R. WI.

VIII.

In Lotionem Pedum Apostolorum.

Solem ex Oceano Veteres exsurgere fingunt
　　Postquam se gelidis nocte refecit aquis :
Verius hoc olim factum est, ubi, Christe, lavares
　　Illos, qui mundum circumire, pedes.

On the Washing of the Apostles' Feet.

The Sun the ancients did devise
Out of the Ocean to arise,

Where his resplendent face he laves
All night within the cooling waves.
More truly was this done by Thee,
O Christ, of Love the boundless Sea;
When washing Thy disciples' feet,
Which girdled Earth with circuit fleet.   G.

IX.

In D. Lucam.

Cur Deus elegit Medicum, qui numine plenus
    Divina Christi scriberet acta manu?
Ut discat sibi quisque quid utile : nempe nocebat
    Crudum olim pomum, tristis Adame, tibi.

On St. Luke.

Why a Physician did God fill with grace
Christ's deeds and death with hand divine to trace?
That what was good for them all men might see;
For raw fruit once, poor Adam, injur'd thee.   R. WI.

X.

Papae Titulus nec Deus nec Homo.

Quisnam Antichristus cessemus quaerere; Papa
    Nec Deus est nec homo : Christus uterque fuit.

The Pope's Title, neither God nor Man.

Search we no more for Antichrist :
The Pope's nor God nor man : God-Man is Christ.   G.

XI.

Tributi Solutio.

Piscis tributum solvit et tu Caesari.
Utrumque mirum est; hoc tamen mirum magis,
Quod omnibus tute imperes, nemo tibi.

The Paying of the Tribute.

A fish for Cæsar brought the tax to shore;
'Twas paid by Thee to him who purple wore.
Both facts are wonderful; but this is more,
That Thou commandest all that swim, walk, soar;
But over Thee none e'er dominion bore.   ·   R. WI.

XII.

Tempestas, Christo dormiente.

Cum dormis, surgit pelagus: cum, Christe, resurgis,
    Dormitat pelagus: Quam bene fraena tenes!

The Tempest: Christ asleep.

When, Lord, Thou sleepest, lo, the sea awaketh,
                    Lifting its waves.
When Thou arisest, lo, its sleep it taketh,
                    No more it raves.
Well o'er the sea His reins the Master shaketh.   G.

XIII.

Bonus Civis.

Sagax Humilitas eligens viros bonos
Atque evehens, bonum facit faecundius,

Quam si ipse solus omnia interverteret,
Suamque in aliis possidet prudentiam.

The Good Citizen.

When wise Humility good men elects
And elevates to honour, she effects
A greater blessing than if one good man
Should change society to suit his plan.
Thus her own wisdom copied out she traces
In many persons and in many places. R. WI.

XIV.
In Umbram Petri.

Produxit umbram corpus, umbra corpori
Vitam reduxit : ecce gratitudinem.

On the Shadow of Peter.

A body gave a shadow, and straightway
A shadow gave back life to mortal clay :
Lo, gratitude is paramount to day ! R. WI.

XV.
Martha: Maria.

Christus adest : crebris aedes percurrite scopis,
 Excutite aulaea, et luceat igne focus.
Omnia purgentur, niteat mihi tota supellex ;
 Parcite luminibus, sitque lucerna domus ;
O cessatrices ! eccum pulvisculus illic :
 Corde tuo forsan, caetera munda, Soror.

Martha: Mary.

Lo, Christ is here! run ye, O maidens, run
Through all the house, let nothing be undone;
Shake out the curtains all, and let the hearth
Glow brightly in the bright fire's dancing mirth;
Tables and couches all be polishèd,
Leave not a speck—by me be admonishèd;
Spare lights—let the whole house a candle be.
O idlers, lo, there some small dust I see:
' In thy heart, Sister, perhaps ?—all else is clean,
        I ween.' G.

XVI.

Amor.

Quid metuant homines infra, suprave minentur
 Sidera, pendenti sedulus aure bibis :
Utque ovis in dumis, haeres in crine Cometae,
 Sollicitus, ne te stella perita notet :
Omnia quaerendo; sed te, super omnia, vexas :
 Et quid tu tandem desidiosus ? Amo.

In Love.

Whate'er skies threaten, or whate'er earth fears,
Thou drinkest in with eager-open ears ;
As sheep on brambles, so thou layest hold
On comet's tail—in trouble manifold—
Lest swift some knowing star thy fate unfold.
All things thou rackest, thyself all things above :
Idler, what wouldst thou learn o' me ? I LOVE. G.

XVII.

In Superbum.

Magnas es ; esto, bulla si vocaberis,
Largiar et istud : scilicet Magnatibus
Difficilis esse haud soleo : nam, pol, si forem,
Ipsi sibi sunt nequiter facillimi.
Quin mitte nugas ; teque carnem et sanguinem
Communem habere crede cum Cerdonibus :
Illum volo, qui calceat lixam tuum.

On a Proud Man.

A Lord art thou ; be also call'd a bubble—
That I will grant thee too without more trouble.
Too hard on Lords you never will find me ;
Dreadfully easy to themselves they be.
Joking apart, let it be understood
That thou possessest the same flesh and blood
As artisans ; that cobbler, if you choose,
Who for your humblest serving-boy makes shoes!   n. wi.

XVIII.

In eundem.

Unusquisque hominum Terra est et filius arvi.
    Dic mihi, mons sterilis, vallis an uber eris ?

On the same.

In every man earth and earth's child we hail :
Wilt be a barren mountain or rich vale ?   n. wi.

XIX.
Afflictio.

Quos tu calcasti fluctus, me, Christe, lacessunt
   Transiliuntque caput, qui subiere pedes.
Christe, super fluctus si non discurrere detur,
   Per fluctus saltem, fac, precor, ipse vader.

Affliction.

The waves Thou troddest, Lord, against me beat,
Over my head they leap, which bore Thy feet.
If o'er the waves, O Lord, I may not glide,
Yet through them bid me pass safe to Thy side.   R. WI.

XX.
In κενοδοξίαν.

Qui sugit avido spiritu rumusculos
Et flatulentas aucupatur glorias,
Felicitatis culmen extra se locat,
Spargitque per tot capita, quot vulgus gerit.
Tu vero collige te tibique insistito,
Breviore nodo stringe vitae sarcinas,
Rotundus in te : namque si ansatus sies,
Te mille rixae, mille prensabunt doli,
Ducentque donec incidentem in cassidem
Te mille nasi, mille rideant sinus.
Quare peritus nauta, vela contrahas
Famamque nec difflaveris nec suxeris :
Tuasque librans actiones, gloriam,
Si ducat agmen, reprime ; sin claudat, sinas.
Morosus oxygala est : Levis, coagulum.

On Vainglory.

Who sucks with greedy breath all light reports,
And windy words of flattery hunts and courts,
His highest happiness outside him places,
And spreads as widely as the crowd counts faces.
Collect thyself, and on thyself rely;
And with a tighter knot life's burdens tie ;
Round as a globe, not handl'd like a cup,
Which thousand snares and quarrels will catch up
And carry off, till thy poor falling helm
A thousand jeers, a thousand smiles o'erwhelm.
Then, like a seaman wise, draw in thy sails ;
Nor suck in fame, nor blow it to the gales.
Balance thine actions well, and if the crowd
Brings glory to thee with applauses loud,
Check them ; but if they stint it, say ' All right!'
Neither morosely sour, nor softly light.[1]   R. WI.

XXI.
In Gulosum.

Dum prono rapis ore cibos, et fercula verris,
    Intra extraque gravi plenus es illuvie :
Non jam ventriculus, verum spelunca vocetur
    Illa caverna, in qua tot coiere ferae.
Ipse fruare licet, solus graveolente sepulcro,
    Te petet, ante diem quisquis obire cupit.

[1] The whey or buttermilk, being sour, is like the morose despiser of praise; the curd, being soft and impressible with the least touch, like the man who is lightly moved by praise or censure.

On a Glutton.

Thou, while with guzzling mouth the plates thou
　　　　clearest,
Within, without, a mass of filth appearest :
A stomach call it not, but a den rather,
That cavern where so many wild beasts gather.
Alone enjoy the stench as of a tomb;
He'll seek thee who would die before his doom.　R. WI.

XXII.

In Improbum disertum.

Sericus es dictis, factis pannusia Baucis :
　　Os et lingua tibi dives, egena manus.
Ni facias, ut opes linguae per brachia serpant,
　　Aurea, pro naulo, lingua Charontis erit.

On a plausible Villain.

Nabob thou art in words, pauper in deeds ;
Thy mouth and tongue are rich, thy hand still needs ;
Unless thy tongue's wealth down thine arms thou shake,
Charon for fare a golden tongue will take.　　　R. WI.

XXIII.

Consolatio.

Cur lacrymas et tarda trahis suspiria, tanquam
　　Nunc primum socii mors foret atra tui ?
Nos autem a cunis omnes sententia Mortis
　　Quotidie jugulat, nec semel ullus obit.

Vivimus in praesens : hesternam vivere vitam
    Nemo potest : hodie vita sepulta prior.
Trecentos obiit Nestor, non transiit annos,
    Vel quia tot moritur, tot viguisse probes.
Dum lacrymas, it vita : tuus tibi clepsydra fletus,
    Et numerat mortes singula gutta pares.
Frustra itaque in tot funeribus miraberis unum,
    Sera nimis lacryma haec, si lacrymabis, erit.
Siste tuum fletum et gemitus : namque imbribus istis
    Ac zephyris, carnis flos remeare nequit.
Nec tu pro socio doleas, qui fugit ad illud
    Culmen, ubi pro te nemo dolere potest.

Consolation.

Why dost thou weep, while slow-drawn sighs
Answer the tears within thine eyes?
As if the sad death of thy friend
No prior death did e'er portend;
Whereas all from the cradle lie
Beneath Death's sentence visibly;
Nor only once may mortals say
We die, for all die day by day.
The present ours—where's yesterday?
Ah, none may yesterday recall,
None may arrest its burial!
Three hundred years died Nestor old,
Not liv'd, so many years enroll'd;
Unless because so oft he perish'd
Thou provest that so long he flourish'd.

Whilst thou weepest, life is going;
Lo, thy hour-glass, tears, fast flowing;
Each drop numbers equal dying,
Therefore vain is thy keen sighing;
Midst so many deaths, o'er one
Waste not admiration.
Too late shall this weeping be,
 If weeping still must comfort thee;
Stanch thy tears, and still thy groaning;
For amid these show'rs, this moaning,
Thou, O weeper, thyself wastest,
And Life's flow'r in fading hastest.
Neither grieve thee for thy friend,
Who to that height doth ascend
Where no tears the eyelids steep,
And where none for thee may weep.   G.

XXIV.

In Angelos.

Intellectus adultus Angelorum,
Haud nostro similis, cui necesse
Ut dentur species, rogare sensum:
Et ni lumina januam resignent,
Et nostrae tribuant molae farinam,
Saepe ex se nihil otiosa cudit.
A nobis etenim procul remoti
Labuntur fluvii scientiarum :

Si non per species, nequimus ipsi,
Quid ipsi sumus, assequi putando.
Non tantum est iter Angelis ad undas,
Nullo circuitu scienda pungunt :
Illis perpetuae patent fenestrae,
Se per se facili modo scientes,
Atque ipsi sibi sunt mola et farina.

On the 'Angels.

The Angels' full-grown keen intelligence
Is unlike ours, which needs must call the sense
To give the forms of things ; and oft until
The eyes unlock the door, and to our mill
Bring corn for grist, unfruitful is the mind,
Out of itself unable aught to grind.
For parted from us by a distance wide
The rivers of enriching knowledge glide ;
Unable but through forms of things are we,
By thinking, to find out what ourselves be.
But no such journey need the Angels take
To reach the waters, no such circuit make
To penetrate into what may be known ;
Wide open always are their windows thrown.
Themselves they know by method short and clear,
And to themselves both mill and meal appear.　R. WI.

XXV.

$$\text{Roma : Anagr.}\begin{cases}\textit{Oram.} & \textit{Maro.}^{[1]}\\ \textit{Ramo.} & \textit{Armo.}\\ \textit{Mora.} & \textit{Amor.}\end{cases}$$

Roma, tuum nomen, quam non pertransiit ORAM,
    Cum Latium ferrent saecula prisca jugum?
Non deerat vel fama tibi vel carmina famae,
    Unde MARO laudes duxit ad astra tuas.
At nunc exsucco similis tua gloria RAMO
    A veteri trunco et nobilitate cadit.
Laus antiqua et honor periit: quasi scilicet ARMO
    Te dejecissent tempora longa suo.
Quin tibi tam desperatae MORA nulla medetur,
    Qua Fabio quondam sub duce nata salus.
Hinc te olim gentes miratae odere vicissim,
    Et cum sublata laude recedit AMOR.

Roma : Anagram.

Thy name, O Rome, has crost to every SHORE,   oram
Since Latium's yoke the early ages bore.

[1] This is one of only two of all these Latin poems that have
hitherto been printed. It appeared in the Parentalia. Cf. with
this of Herbert, Dean Duport's, as follows:

$$\text{Roma}\begin{cases}\text{Maro}\\ \text{Amor}\\ \text{Mora}\\ \text{Armo}\end{cases}\text{Anagram.}$$

Roma Maro: quid enim praeclarius illa Marone
    Unquam, vate sacro, Parthenioque, tulit?
Roma Amor impurus, Venerisque infanda libido,
    Et sitis imperii, et dira cupido lucri.
Roma Mora, oppositusque piis conatibus obex,
    Spemque *reformandi* tempus in omne trahens.
Roma Armo gentes in praelia perque duelles
    Instruo, et in Reges concito regna suos.

    (*Sylvarum*, lib. ii. Musae Subsecivae, pp. 218-19.)

Fame and the songs of fame alike were thine,
Where to the stars on MARO's page they shine.   Maro
But all thy glory, like a wither'd BOUGH   ramo
From that grand ancient trunk, has fallen now.
Thy praise and honour perish, e'en as though
The centuries from their FLANK had hurl'd thee low. armo
To heal thy deep despair comes no DELAY,   mora
Such as great Fabius brought in olden day.
The nations hate thee now which once admir'd,
And with thy glory LOVE too has retir'd.   R. WI. amor

XXVI.

Urbani VIII. Pont. Respons.

Cum Romam nequeas, quod aves, evertere, nomen
    Invertis, mores carpis et obloqueris.
Te Germana tamen pubes, te Graecus et Anglus
    Arguit, exceptos; quos pia Roma fovet.
Hostibus haec etiam parcens imitatur Jesum:
    Invertis nomen, Quid tibi dicit? AMOR.

Pope Urban VIII.'s Reply.

Since Rome you cannot subvert, lo, its name
You invert, and its ways carp at and blame.
But youth of German, Greek, and English race
Rebuke you, welcome made to Rome's embrace.
Her foes she spares, e'en like the Lord above:
Invert her name,—what says it to thee? LOVE.   Amor

R. WI.

XXVII.

Respons. ad Urb. VIII.

Non placet Urbanus noster de nomine lusus
    Romano; sed res seria Roma tibi est:
Nempe Caput Romae es, cujus mysteria velles
    Esse jocum soli, plebe stupente, tibi.
Attamen Urbani delecto nomine, constat
    Quam satur et suavis sit tibi Roma jocus.

Reply to Urban VIII.

Our play upon Rome's name thou wilt not see;
Rome is a serious business unto thee:
Rome's head thou art, and wouldst her mysteries make
A joke thyself, while the crowd fearing quake.
But since thou choosest to be call'd Urbane,
Rome is to thee a pleasant joke, 'tis plain.   R. WI.

XXVIII.

Ad Urbanum VIII. Pont.

Pontificem tandem nacta est sibi Roma poëtam:
    Res redit ad vates Pieriosque duces.
Quod Bellarminus nequiit, fortasse poëtae
    Suaviter efficient, absque rigore Scholae.
Cedito barbaries: Helicon jam litibus instat,
    Squaloremque togae candida Musa fugat.

To Pope Urban VIII.

At last Rome finds a poet for her Pope;
To bards inspir'd power now returns, we hope.

Bellarmine and stern schools could nought effect,
But more from the smooth poets we expect.
Uncouthness, yield : Helicon rolls in sight ;
Vile wrangling gowns the fair Muse puts to flight. R. WI.

XXIX.

Λογικὴ θυσία.

Ararumque hominumque ortum si mente pererres,
    Cespes vivus, Homo: mortuus, Ara fuit.
Quae divisa nocent, Christi per foedus in unum
    Conveniunt ; et Homo viva fit Ara Dei.

A reasonable Sacrifice.

If altars' birth and men's in mind you scan,
Dead earth an altar was, live earth a man.
What droop'd apart, Christ's grace in one hath join'd ;
And man, God's living altar, now you find.   R. WI.

XXX.

In Thomam Didymum.

Dum te vel digitis minister urget,
Et hoc judicium jubes, Redemptor ;
Nempe es totus amor, medulla amoris,
Qui spissae fidei brevique menti
Paras hospitium torumque dulcem,
Quo se condat, et implicet volutans
Ceu fida statione et arce certa,
Ne perdat Leo rugiens vagantem.

On Thomas the Twin.

Thy pierc'd side Thy servant presseth,
Yet, Redeemer, Thou him blesseth ;
For Thou love art—marrow of love ;
Nor may aught Thee from loving move.
To a slow faith and mind shallow
Thou a couch prepar'd didst hallow,
Wherein it might hide, beholding
Thee, and, 'neath Thy love enfolding,
Rest secure, ineffable,
As in some mighty citadel;
Lest the great Lion him destroy,
Wand'ring aside from Thee for joy.   G.

XXXI.

In Solarium.

Conjugium Caeli Terraeque haec machina praestat ;
   Debetur caelo lumen, et umbra solo.
Sic Hominis moles animaque et corpore constat,
   Cujus ab oppositis fluxit origo locis.
Contemplare, miser, quantum terroris haberet,
   Vel sine luce solum, vel sine mente caro.

On a Sundial.

Marriage of Heaven and Earth this dial shows ;
Its light to heaven, its shade to earth it owes.
So soul and body are blended in man's frame,
Whose origin from divers regions came.

Think, wretched one, what fear would o'er thee roll,
If earth lack'd light, or human flesh a soul.   R. WI.

XXXII.

Triumphus Mortis.

O mea suspicienda manus venterque perennis,
Quem non Emathius torrens, non sanguine pinguis
Daunia, non satiat bis ter millesima caedis
Progenies, mundique aetas abdomine nostro
Ingluvieque minor.   Quercus habitare feruntur   5
Prisci, crescentesque una cum prole cavernas.
Nec tamen excludor: namque una ex arbore vitam
Glans dedit, et truncus tectum, et ramalia mortem.
   Confluere interea passim ad Floralia pubes
Coeperat, agricolis mentemque et aratra solutis :   10
Compita fervescunt pedibus, clamoribus aether.
Hic ubi discumbunt per gramina, salsior unus
Omnia suspendit naso, sociosque lacessit :
Non fert Ucalegon, atque amentata retorquet
Dicta ferox : haerent lateri convitia fixo.   15
Scinditur in partes vulgus, ceu compita ; telum
Ira facit, mundusque ipse est apotheca furoris.
Liber alit rixas ; potantibus omnia bina
Sunt praeter vitam : saxis hic sternitur, alter
Ambustis sudibus: pars vitam in pocula fundunt,   20
In patinas alii : furit inconstantia vini
Sanguine, quem dederat spolians.   Primordia Mortis
Haec fuerant : sic Tisiphone virguncula lusit.

Non placuit rudis atque ignara occisio : Morti
Quaeritur ingenium, doctusque homicida probatur. 25
Hinc tirocinium parvoque assueta juventus,
Fictaque Bellona et verae ludibria pugnae,
Instructaeque acies, hiemesque in pellibus actae,
Omniaque haec ut transadigant sine crimine costas,
Artifesque necis clueant et mortis alumni,   artificesque
Nempe et millenos ad palum interficit hostes   31
Assiduus tiro, si sit spectanda voluntas.
Heu, miseri ! quis tantum ipsis virtutibus instat
Quantum caedi? adeon' unam vos pascere vitam,
Perdere sexcentas? crescit tamen hydra nocendi   35
Tristis, ubi ac ferrum tellure reciditur una
Fecundusque chalybs sceleris, jam sanguine tinctus
Expleri nequit et totum depascitur orbem.
Quid memorem tormenta quibus prius horruit aevum
Ballistasque onagrosque, et quicquid scorpio saevus 40
Vel catapulta potest, Siculique inventa magistri,
Anglorumque arcus gaudentes sanguine Galli,
Fustibalos fundasque, quibus, cum Numine, fretus
Stravit Idumaeum divinus Tityrus hostem?
Adde etiam currus, et cum temone Britanno   45
Arviragum, falcesque obstantia quaeque metentes
Quin Aries ruit, et multa Demetrius arte
Sic olim cecidere.

Deerat adhuc vitiis hominum dignissima mundo
Machina, quam nullum satis execrabitur aevum,   50
Liquitur ardenti candens fornace metallum

Fusaque decurrit notis aqua ferrea sulcis :
Exoritur tubus atque instar Cyclopis Homeri
Luscum prodigium medioque foramine gaudens,
Inde rotae atque axes subeunt, quasi sella curulis,   55
Qua Mors ipsa sedens, hominum de gente triumphat.
Accedit pyrius pulvis, laquearibus Orci
Erutus, infernae pretiosa tragemata mensae
Sulphureoque lacu, totaque imbuta mephiti.
Huic glans adjicitur—non quam ructare vetustas   60
Creditur, ante satas, prono cum numine fruges—
Plumbea glans, livensque suae quasi conscia noxae,
Purpureus lictor Plutonis, epistola Fati
Plumbis obsignata, colosque et stamina vitae
Perrumpens Atropi vetulae marcentibus ulnis.   65

    Haec ubi juncta, subit vivo cum fune minister,
Fatalemque levans dextram, qua stuppeus ignis
Mulcetur vento, accendit cum fomite partem
Pulveris inferni properat, datus ignis, et omnem
Materiam vexat : nec jam se continet antro   70
Tisiphone ; flamma et fallaci fulmine cincta
Evolat, horrendumque ciet bacchata fragorem.
It stridor, caelosque omnes et Tartara findit.
Non jam exaudiri quicquam, vel musica caeli,
Vel gemitus Erebi : piceo se turbine volvens   75
Totamque eructans nubem, glans proruit imo
Praecipitata, cadunt urbes, formidine muri
Diffugiunt, fragilesque crepant coenacula mundi.
Strata jacent toto millena cadavera campo

Uno ictu : non sic pestis, non stella maligno   80
Afflatu perimunt : en, cymba Cocytia turbis
Ingemit, et defessus opem jam portitor orat.
Nec glans sola nocet : mortem quandoque susurrat
Aura volans, vitamque aer quam paverat, aufert.

    Dicite, vos Furiae, qua gaudet origine monstrum. 85
Nox Aetnam, Noctemque Chaos genuere priores.
Aetna Cacum ignivomum dedit, hic Ixiona multis
Cantatum ; deinde Ixion cum nubibus atris
Congrediens genuit monachum, qui limen opacae
Triste colens cellae, noctuque et daemone plenum,   90
Protulit horrendum hoc primus cum pulvere monstrum.
Quis monachos mortem meditari et pulvere tristi
Versatos neget, atque humiles, queis talia cordi
Jam demissa, ipsamque adeo subeuntia terram ?

    Nec tamen hic noster stetit impetus : exilit omni 95
Tormento pejor Jesuita et fulminat orbem,
Ridens bombardas miseras, quae corpora perdunt
Non animas, raroque ornantur sanguine regum,
Obstreperae stulto sonitu crimenque fatentes.

    Imperii hic culmen figo : mortalibus actum est 100
Corporeque atque animo.   Totus mihi serviat orbis.

The Triumph of Death.

O hand of mine, to be suspected ever,
And hunger to be ended never, never ;
Which nor Emathian torrent rushing red,
Nor Daunia, nor vast brood of Slaughter bred,

Will satiate ; yea, the whole human family   5
Too small with thy prodigious paunch to vie !

   Man primitive, they say, in oak-trees dwelt,
And caverns which Time's hollowing touch had felt :
There bore they offspring ; there their offspring grew—
Grew too the trees which shelter'd them from view. 10
Nor thence was I shut out ; for from one tree
Acorns gave life, trunk roof, boughs DEATH for me.

   Meantime the youths the floral-feast attend ;
Thither from toil set free the rustics wend ;
The cross-roads ring with the thick-coming feet,   15
Resonant the air as crowd with crowd doth meet.

   Here, as about the grassy slopes they rest,
One turns all things to scorn and bitter jest,
Stinging his neighbour, who retorts with hate ;
Reproaches stick, anon exasperate ;   20
The crowd divides into two sides, and swift
All blindly rage, unknowing of the drift :
Like the cross-roads, they seem at random hurl'd ;
Strange weapons used by Passion and unfurl'd,
Which makes an armory of the whole wide world. 25

   Bacchus sustains the strife ; to those who drink
All things are double, save life—upon that think :
One's fell'd with stones, one 'neath fire-harden'd stake ;
Part i' their cups pour forth their life, part shake
It i' their plates.   Now louder grows the rout ;   30
Immoderate drinking rages all about,
In turn excites the blood, and pours it out.

Such War's first-fruits; such the beginnings be
Of the sharp sports of young Tisiphone.
But such untutor'd and rough killing ne'er   35
Pleas'd DEATH, who sought for skill refin'd and rare;
Approves the clever man-slayer; schools the young,
By dainty diet to high efforts strung,
By mimic fights—rehearsals of true war—
And lines of bristling battle stretch'd afar;   40
And winters spent beneath the raging sky,
While in their goat-hair tents cold-pierc'd they lie;
And all to grow adepts at slaying men
In lawful war, and from red slaughter gain
Fame, as inventors of destruction fell,   45
And foster-sons of Death and yawning Hell.
Yea, the eager youth slays at the mimic stakes
His thousands, and his thirst for glory slakes.
Good gods! for Virtue's self where shall we find
Such zeal as for the slaughter of mankind?   50.
Shall we, who own one life and then must die,
Destroy six hundred lives all wantonly?
    Yet the Hydra, sad of doing hurt, will grow
When men dig iron from earth's depths below;
And brass, of crime prolific and blood-stain'd,   55
Feeds on the world unsated, unrestrain'd.
Why should I reckon-up the engines of war
With which the old times bristl'd wide and far?
Ballistæ, scorpio of Sicilian master,
And English bows, which brought the Gaul disaster; 60

Clubs, slings—by which, on Heaven's high help relying,
When rose the Philistine God's host defying,
Breathless the pious shepherd left him lying;
Add chariots, with British pole scythe-arm'd,
Mowing down all they meet, themselves unharm'd ; 65
The battering-ram, fruit of Demetrius' skill,
Crashing along.   So were men wont to kill.
But still there lack'd that engine most of all
Meet for men's crimes—it no curse can miscall:
The melting iron in the furnace glowing,   70
The metal molten in its channel flowing,
A tube comes forth, a prodigy, one-ey'd—
As if with Homer's Cyclops it had vied—
That deadly orifice its power and pride.
Then upon wheels 'tis plac'd, like curule chair,   75
And DEATH himself triumphant sits down there.
Fire-dust is added—Orcus gave it birth—
A sweetmeat of Hell's table, not of Earth,
Sulphurous, mephitic, to fiends causing mirth.
To this a ball is join'd—not such as grew   80
Within the acorn's cup, before men knew
The ears of corn down-bending in the dew:
A ball of lead, and, as if conscious, livid;
Pluto's red minister—epistle vivid
Of Fate, lead-seal'd—bursting the web of Life   85
With all its threads; cutting sheer as a knife
Held by the wasted Atropos the old,
In many a hoary legend long enroll'd.

These being join'd, behold the gunner stand
With live tow lifted in his fatal hand :⁣   90
Fann'd by the wind, the infernal dust it lights,
And flashing onwards, all the mass ignites.
No more the Fury keeps within her cave,
But, girt with treacherous lightning, doth outbrave
The Day; and flying forth with horrid sound,   95
A dread explosiou thunders all around.
A hiss is heard, which cleaves the sky and Hell.
Nor may be caught beneath the hideous yell
The music of the spheres, or groans of demons fell.
Wing'd with a whirlwind, belching pitchy cloud,   100
The ball tears headlong on with roarings loud ;
Cities fall fear-struck ; huge walls fly asunder ;
Yea, the Earth's chambers, fragile, shake in wonder ;
A thousand bodies stretch'd along the plain,
At one dread blow are found among the slain.   105
Not so the plague, not so a star malign
Did e'er destroy; lo, here the proof, the sign,
Cocytus' skiff groans with its crowding load,
And the tir'd boatman begs help of his god.
Nor hurts the ball alone ; the attendant gale   110
Breathes death, and makes the life it fed to fail.
Say, Furies, whence this monster sprang to light.
Night begot Ætna; Chaos begot Night ;
Ætna fire-breathing Cacus ; Cacus gave
Ixion to Greek song ; he in dark cave   115
Begot a monk, of clouds ; who, his dim cell

Frequenting, shadow'd o'er with Night and Hell,
First made with dust this horrid portent fell.
Who would deny that monks do meditate
On death and mournful dust, and emulate   120
The lowly, unto whom each downward thing
Which dwells beneath the earth can gladness bring?
Nor yet e'en here DEATH's violence endeth all;
There leaps forth, worse than powder-driv'n ball,
The Jesuit, who seeks to blast the world,   125
Scorning explosions which destruction hurl'd
On bodies, not on souls, and seldom found
In king's blood deckt; but with a foolish sound
Obstreperous blazoning their guilt around.

    Here I do fix the summit of my power;   130
Men, ye are done for, body and soul; this hour
Let all the world now serve, and serving cower.   G.

XXXIII.

Triumphus Christiani in Mortem.

Ain' vero? quanta praedicas? hercle adepol,
Magnificus es screator, homicida inclytus.
Quid ipse faciam? qui nec arboreas sudes
In te, nec arcus scorpionesve aut rotas
Gladiosve, catapultasve teneam, quin neque
Alopas nec arietes? Quid ergo? Agnum et Crucem.

The Christian's Triumph over Death.

What dost thou say, O Death? what boasts are thine?
A mighty vaunter thou, and murderer fine.

What shall I do? who neither hedge-stakes wield,
Nor bows, nor scorpions, nor engines wheel'd,
Nor swords, nor catapults, nor battering-ram.
What then? I face thee with the Cross and Lamb!   G.

XXXIV.
In Johannem ἐπιστήθιον.

Ah nunc, helluo, fac ut ipse sugam:
Num totum tibi pectus imputabis?
Fontem intercipis omnibus patentem?
Quin pro me quoque sanguinem profudit,
Et jus pectoris inde consecutus
Lac cum sanguine posco devolutum;
Ut, si gratia tanta copuletur
Peccati veniae mei, vel ipsos
Occumbens humero Thronos lacessam.

To John on the Breast (of Christ).

Ah, let *me* quaff now, thou who drinkest deep:
Unto thyself wilt His whole bosom keep?
Dost intercept the fount open to all?
Nay, for me too the pour'd-out blood did fall;
And thence I claim rights in that breast divine,
And milk roll'd down with blood demand as mine;
Till I, such grace being link'd with sin forgiven,
Stay'd on His arm assay God's throne in heaven.
						R. WI.

XXXV.
Ad Dominum.

Christe, decus, dulcedo, et centum circiter Hyblae,

Cordis apex, animae pugnaque paxque meae :
Quin sine, te cernam ; quoties jam dixero, cernam ;
    Immoriarque oculis, O mea vita, tuis.
Si licet, immoriar : vel si tua visio vita est,
    Cur sine te, votis immoriturus, ago ?
Ah, cernam ; Tu, qui caecos sanare solebas,
    Cum te non videam, mene videre putas ?
Non video, certum est jurare ; aut si hoc vetuisti,
    Praevenias vultu non facienda tuo.

FINIS.

Soli Deo Gloria.

To the Lord.

Christ ! glory, sweetness, Hybla of the mind,
Heart's crown, where my soul's strife and peace I find ;
Nay, let me, let me see Thee, oft I say,
And on Thine eyes expire, my Life,—I pray,—
If I may die ; or if life is sight-born,
Why, soon to die with prayers, live I forlorn ?
Thou Who didst cure the blind, ah, let me see !
Dost deem it sight when I behold not Thee ?
I swear I see not : if Thou forbid'st this,
With Thine own Face prevent me—and 'tis bliss. R. WI.

THE END.

To God alone be Glory.

NOTES AND ILLUSTRATIONS.

I. Passio Discerpta.

i. Ad Dominum morientem. Cf. the Parentalia, i. 6: 'laudibus haud fierem sepia justa tuis.'

xvi. Ad Solem deficientem: l. 1; cf. Psalm xix.

xxi. In Mundi sympathiam cum Christo: l. 4. There is a play on the word quæstio=inquiry by torture, and so suffering as well as search.

II. Lucus.

v. In S. Scripturas: ll. 13-15; cf. Parentalia, ii. 33: 'per angiportus et meandros labitur.'

vi. In Pacem Brit.: ll. 1, 2. A reminiscence of Juvenal, x. 112, 113: 'sine caede et vulnere . . . . sicca morte.'

xi. Tributi Solutio. The tribute-money was not a Roman tax, but the customary offering to the Temple—God's House.

xv. Martha: Maria: l. 2; Tibullus, i. 1, 6, 'Dum meus assiduo luceat igne focus.' The thought is from Juvenal, xxv. 60 seq.

xx. In κενοδοξίαν, l. 7, 'sics'=old form of sis; cf. Epigr. Apolog. 17, l. antepenult, 'siet.' Line 6 (translation), tighter= have fewer incumbrances, lighter baggage.

xxii. In Improbum disertum. See Persius, iv. 21.

xxiii. Consolatio: l. 4, a false quantity, quŏtidie=quŏtidie. So in the Parentalia, vii. 29, and Epigrammata Apologetica, xii. 9. Line 7, a false quantity, trĕcento. The true quantity of the former quŏtĭdiano in the second poem, Ad Auctorem Instaurationis magnae, ver. 2. Lines 5, 6, an echo of Seneca, Ep. 1.

xxiv. In Angelos: l. 2, cŭï, a dissyllable: so in Parentalia, ii. 20, 'suum cuique tempus et locus datur.' In Epigr. Apolog. xxv. 'namque haec jure cuïpiam.'

xxxi. In Solarium: l. 2.   For this pun on caelo and solo, see Ausonius, Epigr. 33 :

> 'Orta salo, suscepta solo, patre edita caelo,
> Aeneadum genitrix, hic habito, alma Venus.'

xxxii. Triumphus Mortis: l. 2, 'Emathius torrens.' Lucan, 'Bella per Emathios plusquam civilia campos' (Pharsalia, i. 1).   Line 3, 'Daunia :' Horace, Carm. ii. i. 34, 35 :

> 'quod mare Dauniae
> Non decoloravere caedes ?'

refers to the battle of Cannæ chiefly.   Line 18, cf. Horace, Sat. ii. i. 25.   Line 23, Juvenal, xiii. 40, 'tunc, cum virguncula Juno.'   Line 41=Archimedes.   Line 44, 'divinus Tityrus. qu. David ?   Line 45, cf. Juvenal, iv. 126-7 :

> 'de temone Britanno
> Excidet Arviragus.'

Line 47 = Demetrius Poliorcetes.   Lines 56-7, cf. Herbert, 'In Obitum Henrici Principis Walliae,' 33-5.   Line 60, cf. Juvenal, vi. 10, 'glandem ructante marito.'   Line 81, a false quantity, Cŏcytia.   These false quantities of Herbert's own make his eager catching at an imagined one of Melville's (in the name Whitaker) somewhat amusing, if only that.   It may be recalled that even Milton allowed himself Iācŏbus, instead of the more accurate Iăcŏbus. (Eleg. Lib. In prod. Bomb.)

The text of 'Triumphus Mortis' from Herbert's own ms., as given by us, corrects various somewhat flagrant mistakes in previously-printed texts of it, under the title of 'Inventa Bellica,' notwithstanding that it has been professedly printed 'e Msto Autog.'   For, not to record the superior punctuation, we have these manifest improvements :

arcus for arces (unintelligible).	cellae for sellae.
huic for hinc.	axes for axis.
juncta for vincta.	crutus for exulis (nonsense).
datus ignis for datur ignis.	primus for primum.

The opening and close have been slightly altered by the Author to suit change of title, and there are other various readings.   G.

GLOSSARIAL INDEX.

Nearly all the references will be found to give more or less full notes on the respective words. Different forms of the same word are placed together. It is only intended to record here words peculiar to Herbert and his contemporaries, or in some way noticeable—not words used in their present and ordinary senses.　　　　　　　　　　　　　　　　G.

Single, market-money, i. 268.
Simpring, i. 14, 53, 186, 245, 308.
Six and seven, i. 26, 269-70.
Sink, i. 36.
Sign, i. 269.
Sigh, i. 82, 289.
Sillie, i. 93, 126.
Silk-twist, i. 101.[1]
Skill, i. 108, 248.
Skipping, i. 275-6.
Slack, i. 15.
Sleight, i. 81.
Sluttish, i. 98.
Sluttery, i. 222.
Smacke, i. 228.
Smooth, i. 87.
Snudge, i. 144, 302.
Sommers, i. 95, 201.
Soure, i. 14, 18, 242-4.
Souldier, great, i. 18, 254.
Sorted, i. 51.
Sowre-sweet, i. 197.
Sophisters, ii. 5.
Sound, ii. 12.
Spider, i. 254.
Sprung-wine, i. 11.
Spittle, i. 40, 276.
Spann'd, i. 116, 146, 303.
Spread, i. 303.
Sphere, i. 311.
Spare, i. 239.
Sport, i. 251.
Staies, i. 10.
Stake, i. 12, 16.
Stormie-working, i. 12.
Stowre. (See under Sowre).
Sting, i. 24, 222.
Stocking, i. 26.
Stroking, i. 40.

Staffe, i. 42, 154, 277.
Straw'd, i. 52.
Stemme, i. 72.
Strongly, i. 297.
Streams, i. 297.
Stormes, i. 303.
Store, i. 294, 307.
Streamer, i. 182, 308.
Strut, i. 182.
Submissiveness, i. 11.
Surety, i. 21.
Superliminare, i. 28.
Subsist, i. 38.
Subtile, i. 58, 282.
Suppling, i. 68.
Surging, i. 107, 131, 197
Surety, i. 258, *et seqq.*
Such, i. 279.
Sycamore, i. 95, 291.
Square, i. 166, 300.

T.

Tallies, i. 82, 289.
Tacks, i. 116.
Take, i. 141.
Tarantulae's, i. 215.
Task, i. 245.
Tentations, i. 81.
Thrall, i. 14, 21, 36, 244; ii. 50.
Then=than, i. 17, *et frequenter.*
Thy=the, i. 42.
This it is, i. 302, 307.
Thirds, i. 112, 294.
Them, i. 242.
Thaw, i. 246-7.
Thorns, i. 275.
Thee, i. 276.
'Tice, i. 52, 203.
Till, i. 143, 302.

---

[1] Cf. with this Joseph Fletcher (our edition, p. 154), in 'Christe's Bloodie Sweate' :

> ' Euen as a man that treades a wearie pace
> In laborinthes, continually in doubt
> To find the center of the curious trace ;
> Once entred, still vncertane to get out,
> Before some skillful maister by a *twist*
> Doth guide him in or out, or as he list.'

=cord or cline, as in Herbert, *not*, as explained by us (in loco), a small twig or branch.　　　　G.

NOTE.

An additional overlooked mispunctuation in Vol. I. page 56, line 34, is here noted, viz. a period (.) for a comma (,). This with the others being, in good old Thomas Larkham's phrase, 'as easily mended as espied' ('Attributes,' 1656), the Reader will of his charity please correct. G.

9 783744 727310